# Meaning Is Everywhere

*Language, Artificial Intelligence, Society*

# Meaning Is Everywhere

*Language, Artificial Intelligence, Society*

Prashant Parikh

Hackett Publishing Company, Inc.
Indianapolis/Cambridge

Copyright © 2024 by Hackett Publishing Company, Inc.

All rights reserved
Printed in the United States of America

27  26  25  24            1  2  3  4  5  6  7

For further information, please address
    Hackett Publishing Company, Inc.
    P.O. Box 44937
    Indianapolis, Indiana 46244-0937

    www.hackettpublishing.com

Cover design by E. L. Wilson and Laura Clark
Interior design by Laura Clark
Composition by Aptara, Inc.

Library of Congress Control Number: 2023946652

ISBN-13: 978-1-64792-161-3 (hardcover)
ISBN-13: 978-1-64792-162-0 (PDF ebook)
ISBN-13: 978-1-64792-163-7 (epub)

The paper used in this publication meets the minimum requirements of American National Standard for Information Sciences—Permanence of Paper for Printed Library Materials, ANSI Z39.48–1984.

∞

*For Avani and Neal*

*Ars Poetica*

A poem should be palpable and mute
As a globed fruit,

Dumb
As old medallions to the thumb,

Silent as the sleeve-worn stone
Of casement ledges where the moss has grown—

A poem should be wordless
As the flight of birds.

\*

A poem should be motionless in time
As the moon climbs,

Leaving, as the moon releases
Twig by twig the night-entangled trees,

Leaving, as the moon behind the winter leaves,
Memory by memory the mind—

A poem should be motionless in time
As the moon climbs.

\*

A poem should be equal to:
Not true.

For all the history of grief
An empty doorway and a maple leaf.

For love
The leaning grasses and two lights above the sea—

A poem should not mean
But be.

—Archibald MacLeish

# Contents

|  |  |
|---|---|
| List of Figures | *xiii* |
| List of Tables | *xiv* |
| Acknowledgments | *xv* |
| Introduction | *xvii* |

## I  MEANING AND LANGUAGE — 1

**1  What Is Meaning?** — 3
    1.1  Meaning, Society, and Artificial Intelligence — 4
    1.2  Semantics — 6
    1.3  My Approach to Meaning — 6

**2  Language and Science** — 11
    2.1  How Many Jokes Work — 11
    2.2  More Examples — 14
    2.3  Why Is Political Speech Often Extreme? — 16
    2.4  Approaching Language Scientifically — 18

**3  Ambiguity and Uncertainty** — 21
    3.1  A Picture of Ambiguity — 21
    3.2  Beyond Intended Meanings — 24
    3.3  An Overall Picture — 26
    3.4  Ambiguity and Artificial Intelligence — 27

**4  Vagueness and Value** — 33
    4.1  Words and Concepts — 33
    4.2  Toward a Scientific Account — 34
    4.3  Essentially Contested Concepts and the Emergence of Value — 36
    4.4  Vagueness and Artificial Intelligence — 38
    4.5  Can Computers Think? — 40
    4.6  The Story So Far — 43

## II  SITUATIONS AND GAMES — 45

**5  The Ubiquity of Context** — 47
    5.1  Analog and Digital — 49

|   |     | 5.2 Ways of Being | 50 |
|---|---|---|---|
|   |     | 5.3 What Does the World Have in It? | 51 |
|   |     | 5.4 Information | 55 |
|   |     | 5.5 Natural and Artificial Meanings | 55 |
|   |     | 5.6 Context and Calculability | 58 |
|   |     | 5.7 Context and Partiality | 59 |
|   |     | 5.8 Internal Contexts, Concepts, and Reduction | 61 |

## 6 What Is a Game? — 65

- 6.1 A Simple Example — 66
- 6.2 Solving Games — 68
- 6.3 Situated Games — 69
- 6.4 Situated Games and Conversation — 72
- 6.5 Situated Games and Common Knowledge — 73
- 6.6 Situated Games and Power — 74
- 6.7 Rationality, Irrationality, and Existence — 75
- 6.8 Situated Games and Heidegger — 78
- 6.9 Situated Games and Complexity — 81
- 6.10 The Story Further Along — 82

## III MEANING AND MODERNITY — 85

## 7 How We Communicate — 87

- 7.1 The Key Ideas — 87
  - 7.1.1 Fixed and Variable — 87
  - 7.1.2 Parts and Wholes — 88
  - 7.1.3 Networks — 91
- 7.2 Communication and Jokes — 93
- 7.3 Communication and Political Speech — 94
- 7.4 Utterance Meaning and Discourse Meaning — 95
- 7.5 Referential Meaning — 96
- 7.6 What Is Understanding? — 97
- 7.7 Some Consequences of the Framework — 102

## 8 Language at Large — 105

- 8.1 How Conventional Meanings Emerge — 105
- 8.2 How Conventional Meanings Change — 108
- 8.3 Convention — 109
- 8.4 The Social Nature of Language and Convention — 112

|  |  |  |  |
|---|---|---|---|
|  | 8.5 | The Public Sphere | 113 |
|  | 8.6 | Language Games and Artificial Intelligence | 122 |
| **9** | **Images, Actions, and Objects** | | **125** |
|  | 9.1 | Images | 126 |
|  |  | 9.1.1 Pictures | 127 |
|  |  | 9.1.2 Motion Pictures | 131 |
|  | 9.2 | Actions | 133 |
|  |  | 9.2.1 International Relations | 134 |
|  |  | 9.2.2 *Waiting for Godot* | 135 |
|  | 9.3 | Objects | 137 |
|  |  | 9.3.1 Rocks, Toasters, Cats, and Persons | 137 |
|  |  | 9.3.2 Modernity | 141 |
|  | 9.4 | In the Center of the Story | 145 |
| **IV** | **MEANING AND CIVILIZATION** | | **147** |
| **10** | **The Meta-Structure of Society** | | **149** |
|  | 10.1 | Persons and Groups | 150 |
|  | 10.2 | Social Institutions | 151 |
|  | 10.3 | Situated Games and Social Roles | 156 |
|  | 10.4 | Self and Society | 158 |
|  | 10.5 | Preferences and Values | 161 |
|  | 10.6 | Power | 162 |
|  | 10.7 | Social Change | 165 |
|  | 10.8 | Meaning, Society, and Artificial Intelligence Revisited | 167 |
| **11** | **Situated Artificial Intelligence** | | **171** |
|  | 11.1 | Informational Transforms | 172 |
|  | 11.2 | Situated Actions | 173 |
|  | 11.3 | Technology | 174 |
|  | 11.4 | Situated AI | 175 |
| **12** | **What Is a Partial Utopia?** | | **179** |
|  | 12.1 | Human Suffering | 179 |
|  | 12.2 | Scarcity | 181 |
|  | 12.3 | Inclusion and Exclusion | 185 |
|  | 12.4 | Partial Utopias | 189 |
|  | 12.5 | The Meaning of Life | 192 |

*Appendix A: A Concrete Example of Communication*   199
*Appendix B: Situation Theory*   203

*References*   209
*Name Index*   219
*Subject Index*   223

# List of Figures

| | | |
|---|---|---|
| A | A Map of the Book | xx |
| | | |
| 3.1 | Classification of Intended Meaning | 21 |
| 3.2 | Classification of Communicated Meaning | 22 |
| 3.3 | Classification of Direct Meaning | 22 |
| 3.4 | Classification of Indirect Meaning | 23 |
| 3.5 | Classification of Extracted but Unintended Meaning | 24 |
| 3.6 | Classification of Discourse Meaning | 26 |
| | | |
| 4.1 | A Precise Concept | 34 |
| 4.2 | A Vague Concept | 34 |
| | | |
| 5.1 | What Is It Like to Be a Bat? | 63 |
| | | |
| 6.1 | A Coordination Game $G$ | 66 |
| 6.2 | A Mixed-Motive Game $G'$ | 67 |
| 6.3 | Classification of Human Actions | 77 |
| | | |
| 7.1 | Classification of Discourse Meaning | 95 |
| 7.2 | Two Crosscutting Distinctions | 100 |
| | | |
| 8.1 | A Language Game with a Network of Two Communication Games | 106 |
| 8.2 | Language Games in Society | 107 |
| 8.3 | A Network Game with Two Local Games | 111 |
| 8.4 | A Hegemony Game | 119 |
| | | |
| 9.1 | A Visual Joke | 127 |
| 9.2 | Paul Cézanne, *The Card Players*, 1890–92, The Metropolitan Museum of Art Collection | 129 |
| | | |
| B | A Map of the Book | 145 |
| | | |
| 10.1 | Linguistic Instance of Structure and Agency | 153 |
| 10.2 | Linguistic Instance of Structure and Agency Simplified | 153 |
| 10.3 | Structure and Agency | 154 |
| 10.4 | Structure and Agency with Namaste | 154 |
| 10.5 | Structure and Agency with a Traffic System | 154 |
| 10.6 | A Mixed-Motive Game | 157 |
| 10.7 | A Coordination Game | 159 |

| | | |
|---|---|---|
| 10.8 | Hegemony Game between Ann and Bob | 164 |
| 10.9 | Hegemony Game between Ann and Cathy | 164 |
| 10.10 | Hegemony Game between Bob and Fred | 164 |
| 10.11 | Hegemony Game between Cathy and Oscar | 164 |
| 10.12 | The Hierarchy of Power | 164 |
| 11.1 | An Informational Space with Informational Transforms | 172 |
| 12.1 | A Possible Space of Human Relationships | 190 |
| 12.2 | A Mixed-Motive Game | 195 |
| 12.3 | A Coordination Game | 195 |
| 12.4 | A Different Coordination Game | 196 |
| A.1 | The Lexical Semantic Game $g_1$ | 199 |
| A.2 | The Lexical Semantic Game $g_2$ | 199 |
| A.3 | The Sentential Semantic Game $g_{12}$ | 200 |

# List of Tables

| | | |
|---|---|---|
| 2.1 | Common and Rare Meanings in the *Saturday Night Live* Joke | 12 |
| 2.2 | Common and Rare Meanings in the Groucho Marx Joke | 14 |
| 2.3 | Common and Rare Meanings in the Laurel and Hardy Routine | 15 |
| 2.4 | Common and Rare Meanings in the Mulla Nasruddin Joke | 16 |
| 4.1 | Judging Whether Fred Is Bald or Not Bald or Borderline Bald | 35 |
| 9.1 | Common and Rare Meanings in a Visual Joke | 128 |
| 10.1 | A Rudimentary Representation of a Self | 159 |

# Acknowledgments

This is an unusual book. It emerged imperceptibly over many decades from conversations and interactions with my wife, Avani. Her example and our reciprocal insights gave birth to the germ of its idea. Without her, it would have been impossible, unthinkable.

My son, Neal, also contributed in indispensable ways—through innumerable discussions of artificial intelligence, with helpful references to the literature, and just by always being there.

Likewise, my father, Jagdish, who is currently ninety-four, was the source of some key ideas as many of our interests overlap.

I am immensely grateful to the many people who offered comments on earlier drafts. I would like to thank Kalyan Chatterjee, Nelson Correa, Paul Freedman, Pramod Khargonekar, Peter Ludlow, Sudhir Patwardhan, Jyoti Narula Ranjan, Rajat Ranjan, Suhrud Sardesai, Sunil Shah, Ennio Stacchetti, Michael Stevenson, and Jiye Yu.

I would also like to acknowledge extended, helpful conversations over the years with Anjum Altaf, Parag Amladi, Ken Arrow, Jon Barwise, Anton Benz, Akeel Bilgrami, Noël Carroll, Robin Clark, Jack Copeland, Nelson Correa, Michael Devitt, Fred Dretske, Dan Flickinger, Dagfinn Føllesdal, David Israel, Geeta Kapur, Julie Maybee, Ravi Mazumdar, Gieve Patel, Sudhir Patwardhan, Suhrud Sardesai, Richard Schechner, Sunil Shah, Ennio Stacchetti, Robert Stalnaker, Tom Wasow, Scott Weinstein, and Ed Zalta.

Jeff Dean, my editor at Hackett, was extraordinary. I owe him everlasting thanks. All my books have been edited by Alice Peck, my editor of over twenty-five years, to whom I remain deeply grateful.

# Introduction

Our planet has just emerged from the uneven impact of the SARS-CoV-2 pandemic, some global elites thriving and the rest of humanity struggling to maintain a foothold. The future remains profoundly uncertain, dependent as it is on what so many feel is a troubled, insecure, and increasingly arbitrary and authoritarian world. Everywhere, there appears to be deepening economic inequality despite an overall reduction in poverty, a polarized civil society that flares up into spasms of violence, the rise of a militant majoritarianism, and the spread of fake news exacerbated by social media. This has undermined democracy itself because democracy requires reasonable equality, a civilized public sphere, a balance between majorities and minorities, and, perhaps most critically, a social order that respects the truth. Without these things, democracy's very nature is distorted.

The confidence many shared in the old pieties of the left or the right has been shaken to its roots, and public intellectuals of various persuasions, often relying on the old models, find themselves taken more or less completely by surprise, especially when they have to face the fact that many contemporary authoritarians are democratically elected. Despite many insightful attempts at understanding, the global conversation—if it can be called that given the level of acrimony that prevails—tends not to be *radical* enough and *general* enough. It is necessary to formulate the seemingly intractable questions that confront us with a fresh and foundational clarity and then answer them with an equally daring and innovative rigor. Only then can we find a way into the future.

This implies that we cannot approach these matters by the usual routes: either economics or political science or sociology, or, more academically, via one or another grand social theory. We have to find a radically new angle, taking the risk that that always entails. We have to dig deep under those seemingly intractable questions, and unearth possibly a new foundation altogether, a foundation that can help us build what I call, cautiously, a *partial* utopia, a vision for a not-so-distant future society within our practical grasp for collective human flourishing. Such a practical topos cannot simply be described by a list of desiderata, it must be accompanied by a grounding vision of the world we live in so that the desiderata may be actualized: it must be brought down to earth.

First among these intractable, foundational questions—because it is humanity's oldest and remains unsatisfactorily answered—is whether and how humanity should seek meaning, and what its place in civilization is. It provides the architecture, the frame, the very *ground* for all of life. The advent of modernity around 1500 CE has uprooted this traditional inquiry in all sorts of unforeseen if not astonishing ways, and it is in this still ongoing context that the question must be asked anew.

One consequence of this uprooting has been that almost no one asks the large questions about meaning any more. Indeed, philosophers typically see its different manifestations as distinct phenomena and consider such questions as belonging to a quaint bygone era. To ask about the meaning of life without irony today is a mark of ignorance or naivete or both.[1] The subject has also been divided among so many specializations other than philosophy even though philosophy remains the master discipline in this one area. But philosophy itself has broken it down to its many branches so that few ask what is common to its various applications, whether we are asking for the meaning of a verb, the meaning of a play, or the meaning of modernity itself.

But if we are to provide a grounding vision of the world that will enable us to fashion an image of possible partial utopias by answering the large questions about meaning—one of the few fresh and radical avenues available to us—it is crucial to try to stitch its swatches back together, especially with the threads of several new ideas, some of which have appeared in greater detail in my earlier academic books.[2]

Meaning, then, is what I start with, and I will try to show how it permeates literally everything, not only language, its most obvious site, but also signs and symbols at large, actions from the simple to the complex, and objects of many different kinds including modernity itself. Based on these foundational building blocks, I will sketch the "meaningful" construction of society and civilization from the ground up. Weaving through this narrative is another that forms in many ways the heart of modernity, the emergence of modern science and technology with its most potent promise of a truly general artificial intelligence (AI). It is this enframing complex, this grounding vision of the world as it is today, that will enable us to speculate about the possibility of *partial* utopias, that will

---

1. Eagleton (2008b).
2. Parikh (1987/2020, 2001, 2010, 2019).

equip us 'to show the fly the way out of the fly-bottle', to borrow a phrase from the Viennese philosopher Ludwig Wittgenstein.

So, rather than begin with one of the social sciences, I will be setting about the intractable questions that perplex and oppress us with language and symbols, as unlikely a point of departure for social issues as any. Upon further reflection, however, it may seem apt to be opening our inquiry with the very institution that makes us human, that enables our being with others in unfathomably varied ways, that gives us some of our loftiest civilizational achievements.

It is also because of these qualities that language is an essential starting point for figuring out whether and how a general AI might be possible. The recent advances of machine learning have startled everyone, even the experts. There are extravagant claims on all sides of the debate it has set off, and there are questions about meaning that must be answered before we can begin to dream about partial utopias.

To do my best to maintain the twin virtues of clarity and rigor in telling these intersecting and interdisciplinary stories about meaning and modernity, I will draw upon my version of situation theory and what I call situated game theory, two elementary mathematical frameworks described in plain English that I believe provide an *indispensable* language in which to express my novel argument. I urge you to be sufficiently patient so that you can see how potentially far-reaching conclusions emerge naturally from fairly commonsense assumptions, so that you can glimpse the way forward from our shared confines toward human emancipation.

## A Map of the Book

The central argument of the book is that the world is full of meaning, that everything is meaningful, and understanding this key fact in some interconnected detail can help us realize a better society, even a partial utopia, if certain preconditions are satisfied. This requires spelling out in a foundational way what meaning is, what society is, what a better society might be, and what its preconditions are.

Our exploration of meaning will begin with language and then move on to society and artificial intelligence and ultimately to the possible formation of partial utopias. I begin this way not only because language presents us with the clearest and most familiar site of meaning. It is also because language is a social institution and it *mirrors* other social institutions—and society itself—as I will show in later chapters (Chapters 7, 8, and 10).

Understanding the details of language (Chapters 1, 2, 3, 4, 7, and 8) will, in fact, prepare us in two ways. First, we will grasp a key social institution concretely and this groundwork will give us an analogical insight into how other social institutions can be understood via meaning as well (Chapters 9 and 10). Second, language and meaning play a deep role in the challenges and possibilities for AI (Chapter 11). Together, an appreciation of society and AI will allow us to speculate about the form and content of partial utopias and their preconditions (Chapter 12). Figure A is a road map of these connections.

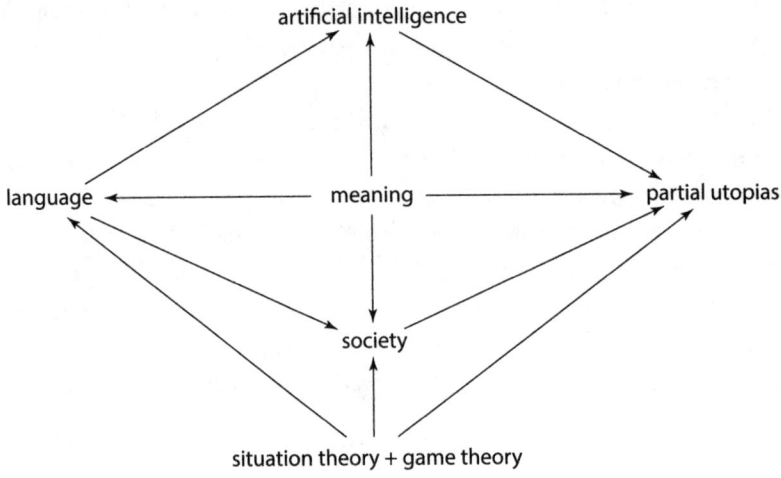

Figure A  A Map of the Book

As Figure A shows, meaning lies at the center of the four elements of language, society, AI, and partial utopias, and arrows lead from language to society and AI and from there on to partial utopias. The combination of situation theory and game theory is the framework that undergirds the whole exploration (Chapters 5 and 6). The entire structure indicated by the map is, indeed, a new way of conceiving meaning and its relation to civilization, as will become clearer once the story begins.

We will examine the difficulties that plague language—ambiguity, vagueness, and context—and how these three aspects intersect with corresponding aspects of society and AI, and then move on to the heart of language—which is communication. Along the way, I will introduce situation theory and situated game theory, the elementary mathematical frameworks that will enable me to express the argument. I will then indicate how meaning operates in the case of images, actions, and objects as they are central to civilization. And because our study is foundational, I will show how meaning relates to reduction and rationality and related notions that are key to acquiring a clear sense of how the whole picture is grounded. In the last part of the book, based on our earlier insights into language, meaning, and communication, I will look at the structure of society, offer my thoughts about the prospects for a situated artificial intelligence, and end with a discussion of partial utopias that will rest on both the nature of society and the possibilities for a situated AI.

Most emancipatory writing today offers helpful hints toward solving this or that social problem but fails, despite its best intentions, to provide a vision for life itself, its very meaning, what it is for. Without such a telos, however fragmentary, civilization becomes unmoored. I come to this challenge aslant: from language, the very elusive thing that makes us human, to the complexities of AI and society, and thence to the delicate possibility of partial utopias, which culminates with a sketch of the meaning of life itself.

Who is this book for? It is for anyone curious about meaning and its connection with our modern civilization, but it is especially for those interested in seeing how the fly may find its way out of the fly-bottle; for those prepared to grapple with things that may be unfamiliar and to add what they know to my thoughts. All books are collective endeavors in this sense, but this one is more so than most.

Paraphrasing Gandhi—in a gentle way, we can together shake the world.

# PART I
## MEANING AND LANGUAGE

# CHAPTER ONE

# What Is Meaning?

One way to interpret Fyodor Dostoyevsky, possibly the greatest novelist and sincerest romantic of all time, is to say he craved meaning above all else—whether the new ideals of humanism and the centrality of humanity sweeping in from the West in nineteenth-century Russia, or, when they fell short, a wavering between, on the one hand, a displaced god and disenchanted religion, and on the other, a grasping for an impotent egoism, modern man as Faustic man.

His failure to find meaning in modernity points to, of all things, a *methodological* flaw in much romanticism, philosophical and aesthetic, the desire to pursue what is complex and whole *directly* rather than starting with the simple and partial. After all, as the Chinese philosopher Lao Tzu put it, the journey of a thousand miles begins with a single step.

Indeed, although this insight has been known since antiquity, it has been codified as part of the scientific method only since modernity. Asking why an apple falls to the ground may lead to bigger questions and possibly answers. In a book attempting to address humanity's oldest question, we must start with what meaning is in the first place.

For many of us, our first self-conscious encounter with meaning occurred when a parent or caregiver told us a story and we asked, "What does that mean?" As we grew up, we learned indirectly that lots of things have meaning—not only words but also images and actions and objects (like *smoke* meaning *fire*) and possibly even our lives. We seem to be surrounded by meaning and even seek it in order to feel fulfilled as human beings.

Like other animals, we are exquisitely attuned to meanings in our environment, especially as they relate to human interactions. We can generally distinguish a compliment from an insult and friend from foe, although there are also times when we are stymied by ambiguity. Our physical environments, too, are full of meaning and we can often infer when smoke means fire or dark clouds mean rain. It is this constant immersion in one meaning or another that largely constitutes our lives.

Nevertheless, even if our curiosity is aroused by its apparent ubiquity and relation to human affairs, most of us would find it quite difficult to say what this hazy awareness of meaning consists of. We can usually identify the meanings of simple words and images and other objects, but if asked about more complex things—like the meaning of Samuel Beckett's play *Waiting for Godot* or the meaning of modernity—we are likely to be at a loss. We sense there is a whole range of meaning from the superficial and mundane to the deep and transcendent. In a strange, even mysterious, way it seems connected with everything. It is everywhere and nowhere. And so the more profound questions—like what meaning is generally and how it is that all these varied things come to signify— seem to lie beyond our ken.

## 1.1 Meaning, Society, and Artificial Intelligence

It might appear that meanings are relatively private and belong entirely to individual perceptions of the world, but they turn out to be predominantly social, although private meanings certainly also exist.

Perhaps most obviously, language is a social institution. If we did not— at least to a great extent—share the meanings of words, we would not be able to communicate. However, this sharing of meanings goes far beyond language. Society is full of social institutions, such as civil society, the economy, and the state, each of which is made up of many component institutions, such as the family and the public sphere, technology and various sectors of industry, and political elections and governments, respectively. The myriad institutions in society exist and function because people share the meanings that constitute them. For example, in presidential democracies, people collectively know that a presidential election means that the winner will be the chief executive of the country for a specified term. Here, meaning and society are intertwined.

Consider our shared technological systems in the twenty-first century as they continue to form the heart of modernity. AI agents are rapidly beginning to do all sorts of amazing things like drive cars, diagnose illness, and translate languages, tasks that were once the exclusive preserve of humans. This could augur a watershed in the history of humankind, surpassing the scientific revolution of the sixteenth and seventeenth centuries in the West that built upon smaller breakthroughs in multiple cultures in the East and West stretching back to ancient times. Such progress has the potential to radically alter society in ways that are hard to imagine. How has this been possible and could these artificial agents take over the world one day?[1] How do we respond with nuance and insight and what do these agents' abilities have to do with the apparently unrelated subject of meaning?

In 2012, Google used *deep learning*—a new technique based on a neural network—to recognize the picture of a cat in unlabeled images from YouTube videos with a fairly high accuracy (about 85%), something that had for a long time been quite hard to do.[2] This remarkable feat has been repeated to recognize thousands of other objects, and with increasing accuracy. Getting an inanimate computer to identify cats and dogs and tables and chairs—and human faces—can be put to, indeed, is already being put to, many powerful uses, both good and bad. This raises the question: Does the AI system know what a cat is the way we do? And, indeed, what is the meaning of a cat? And further, is our understanding individual or social and can it be acquired by an artificial agent such as a driverless car?

Given such ambiguous advances in AI and similar fields, it seems that technology, too, instead of emancipating humanity from labor and ushering in a truly free society may in fact abet various contemporary global tendencies and create a heaven for the few at the expense of a hell for the many. Viewed historically, humans seem to be inherently flawed creatures, capable of great good and great evil, and barely able to solve the problems they set themselves. Yet in many respects, considering where *Homo sapiens* began, modern civilization is a towering achievement.

Can understanding what meaning is throw some light on this dual nature of humanity? And, based on this understanding, can we nurture its better angels, realize that we could be engaged in building a meaningful world, and work toward a cluster of partial utopias—*partial* to preempt totalitarianisms of all kinds, *partial* to allow a variety of societies to flourish, and *partial* to cultivate a radical openness to life?

---

1. Bostrom (2014), Boden (2016), Mitchell (2019). See also the Stanford University 2016 report *Artificial Intelligence and Life in 2030: One Hundred Year Study on Artificial Intelligence* at https://ai100.stanford.edu/2016-report and the 2021 report *Gathering Strength, Gathering Storms: The One Hundred Year Study on Artificial Intelligence (AI100) 2021 Study Panel Report* at https://ai100.stanford.edu/2021-report.
2. Goodfellow et al. (2016, p. 24).

## 1.2 Semantics

To think about what insights meaning may offer our personal and social quests, we need to step back and start with relatively smaller and seemingly remote questions. What is meaning and where is it? How does it originate? How does it relate to value? And why is it important? I will start with verbal language as it is both most familiar and in some ways the simplest example of meaning.

As revealed by four quite different traditions—Sanskrit, Greek, Hebrew, and Arabic—the study of meaning emerged as an independent discipline roughly three thousand years ago from the exegesis of mostly religious texts and concerned the relationship between language, reality, and knowledge.[3] The discipline's original context was communicative, initially between people and divine powers when the world itself was largely read as signs from above. Today, the field, variously called semantics, semiotics, or semiology, belongs primarily to philosophy, linguistics, psychology, sociology, and artificial intelligence, as well as derivatively to many other disciplines, each studying meaning from different points of view and with different goals.

## 1.3 My Approach to Meaning

Physicists these days frequently refer to a 'theory of everything'.[4] While this is a welcome development, it also embraces a reductionist vision, seeing our meaningful *world* as nothing over and above the physical *universe*, just as water was discovered to be nothing over and above $H_2O$. I take this view to be ultimately correct: our minds and therefore the cultures and communities we create cannot be fundamentally different from the rest of the universe. That would be a strange kind of exceptionalism. Everything is nature or patterns in nature—that is, everything is either inanimate or made out of inanimate stuff. In other words, dualisms in terms of mind and body or culture and nature are false

---

3. See van Bekkum et al. (1997, p. 286). See also Deutsch and Bontekoe (2007) for other traditions besides these four.

4. However, see the recent article on the future of physics in *The Economist* at https://www.economist.com/science-and-technology/physics-seeks-the-future/21803916.

doctrines.[5] However, this physicalism seems only *ultimately* correct because our private and public worlds are strangely resistant to this idea: everything we experience—such as a thought or feeling—suggests a radical dichotomy.[6]

How do we account for this discrepancy between the way physical reality is and how we experience it? My view is that it has to do with the nature of context. The situations we occupy affect us in deep and as yet poorly understood ways. The realm of biology (where our minds and bodies meet) and the social sciences and humanities (where culture and nature meet) are precisely the points where these contexts are the hardest to discover. We are situated beings. There are internal contexts in our minds as well, which is probably part of the reason why we feel our consciousness is cut off from the universe. This is just a hunch, and I will say more about it later.[7]

Whatever the correct explanation, just as we are situated so are atoms and quarks, even though the language of the physical sciences has generally omitted the word "context" as it can be vague and has many uses. However, when we state the *conditions* under which a phenomenon occurs—such as a solar eclipse—we are merely using a different word for the context *in which* it occurs. Conditions, contexts, situations, ecological niches, frames, fields, systems, environments, backgrounds, and worlds are all terms that identify roughly the same thing: the natural, surrounding wholes in which all entities exist and function.

The particular fact about context that makes it so special is that it is invariably *connected* to other contexts via the entities that inhabit each context. Situations with smoke are generally connected to situations with fire and likewise dark clouds with rain. It is these connections that enable one situation to carry information about another situation. An agent who sees the first situation and who is aware of the connection can infer the existence of the second situation. Such connections don't always involve causality narrowly interpreted; they might even occur via a social convention like greeting a person with palms held together in an Indian namaste. It is such connections between contexts that

---

5. For a fascinating social and intellectual history of one manifestation of such dualisms (and a great deal more), see Janik and Toulmin (1973).
6. Chalmers (2002) is a useful collection of papers on this and related topics. See also Robbins and Aydede (2009), Mesquita et al. (2010), and Montero and Papineau (2016).
7. See Section 5.8.

make all the difference in both our physical and social worlds: all life depends on them. Indeed, they *constitute* our civilizations. Another name for these connections is *meaning*.[8]

Meaning is closely related to causality broadly considered—the connection between a namaste, a kind of gesture, and its conveying a greeting is also causal in a broad sense—although sometimes the causes themselves are more pronounced in our language, as in "dark clouds mean rain," and sometimes their effects, as in "smoke means fire," depending on what we are more likely to observe and find useful to infer from our observations. Meanings are regularities in (physical and social) nature, not just accidental correlations, and can be deterministic or probabilistic.[9]

The language of meaning—and, indeed, of its enabling substrate, information—makes it possible for us to contemplate reducing a phenomenon to something simpler, but also allows us to communicate at higher levels when we wish to. We can reduce a social convention to the persons who comprise it and the relations between them in a special sort of way I discuss later.[10] Beyond this, we can also see (although only in principle because such reductions appear difficult if not impossible to carry out in practice) persons and their interrelations as nothing over and above their physical bodies and their interrelations, and, further, their bodies as just chemicals and electrical impulses and finally atoms and quarks and strings and membranes—whatever the ultimate constituents of the universe turn out to be—and their interrelations through the fundamental forces that bind them.[11] But we can also talk about what the namaste meant at our everyday level and whether or not the addressee understood the greeting. In other words, the language of meaning and information makes it possible for us to be true to the physical universe we live in—the electrons and quarks and fields and forces—*and* to our everyday experience—the gesture grasped as a greeting. It is a different

---

8. Hume (1748/1988), Peirce (1867–1913/1991), and Heidegger (1927/1962) anticipated this idea of meaning. Barwise and Perry (1983) first developed it, and my version of it and its further development are contained in Parikh (1987/2020, 2001, 2010, 2019). The technical term for "connection" is "constraint."

9. See Pearl and Mackenzie (2018) for a lucid account of causality and causal inference. See also Dretske (1981, chap. 1) for a discussion of the difference between causality and "the flow of information." Meaning straddles both.

10. See Section 8.3.

11. Of course this may not be the best way to describe this ultimate layer of reality as it is just our currently commonsense way of understanding it.

and in a certain sense more accessible way to express a theory of everything, as meaning and information are what is common to the different levels of reality.

Because everything is situated and the entities in different situations are connected with other entities, everything is meaningful and meaning can be said to be everywhere. From commonplace occurrences like a wisp of smoke in one situation indicating a fire in another, to the waggle dance of a honeybee signaling to other honeybees where and how far the flowers are, to people engaging in acts of situated communication to ask for a coffee in a restaurant or to convey the meaning of life in a funny or solemn situation, the whole universe is immersed in meaning. We can say in each instance either that the meaning is the connection between some situated $x$ and situated $y$ or, more colloquially, that the meaning of $x$ is $y$.

Now that we have a preliminary grasp of what meaning is, let us turn to its instantiation in language.

# CHAPTER TWO

# Language and Science

As I have said, our most familiar self-conscious encounter with meaning is through verbal language. Despite this, even many of the simplest ideas involving linguistic meaning are quite complex. For example, it is easy to look up a dictionary to see what a word means, but it is incredibly difficult to define word meaning, that is, say what it is in general. Likewise, it is easy to refer to a table by saying "this table" but a real challenge to define reference. And this applies to many other such problems involving the relation between language, reality, and knowledge that forms the core of semantics as we saw earlier.[1]

Because of this, I will proceed from surface phenomena to deeper concepts, and to smooth this transition, I will start with a new account of how some jokes work as they are not only among the more entertaining uses of language but also embody both surface phenomena and deeper concepts. I will then briefly provide a novel explanation of a ubiquitous aspect of political speech as it will help set the stage for some of the social phenomena I explore later. These more practical domains will help us begin to grasp the different ways in which meaning suffuses everything from the concrete to the abstract.

## 2.1 How Many Jokes Work

Imagine two friends Ann and Bob engaged in an everyday conversation where Ann narrates the following joke to Bob from a *Saturday Night Live* episode from the 1970s:

> "Every ten minutes a man gets mugged in New York. Tonight we are going to interview him."

---

1. Section 1.2.

Bob is momentarily puzzled and then laughs. The pause before he gets the joke is not gratuitous, as we will see.

A discourse consists of two or more sentences uttered in succession, so what we have here is indeed a discourse. It raises a multitude of questions. First, how does the joke work? More abstractly, how do spoken sounds carry one or more meanings from speaker to addressee? How did the words uttered get their individual meanings in the first place? How are these individual meanings put together to create a meaningful whole?

Consider the first sentence. It has nine words ("New York" is treated as a single unit), each of which has a conventional meaning. A conventional meaning is like a dictionary meaning, but only in part because the latter is given with other words and if one sought the meanings of those words, they would lead to still more words, until we realize that a dictionary is ultimately circular. So, conventional meanings are not other words in a dictionary but in fact properties or attributes that we have to describe in words. For example, "man" has the conventional meaning or property *male person*. For the moment, assume such meanings are fixed and given for each of the words in Ann's joke.

The next thing to realize is that the noun phrase "a man" is ambiguous. It could mean either *some man or other* or *a particular man* as in the usual interpretations of the phrase in "She does not have a man in her life" or "She met a man." This makes the whole first utterance of the joke potentially ambiguous. Its commonplace meaning would be that *every ten minutes some man or other gets mugged in New York* whereas its rarer meaning would be that *every ten minutes a particular man gets mugged in New York*.

| common meaning | some man or other gets mugged |
|---|---|
| rare meaning | a particular man gets mugged |

Table 2.1 Common and Rare Meanings in the *Saturday Night Live* Joke

When Bob hears the first sentence, he chooses its more common meaning, but when he hears the second sentence, he gets stuck because there is no place to anchor the singular pronoun "him" as the only plausible candidate would be *some man or other*, which does not provide a single object. He is forced to shift to the second, rarer interpretation, *a particular man*, which does, indeed, provide a single object for the singular pronoun. By switching from the common to the rare interpretation, he is able to solve his momentary puzzlement and make sense of the discourse.

This switching between meanings is part of what causes Bob to laugh if the second sentence also builds upon the rare meaning to create an amusing overall interpretation. And the switching takes some time. Hence the slight pause before the laughter. The amusing overall interpretation does not by itself create the humor. The switch from an unremarkable interpretation to an amusing one is what is responsible. Consider the following:

> "Every ten minutes a particular man gets mugged in New York. He was interviewed on TV today."

This is decidedly not funny. It may have a certain offbeat interpretation that may be marginally amusing in itself but that does not make it a joke. It is because Bob had to switch interpretations to something amusing that the discourse became funny.

On the other hand, the switch does not make up the joke by itself either. To see this, consider the following:

> "Every ten minutes a man gets mugged in New York. He lives on the Upper West Side."

This is also not funny, or may only be marginally so, because the second sentence does not build upon the preceding utterance in an amusing way. That the man will be interviewed on TV tonight does build upon his unhappy and extraordinary situation in an amusing way.

In other words, a switch in meaning is a necessary condition for the discourse to be a joke, and adding an amusing buildup makes the two jointly sufficient.[2]

---

2. A condition is necessary for something if that thing cannot exist without it. And one or more conditions are sufficient for something if their presence enables it to exist. I will use these concepts of necessary and sufficient conditions often.

## 2.2  More Examples

Does this insight apply only to the *Saturday Night Live* joke or to others as well? Can we explain the following Groucho Marx joke in the same way?

> "Last night I shot an elephant in my pajamas. How he got into my pajamas I'll never know."

This joke exploits the fact that a sentence is not solely a linear string of words. It has a more complex structure. "In my pajamas" in the first sentence forms a prepositional phrase that would ordinarily attach to the verb "shot" but could also attach to the noun phrase "an elephant." Once again, the utterance is potentially ambiguous. Its commonplace meaning would be that *the shooting happened in the person's pajamas* whereas its rarer meaning would be that *the elephant was in the pajamas*. And the second sentence forces the addressee to switch from the common to the rare interpretation and also presents the amusing picture of an elephant in someone's pajamas.

| common meaning | shooting in my pajamas |
|---|---|
| rare meaning | elephant in my pajamas |

Table 2.2  Common and Rare Meanings in the Groucho Marx Joke

This second joke is somewhat similar to the first one. Could this pattern of a switch of interpretation accompanied by an amusing buildup be even wider? It turns out that it is in fact applicable to many types of jokes including clever puns such as "What is Beethoven doing in his grave? Decomposing." It can describe even slapstick humor like that of early Hollywood's comedy team of Laurel and Hardy where no spoken language is involved.

Imagine Laurel carrying a long plank horizontally in a situation where Hardy calls out to him from behind. Laurel turns around to look, swiveling the plank with him, and this knocks down Hardy. Here there is a more commonly expected situation—a meaning—with no mishap, and another rarer situation—a second meaning—where there is a mishap. The actual accident provides the amusement. And such situations can be repeated where Hardy is knocked down several times with Laurel's whirling back and forth, each time subverting the common meaning and switching to another that is rare and amusing—until the accidents are no longer funny because they come to form the expected common meanings and there is no switch to make us laugh.

| common meaning | no mishap |
|---|---|
| rare meaning | mishap |

Table 2.3  Common and Rare Meanings in the Laurel and Hardy Routine

Incidentally, this sort of insight about humor seems to be wonderfully captured in one of Woody Allen's finest films *Crimes and Misdemeanors* where a sitcom producer says: "If it bends, it's funny. If it breaks, it's not funny." The bending would correspond to the switching between meanings with an amusing buildup, the breaking to a switch without an amusing buildup like the case of the man living on the Upper West Side. The common element in the bending and breaking is the switching.

In some sense, that is all there is to how so many jokes work and how we come to understand them. In fact, if I stretch the point, the model may apply to practically every joke as there is always a switch between a meaning we expect, possibly hazily, and an unexpected and funny *punch line*. Here is a joke where the expectation is hazy.

> Mulla Nasruddin[3] was in the British Museum and followed a group of tourists led by a guide.
>
> Arriving in one room the guide said, "This vase is twenty-five hundred years old."
>
> The Mulla said at once, "Twenty-five hundred and three!"
>
> Everyone was impressed by the Mulla's expertise.
>
> "And how do you know?" asked the guide.
>
> The Mulla replied, "Oh, I was here three years ago and you said then that the vase was twenty-five hundred years old!"

---

3. Mulla Nasruddin probably lived in the thirteenth century in Persia or Turkey and was known as a wise man full of humorous stories with an insightful angle.

| common meaning | something vague involving expert knowledge |
|---|---|
| rare meaning | overly precise interpretation of "twenty-five hundred years old" |

Table 2.4  Common and Rare Meanings in the Mulla Nasruddin Joke

Thus, much humor, even slapstick, trades on ambiguity.[4] Of course, ambiguity can be a very serious issue as well, as we will see throughout this book.

## 2.3 Why Is Political Speech Often Extreme?

It is well known that political speech is often extreme and, as a result, risky not only for the speaker but also for their audience. Extremism creates suspicion, acrimony, fear, and hatred. The deepening authoritarianism I have mentioned has only exacerbated this general tendency. Initially, we are apt to think that only politicians or others we disagree with engage in such behavior, but the disturbing fact is that almost everyone does. Indeed, are we sufficiently aware of our own ways of speaking when we discuss politics?

Let me start with a simple recent example. In late 2018, devastating fires raged in California. In my view, they were caused primarily by global warming but were also possibly triggered by local mismanagement. Planetwide, changes in our climate have destroyed many lives, and yet many politicians and their affiliates continue to cite other reasons for these catastrophes.

An accurate and nuanced description of the state of affairs in California might have been: "Very likely, climate change is primarily responsible for the fires." In political contexts, especially divisive ones of the kind that prevail today, such a statement would have been self-defeating, as dishonest politicians would have seized on the slight uncertainty expressed not only to discredit the statement but also to offer entirely different explanations. Indeed, the more brazen

---

4. Some ultrasophisticated theorists who have treated Ambiguity as having a capital $A$ and have tried to frighten neophytes into thinking that communication is impossible have perhaps never understood such jokes.

among them did this anyway, suggesting, for example, that poor forest management was the only significant cause.

Because the stakes are high in most political situations, it becomes impossible to maintain such subtleties in one's speech. Honesty turns out not to be the best policy. So, willy-nilly, even ethical observers are often forced to switch from "Very likely, X" to "Certainly, X" whatever X may be. And if this is so for the upright, what hope is there from most in the political arena?

Let's examine the informal details of the mechanism by which this happens. Start with a high-stakes situation; consider an informationally weaker statement like "Very likely, X" rather than a bolder "X"; discover that your opponents will deliberately distort your meaning to "Not X" because "Very likely, X" leaves room for doubt and can be interpreted as weakness rather than truthfulness; and so discard the weaker statement and choose the informationally stronger but slightly dishonest "Certainly, X" or just "X". Here, X stands for a sentence like "Climate change is primarily responsible for the fires."

This would explain why political language in the public sphere tends to be less nuanced than one might wish. Basically, weak statements are spurned and turned into their opposites, and to avoid this, even well-meaning people become extreme because the stakes are high. When societies are as deeply divided as they are today, this tendency can become vicious and not only make everyone insecure but also sow fear and hatred, deepening the divide in an escalating spiral of mistrust.

This negative finding, however, points to a deeper positive truth. The key reason for this phenomenon is that in politics the stakes are often high. Why are they often high? Because, as Aristotle said, man is a political animal. We can become fully human and lead fulfilling and meaningful lives only within the context of other human beings. We are at least implicitly aware of this, and so tend to value political outcomes greatly. The kinds of societies we create, whether partial utopias or partial dystopias, determine to what degree we can actualize our potential and experience a higher level of freedom and happiness collectively and individually. Simply put, we need one another to realize ourselves.

## 2.4 Approaching Language Scientifically

I have given an informal account of how many jokes work and also why political speech lacks nuance. For the first, while there are many reasons why a more scientific description is desirable, a simple practical motivation is whether such an explanation can be used to make computers understand jokes. The idea of switching from a commonplace meaning to a rarer one seems prima facie implementable. And for the second, we can be better prepared to grasp what is going on in political communication if we know its underlying structure.

Going beyond jokes and politics, what are some of the difficulties in understanding how linguistic meaning works? I will highlight three that I consider central and that are intimately linked to AI and society. The first and most familiar is, in fact, ambiguity. Broadly understood, it enters whenever we communicate. The second, of which we are less aware although it is as common, is vagueness. If you think about it, practically every word—such as "bald" or "language"—is vague, although some words are vaguer than others. The third is even more fundamental: the presence of context in everything we say and do. It is partly because of these three phenomena that it is difficult to define things like word meaning and reference and, indeed, for computers to participate in a dialogue or for us to pin down what social structure actually is. Notice how all three are present in both jokes and political speech.

Underlying all three difficulties is the key fact of communication in society. It is a complex, circular process involving multiple conversations that both depend on existing conventional meanings and allow these very meanings to come into being. These conversations are beset by ambiguity, vagueness, and context. As a result, it has not been clear how to study communication and its counterpart, meaning. Writers like Noam Chomsky and Jerry Fodor have even said it is impossible to do so.[5]

What is required to tackle these problems is a framework that is philosophically sound and empirically adequate. To the extent that it is mathematical, the mathematics must be solid and lead to computationally tractable results because we are finite creatures who are able to communicate to a reasonable extent despite the pervasiveness of ambiguity, vagueness, and context.

The analytic tradition in philosophy—represented by figures such as Peirce, Frege, Russell, Wittgenstein, Austin, Grice, Strawson, Lewis, Kripke, Dretske,

---

5. Chomsky (2000). Personal communication with Fodor.

Barwise, Perry—has attempted to study the *form* of language and its use and the *form* of reality and the relation between the two. However, while its two main strands—so-called ideal language and ordinary language philosophy in the first half of the twentieth century and their later mixtures in the second half—have made great strides in understanding some particular aspects of verbal meaning, it hasn't gotten close enough to solving these problems, and it has yet to create a satisfactory account of the three phenomena of ambiguity, vagueness, and context, and also to generate sufficiently effective frameworks implementable on a computer. This indicates a big gap in our understanding. These philosophers have generally favored logic over other tools, and, in my view, this is why there is a gap—because logic as currently conceived does not seem to have the resources to understand communication, the origin and heart of linguistic meaning.

One of the analytic tradition's results has been a far better and deeper insight into *structure*—the understanding of which is the object of all foundational inquiry—than offered by continental structuralism or other continental traditions. But its approach has made it abstract and remote from social issues for readers who want a direct, almost visceral, connection with human emancipation as continental thought has often offered.

The continental theorists—figures such as Husserl, Heidegger, Merleau-Ponty, Sartre, Barthes, Foucault, Derrida, Bourdieu, Habermas, Taylor—have often acknowledged ambiguity and context more fully, although not vagueness, by looking beyond single sentences to texts like novels and plays and, indeed, society at large, but seldom in a scientific spirit, often claiming their structures and meanings lie beyond science but within some broader and vaguer notion of reason. There is a great diversity in these approaches so it is hard to summarize them, although it could be said that more or less all of them trace their ancestry to Descartes, Kant, and Hegel and to reactions to these philosophers. Despite some deep insights, their frameworks tend to be philosophically questionable and empirically idiosyncratic, and some of them rely on broad statements that lack the kind of detailed argument and rigor commonly found in analytic approaches. As a result, the whole enterprise becomes a bit of a hit-or-miss affair.

A consequence of the analytics' focus on single sentences and use of relatively plain language to express their arguments and the continentals' focus on whole texts and use of relatively obscure but occasionally poetic language is that the former tend to appear less interesting with respect to the common concerns we share in having meaningful lives whereas the latter appear more attractive by relating to fiction and art and society, which are intrinsically about how the world affects us in both trivial and profound ways. However, this difference in their emotional appeal should be set aside.[6]

I borrow ideas from both these traditions, and from other fields, and add ideas of my own, deploying them with the help of two highly useful mathematical tools: situation theory and game theory. I have used these tools over the past forty years to develop a framework for the understanding of communication and meaning. Situation theory was created by Jon Barwise and John Perry in the 1980s and is a qualitative account of information and context.[7] Game theory originated informally in the writings of Machiavelli and Hobbes in the sixteenth and seventeenth centuries and was formalized in the twentieth century by many mathematicians and economists, especially John von Neumann.[8] In this context, a game is a model of the core of an interaction between two or more people. I have combined the two tools in my own way, adding to each of them individually as well, in order to build a framework for meaning that is philosophically sound, empirically adequate, mathematically solid, and computationally tractable. Situation theory provides a way to understand contextual information, game theory provides a way to understand human behavior, and by putting the two together, one acquires a way to understand contextualized human behavior as it relates to information, which, as I will try to show, forms the essence of all meaning.

---

6. An example of this difference is offered by Krishna (2016): "When the French philosopher Gabriel Marcel announced impressively to one of Oxford's philosophical clubs that human freedom was the 'ontological counterweight to death', Austin invited him to explain what he meant. The request, made with his characteristic courtesy, was followed up repeatedly with appeals for further clarification. Marcel ended up saying he meant that the fact we are going to die makes all our earthly doings ultimately futile, but we carry on in full awareness of this by investing some things with value by an exercise of free will. Was this true? Maybe, maybe not, but at least that question could now be intelligibly posed."

7. Barwise and Perry (1983). They draw upon Shannon and Weaver (1949), Austin (1961/1979a), and Dretske (1981).

8. John von Neumann and Oskar Morgenstern (1944/1947).

# CHAPTER THREE

# Ambiguity and Uncertainty

Whenever there are multiple possible interpretations, as happened with the jokes in the previous chapter, there is ambiguity. The main problem ambiguity poses is that it makes it harder to infer the intended interpretation(s) in a context.

In this chapter, I will classify the many different types of ambiguity that occur in verbal language mainly to show why it is difficult to handle. These classifications will prove helpful as similar ambiguities often occur in visual and gestural symbol systems as well, not to mention other social institutions.

## 3.1  A Picture of Ambiguity

Figure 3.1 shows a picture of two types of intended meaning where ambiguities occur and have to be routinely disambiguated.

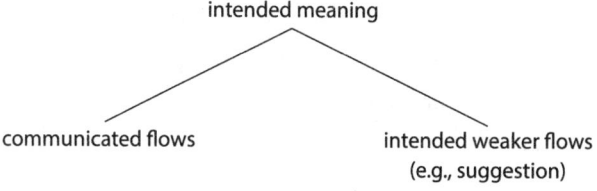

Figure 3.1  Classification of Intended Meaning

At the top, we have the category of intended meaning which divides into communicated and intended weaker flows of information from speaker to addressee. Communication is a type of transfer in which all the intentions involved are shared between the interlocutors. Weaker flows generally have some things that remain private as happens when a speaker merely suggests a meaning rather than communicates it. This kind of suggestion often occurs in the realm of art: Picasso's *Guernica*[1] may only suggest the horror of war rather than state or communicate it.

Communicated flows divide into direct and indirect meanings as shown in Figure 3.2.

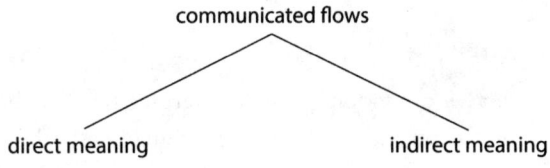

Figure 3.2  Classification of Communicated Meaning

Direct meanings can be described roughly as those meanings that come "directly" from the words in an utterance (and its context) as opposed to being implied by them. It should be apparent that such direct and indirect meanings occur not only with verbal language but also with actions and social institutions generally. They can be further classified as shown in Figure 3.3.

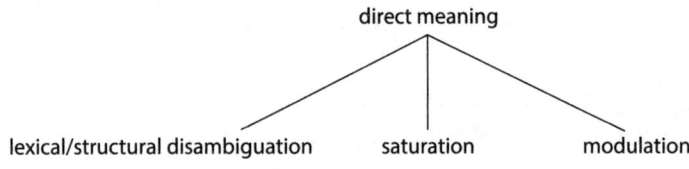

Figure 3.3  Classification of Direct Meaning

Let me briefly note the meanings of the terms "lexical ambiguity," "structural ambiguity," "saturation," and "modulation." Words like "bank" and "eye" give rise to multiple meanings in different ways. The first involves several unrelated senses such as *a financial institution of a certain kind* and *the land alongside a river*. The second involves several related senses such as *the organ of sight* or *the hole in a needle*, both involving a kind of aperture. "Bank" and "eye" also function as verbs.

---

1. The 1937 painting was a response to the bombing of Guernica, a Basque Country town in northern Spain, by Nazi Germany and Italian warplanes at the request of the Spanish Nationalists. See Wikipedia at https://en.wikipedia.org/wiki/Guernica_(Picasso).

Such ambiguities are all called *lexical*.[2] Likewise, there are ambiguities arising from sentence structures as I showed with the Groucho Marx joke.[3] Another such ambiguity occurs in the sentence "Flying planes can be dangerous." When uttered, it could mean *planes that are flying* or *to fly planes*. Such ambiguities are *structural*. A third direct type involves the reference of pronouns like "he" or "she" or "this" or "that." Along with seemingly incomplete utterances (like "Jack is taller" that can be contextually completed by something like *than Jill*), they form the category of *saturation*. I will address modulated meanings below.

Figure 3.4 shows how indirect meanings are structured.

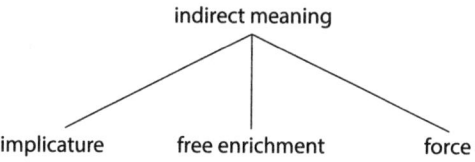

Figure 3.4   Classification of Indirect Meaning

There are indirect meanings such as an ironical utterance of "He is a fine friend" where the intended meaning is exactly the opposite of what was directly stated. There is a large class of such *implicatures*, so named by Grice[4] who attempted the first systematic way to derive them. Another example is Ann saying to Bob, "It is two p.m.," in a suitable context, implying that *it is time to go to the matinee*. There is also *free enrichment* where an utterance like "He weighs 150 pounds" is often enriched by a meaning like *in the morning before breakfast* in special contexts like, say, a doctor's clinic. Many sentences need such optional completion relative to a context for the addressee to infer a fuller intended meaning. Thirdly, as Austin,[5] building on Frege, pointed out, utterances do not just convey information but also inflect it by a *force*. So, telling a pedestrian not

---

2. That is, "relating to words." The first involving "bank" is called homonymy and the second involving "eye" polysemy.

3. Section 2.2.

4. Grice (1975, 1989). See also Ingalls (1990, Introduction) for what might have been the first *theory* of implicature and suggestion developed by Anandavardhana and Abhinavagupta who lived in the ninth and tenth centuries CE in India.

5. Austin (1961/1979b).

to cross unless the light is red also involves a warning or an order, just as asking a waiter to get you some water involves a request.

And there are mixed cases such as occur in uses of a phrase like "the stone lion" where the ordinary meaning of "lion" gets *modulated* to convey something like *an artificially made lion*. Think also of how an adjective such as "large" gets differently modulated in phrases like "the large mouse" and "the large elephant." I have grouped this under direct meanings in Figure 3.3 although it has elements of both direct and indirect meaning.

In all these instances, there are always multiple possible interpretations available that have to be disambiguated by the addressee to get at the speaker's intended meaning. They have posed significant challenges to analytic semantics owing to their contextual nature, and possibly as a result, they have often been sidelined despite the work of Austin and Grice and their followers.[6]

## 3.2 Beyond Intended Meanings

There are also meanings that go beyond intended meaning altogether and become part of the utterance meaning and discourse meaning, such as the meanings of plays like *Waiting for Godot* where the addressee may supply their own context to a greater degree than with ordinary utterances. All of these meanings, shown in Figure 3.5, involve multiple possibilities that rely even more than intended meanings on the context of utterance for their partial disambiguation.

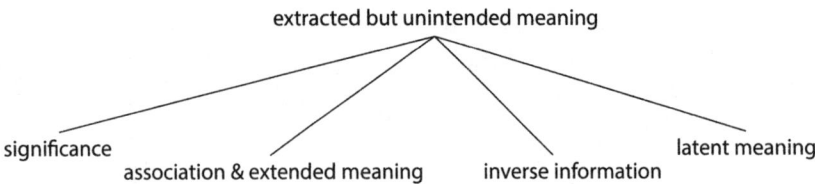

Figure 3.5 Classification of Extracted but Unintended Meaning

Such meanings, especially latent ones, have been much explored by continental theorists as they typically arise in larger discourses and texts and are often

---

6. My books, especially Parikh (2010, 2019), address the resolution of all such ambiguities.

of interest in literary criticism. There is the old joke of the three psychoanalysts stepping into an elevator one morning with the first saying "Good morning" to the other two, and the second asking the third, "What do you think he meant?" (Incidentally, this joke, too, works via the switching mechanism discussed in the previous chapter. See if you can explain it.) Freud and his followers revel in such hidden and repressed meanings and some literary critics[7] have a special instinct for this kind of meaning. These are meanings that get disclosed *despite* their author.

Latent meanings are often inferred relative to beliefs external to an utterance's context. When critics engage with a text, they may bring a theoretical framework (e.g., a Freudian one) to bear on it and this framework would then combine with the narrower contents of the text to allow such meanings to emerge. One reason why continentals and critics focus on these meanings is because the mundane intended meanings are often more straightforward for human beings to discern. Theoretically, it *is* an accomplishment to show how an intended meaning can be derived from first principles and this has occupied researchers for millennia, but critics and continental philosophers are not particularly interested in this challenge. On the other hand, the analytics have exhibited their own insularities and have failed to appreciate these richer unintended aspects of meaning. What is required is to marry the rigorous methods of semantics with this broader scope of meaning.

Here is an example of association.[8]

"He was pounding the nail when . . ."
"He was looking for the nail when . . ."

The first sentence is likely to be associated with something like a hammer. This is less likely with the second utterance. Such inferences may not be easily separable from the intended meaning of the utterance. In fact, addressees are frequently mistaken about precisely what they have heard because such associations are mixed in with the intended meaning.

I will not go through the other types of unintended meaning as they are less relevant to my goal, which is to exhibit some of the varied sorts of intended

---

7. Barthes (1957, 1968, 1977), Eagleton (2008a), etc.
8. Fernández and Cairns (2011, pp. 244–245).

and unintended meanings that complicate language and communication, and by analogy, other symbol systems and social institutions.

## 3.3 An Overall Picture

We can gather intended and unintended meanings, which together constitute utterance meaning. These lead to the larger category of discourse meaning as shown in Figure 3.6.

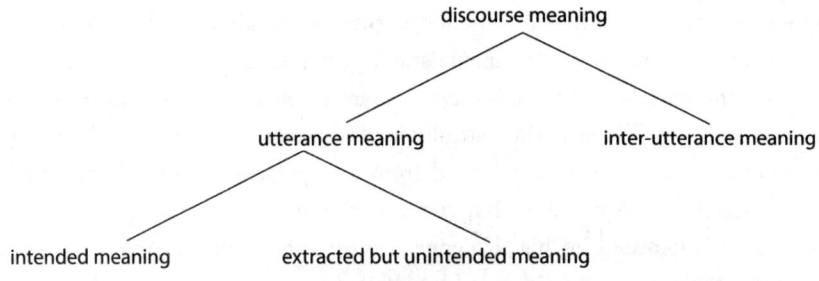

Figure 3.6 Classification of Discourse Meaning

In *Getting Even*, Woody Allen says, "Can we actually 'know' the universe? My God, it's hard enough finding your way around in Chinatown." The humor in this works partly because of the contrast between the scale of the universe and the scale of Chinatown and partly because of the bathetic fall from the loftiness of cosmological inquiry to merely getting around. This contrast and bathos—also involving a switch—are not directly present in either sentence taken by itself. It is their *juxtaposition* as part of a single discourse that gives rise to such inter-utterance meanings.

I have already briefly mentioned irony as an example of implicature.[9] Figures of speech like metaphor, metonymy, synecdoche, hyperbole, and others can all be seen as instances of modulation. For example, an utterance of "The pen is mightier than the sword" would result in a modulation of both nouns. In other words, these fancier uses of language can all be reduced to the kinds of meanings

---

9. Section 3.1.

introduced above. This, then, provides a more or less complete account of the many types of meaning that occur in language.

Although I have classified all these varied meanings into seemingly separate categories, there can be considerable overlap between them in an actual utterance. The diagrams are still helpful as they enable us to understand the different ways in which ambiguities arise and create uncertainty. As should be evident from the foregoing, disambiguation is a formidable task. We are still far from figuring out how we do it but I will show one way to approach it when I discuss communication.

Many such ambiguities also occur in images, actions, and objects generally as well as in most social institutions. For example, a namaste carried out with a bow may indicate excessive formality or a show of respect. This might be seen as an instance of a structural ambiguity in the composite gesture or a case of modulation. This is one reason for understanding ambiguity in some detail as it occurs in language. Another is the challenge it poses to AI.

## 3.4  Ambiguity and Artificial Intelligence

Given this somewhat bewildering array of interpretive possibilities, could an AI agent ever understand language? There are actually two questions packed into this single query, one relatively straightforward and the other quite subtle. The first: Could an AI agent disambiguate such ambiguities as we are generally able to, that is, could it identify the intended meaning in an utterance of something like "Fred went to the bank" or "Fred ran"? The second: Could it *understand* what it has disambiguated? What does "understand" even mean?

Many simpler ambiguities (e.g., words like "bank" and "ran") can be disambiguated just by relying on large amounts of training data. This is what search engines and chatbots are often able to do. Here is how the stunning new language model ChatGPT[10] released by the company OpenAI in late 2022 responded to an ambiguous question:

---

10. See the Wikipedia article at https://en.wikipedia.org/wiki/ChatGPT. "ChatGPT" stands for "Chat Generative Pre-trained Transformer." See also the original paper on transformers by Vaswani et al. (2017) and OpenAI's paper on reinforcement learning with human feedback by Ouyang et al. (2022). Finally, see the recent article by Cade Metz and Mike Isaac

Me: Can you fish at the bank?

ChatGPT: It depends on where the "bank" is located. If the "bank" is referring to a financial institution, then no, it would not be possible to fish there. However, if the "bank" is referring to the edge of a body of water, such as a river or lake, then it may be possible to fish there, as long as it is legal and done in a responsible manner.

It's important to check whether the area is designated for fishing, and if it requires any specific permit or regulations. Furthermore, it's also important to be aware of the local fishing laws and regulations regarding the type of fish that can be caught and the methods that can be used, as well as any seasonality and size limits.[11]

This is impressive although a human would probably have been less literal about the ambiguity and would have assumed that something like a riverbank was intended. This is because the context of the ambiguous word "bank" in the question has two components, a linguistic context (the rest of the sentence "Can you fish at the") and a situational context (what I will later call an utterance situation), and ChatGPT, being a language model, has no access to the latter the way a person would.[12]

Now consider the humdrum sentences below spoken to ChatGPT or even to a robot:[13]

"The weight went through the wall because it was made of iron."
"The weight stopped at the wall because it was made of iron."

How would the robot know whether "it" referred to *the weight* or *the wall* in these utterances? *We* know that in the first, "it" refers to *the weight*, and in the second, to *the wall*. Clearly, no simple grammatical rule such as preferring

---

in the *New York Times* at https://www.nytimes.com/2023/02/07/technology/meta-artificial-intelligence-chatgpt.html on similar chatbots developed by Meta and Google as well as a transcript of the dialogue Kevin Roose of the *New York Times* had with ChatGPT at https://www.nytimes.com/2023/02/16/technology/bing-chatbot-transcript.html.

11. Keep in mind that ChatGPT keeps learning so its response to the same question later may be different from what I got.

12. The situational context also contains the "world knowledge" humans have.

13. The AI pioneer Terry Winograd probably first set up similar sentences.

the subject (i.e., "the weight") would suffice because the reference changes to *the wall* in the second sentence. It is possible that exposure to data would help here as well but it is likely the accuracy of the predictions would suffer. Indeed, ChatGPT assigned the same referent (*the weight*) in both utterances, getting the second one wrong.

In the following discourse, the situation is even more complex:

> John's spaghetti spilled on Fred's jacket. He didn't notice. His jacket, however, was ruined."[14]

In the second sentence, whom does "he" refer to? Even we would not know whether "he" means *John* or *Fred* until we encountered the third sentence. Initially, the reference is indeterminate (or probabilistic) and later it gets resolved to *Fred*. Would an AI agent be able to manage such delicate discriminations as we easily do?

Here is a third example of a commonplace type:

> "Fred got into a cab. The radio was blaring."

Notice that the speaker has said "The radio," not "A radio," implying some particular radio available from the utterance, but no radio has been mentioned explicitly, and so it has to be inferred from the fact that cabs generally have radios. We know such facts or can guess them from the context, but could a computer? Just like the case of the weight and the wall, this requires some general knowledge of the world, a tacit awareness of the speaker's rationality, and the further ability to make appropriate inferences from these items. However, such examples could also potentially be tackled partially with training data but the way a language model would manage them would be fundamentally different from the way we do, our way being based on *understanding* them, a notion I will discuss later.[15]

There is a great deal of complexity even in such seemingly trivial utterances, and the kind of fine-grained disambiguation we are able to carry out effortlessly is currently beyond the reach of AI. There are information extraction engines and related applications that may partially succeed in *correlating* the right

---

14. This and the next example are from Clark and Parikh (2007).
15. See Sections 4.4, 4.5, 7.6, and 11.4.

interpretations with one or more sentences, but they lack the flexible understanding humans exhibit and, like ChatGPT, are not as reliable as humans typically are. I will presently sketch a way that comes closer to solving this difficulty for AI in a theoretically principled way.

This is not all. We are frequently able to infer various sorts of indirect and unintended meanings from single utterances and larger texts by bringing more complex interpretive mechanisms as well as our personal worlds and frameworks to bear on the task. Could an AI agent tell the difference between an implicit request and an implicit order? And could it ever *understand* the open-ended *Waiting for Godot* when even we cannot do it satisfactorily?

Interestingly, ChatGPT performed spectacularly well in synthesizing a response to this very question although with occasional errors:

> Me: What is the meaning of the play *Waiting for Godot*?
>
> ChatGPT: *Waiting for Godot* is a play written by Samuel Beckett in the 1950s, and it is considered one of the most important works of the 20th century. The play is a two-act tragicomedy in which two characters, Vladimir and Estragon, wait for the arrival of a person named Godot, who never arrives. The two characters spend their time discussing their situation, playing games, and engaging in various activities while they wait.
>
> The play is often seen as a commentary on the human condition, and it raises many questions about the nature of existence, the meaning of life, and the possibility of salvation. The play explores themes such as the passage of time, the human need for meaning and purpose, and the nature of human relationships.
>
> The play is considered as a masterpiece of absurdist theatre, which is a genre that emphasizes the meaningless of human existence. The play's characters are waiting for someone or something that never appears, which reflects the human's quest for purpose and meaning, and the frustration of waiting for something that may never happen.
>
> Many interpretations have been made of the play, and some see it as a metaphor for the human condition, the search for meaning and the sense of waiting for something that may never come. It can also be seen as a commentary on the human need for hope, even in the face of despair, and the importance of human connections in the

face of the void of existence. The play's open-endedness and lack of a clear resolution has also been seen as a reflection of the human search for answers and the fact that life is ultimately uncertain and unknowable.

Remarkable as this answer is, it nevertheless raises the deep and difficult question about whether it knows what any of this *means*, whether this isn't just a *pattern* of lexical symbols that *we* find meaningful, reminiscent of the infinite monkey theorem, different though it is, which states that a monkey typing randomly for infinitely long will almost surely eventually produce Shakespeare.

# CHAPTER FOUR

# Vagueness and Value

Except perhaps for certain technical words like "electron" and "photosynthesis," practically every word in a natural language is likely to be vague. What is vagueness and why does it arise? With words like "electron," for which we develop progressively more accurate definitions, one knows exactly whether or not something is an electron. There is no room for doubt, even if we later discover we were wrong in our identifications. It is presumably the same with "photosynthesis." Such words are precise. Vagueness arises when words are not precise and borderline cases can occur. A completely hairless person is certainly bald and a person with a full head of hair is certainly not bald, but there are many cases in between where we cannot be sure and where different people may have different judgments. Even we ourselves may judge differently on different occasions. This makes "bald" vague. A little reflection on varied words like "chair," "art," and "democracy" shows that most words do not have crisp boundaries.

## 4.1 Words and Concepts

Earlier, I said that the conventional meanings of words were not other words as found in a dictionary but properties or attributes. More precisely, they are *concepts*, mental stores or representations of collections of things in the world. So the concept *electron* is a mental portrayal of the collection of electrons and the concept *bald* is a mental portrayal of the collection of bald persons. Each of us has a concept for words like "electron" and "bald." In the case of precise words, there is one right concept, but in the case of vague words, there is a certain fuzziness. Your concept can be a little different from mine and we can all still get along fine when we communicate.

Why does vagueness arise? The properties of things in the world—such as their color, shape, and size if they are physical objects—often occur along a continuum rather than discretely. When does a hairy person shift into being bald and when does a quiet space become noisy? So, when different people group things together in a concept, they draw the boundaries in different places and do this in an imprecise way. We need sharp concepts for scientific work as we need to identify their necessary and sufficient conditions but for everyday life it is the efficiency of communication that matters. Vagueness allows us to get by with relatively few concepts for many different collections of things. So we need to know fewer words and store less information in our heads. The price for this is occasional misunderstanding because interlocutors may demarcate their concepts differently.

## 4.2 Toward a Scientific Account

I offer an outline of my own account that draws upon ideas from cognitive psychology.[1]

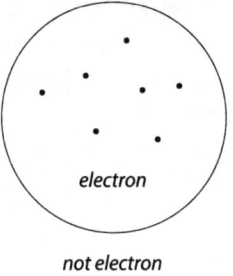

Figure 4.1  A Precise Concept

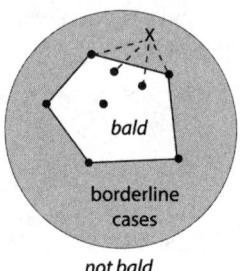

Figure 4.2  A Vague Concept

Every person starts with exemplars for concepts like *electron* and *bald* that are learned from the wider community in which they participate. The dots inside Figures 4.1 and 4.2 indicate such exemplars. Ann may call someone bald and Bob may pick up this exemplar from her. Each exemplar of a concept has multiple properties or attributes that take on particular values. *Bald* may involve

---

1. Parikh (2019, chap. 11).

attributes such as the number of hairs on the scalp, the number of completely hairless patches on the scalp, the fraction of the scalp that is hairless, and so on.[2]

The basic new idea is to see how "far" a candidate, say Fred, is from all the exemplars an agent like Ann has for *bald*. The x in the gray area in Figure 4.2 represents Fred and the dashed lines to the exemplars represent the relevant distances. This calculation is done through the relevant attributes of the exemplars. If the candidate is "near" the exemplars, he can be judged to be bald. If he is far from them, he can be judged to be not bald. If he is neither too near nor too far, he would have to be treated as a borderline case, neither clearly bald nor clearly not bald.

| Fred near exemplars | Fred is judged to be bald |
| --- | --- |
| Fred far from exemplars | Fred is judged to be not bald |
| Fred neither near nor far from exemplars | Fred is a borderline case |

Table 4.1  Judging Whether Fred Is Bald or Not Bald or Borderline Bald

Since different agents will have picked up different exemplars from time to time from their interactions with the community, their judgments about who is bald or not bald or borderline bald will naturally differ somewhat. Moreover, such decisions could change even for the same agent, as Ann may invoke more or less stringent criteria in different situations to suit her purposes. For example, on one occasion she may be more stringent and say, "I wouldn't date Fred—he's bald"; on another she may be lax and say, "Fred isn't bald—he needs a haircut." So the sentence "Fred is bald" may be true for Ann in one situation, false for her in another, and indeterminate in a third.

This idea of distance from exemplars allows us to define a concept as vague for an agent in some situation just when it has borderline cases in that situation. Otherwise, it is precise like *electron* because such concepts have no borderline cases. We can extend this to properties which can be thought of as averages of

---

2. There are, in fact, "objective" rankings for some concepts like *bald* and *democracy* that are implicitly based on a similar idea as can be seen from the Norwood scale (https://www.healthline.com/health/norwood-scale) and the Democracy Index (https://en.wikipedia.org/wiki/Democracy_Index).

the concepts of members of the community: a property is vague when the community's corresponding concepts are vague.

There is a lot more to say about the account I have sketched including how it can help us resolve paradoxes like the sorites.[3]

## 4.3 Essentially Contested Concepts and the Emergence of Value

A consequence of my approach is that what may be true or false or indeterminate for Ann may not be so for Bob or Cathy. In other words, there is *no* agent-independent or objective truth when vague words are used. However, because the agents belong to the same linguistic community and the exemplars each agent draws upon are generally shared through communication, the agents are likely to agree most of the time. Indeed, for a concept or conventional meaning to be socially useful, its exemplars *must* be sufficiently shared by the community. This is nevertheless part of the reason why certain types of fake information are difficult to dispute as someone may deliberately distort the prevailing meaning of a word. For example, a politician may describe their country as secular even though religious minorities are persecuted by the state or affiliated organizations. Here the word "secular" is vague and different states can be judged secular in different ways.

Because practically every word in a natural language is vague, practically every word involves our judgment. These judgments result from the exemplars more or less shared by us and the calculation of distance from them. This observation applies not only to mundane concepts like *bald* and *tall* but also to weighty ones like *art, science, politics,* and *good*. Vague concepts are inherently *contestable*[4]

---

3. The sorites paradox, also called the heap paradox ("sorites" derives from the Greek word for "heap"), is generally attributed to Eubulides, a Greek philosopher from the fourth century BCE.

4. My use of the term is wider than Gallie's (1956) as he restricts it to traditional areas of philosophy such as ethics, aesthetics, and political philosophy where contests over the meaning of a word are endless and conceptual differences are greater. But transitory and less material contests also occur over everyday concepts such as *bald* that can therefore be assimilated to the same idea.

because individual and group agents may have different exemplars, may consider different attributes for each exemplar, or may calculate distance differently, and, as a consequence, arrive at potentially different concepts with substantially less overlap than I have discussed so far.

Since most concepts are vague and involve judgment, language emerges as an agonistic site of innumerable large or small potential contests against a background of partially shared conventional meanings. The actual differences that occur over the meaning and use of words reflect the large or small differential *interests* of the members of the linguistic community. Two individuals or groups may diverge over whether someone is bald or, more significantly, over whether some policy is democratic or some action is good.[5] Thus vagueness has an extremely important consequence: it unexpectedly gives language a *normative* and even a *moral* dimension. The fine structure of meaning partially constitutes the contrasting *values* that prevail in society.

Because properties may be viewed as averages of the individual concepts in a community, it is not just vague language but also vague properties that are normative. Since most concepts are vague, most properties are vague, and thus we get the somewhat startling view that the world itself is largely based on human values and judgments. This is one novel way in which values emerge naturally through communication in society without requiring anything otherworldly.[6]

It is also possible to begin to appreciate how language and meaning are both individual and social. Neither are we locked into our minds solipsistically nor are we wholly public. Through sharing our exemplars, each one of us builds their own overlapping concepts. I will later extend this idea to the more encompassing notion of a language game, a term I borrow from Wittgenstein but use in my own way.

---

5. Connolly (1993) offers an illuminating discussion of the contests surrounding such fundamental concepts in political theory as *politics, interests, power*, and *freedom*. He shows how these debates are constitutive of politics itself and therefore how conceptual revision is a necessary condition for political change.

6. Vagueness is not the only language-related source of values. The Romantic conception of language (e.g., Taylor 1985/1999) provides another way for norms to arise through language. A third somewhat controversial way is based on the speech act theory of Austin (1975) and especially Habermas (1976/1998, 1988/1998).

## 4.4 Vagueness and Artificial Intelligence

The natural question that arises is whether a computer might be able to handle vague concepts and properties. This would seem to be an essential requirement especially for tasks like creating a flexible chatbot that can converse but also to enable wider object recognition as when there is a chair in a room.

My approach to vagueness has some affinity with contemporary machine learning because both involve the use of exemplars to construct a concept, the latter through training data. There are interesting differences as well, because my method involves the calculation of distance from these exemplars to give a definition of vagueness.

Equally important, our exemplars for concepts like *bald* or *democracy* are more or less shared with the community and so our individual concepts or conventional meanings also overlap sufficiently to generally allow us to communicate. If computers were inducted into the community in the same way, they could presumably also judge whether Fred is bald or whether the United States is democratic today in roughly the way Ann and Bob do. If this were done across all the words in a language, an AI agent could potentially acquire the same sort of concepts or conventional meanings we do. To a certain limited degree, it would share our world, although a lot more is required for the agent to act in it as we are able to.

There seem to be two general sorts of difficulties with carrying out this kind of procedure. The first difficulty is that our knowledge of the external world minimally involves many *interlinked* (as opposed to isolated) concepts and is bound up with the kinds of actions we undertake. As we saw earlier, on one occasion, Ann may not want to date Fred because she finds him bald, and on another, she may tell him to get a haircut because she doesn't find him bald. This isn't inconsistency but context-dependence. It makes realizing the task of sharing our conceptual world more challenging for a robot because it would have to be endowed with contextual linkages among concepts and actions.

The second problem should bring to mind Google's getting a neural network to recognize the picture of a cat. The network can perhaps even recognize a real cat but it does not have the web of belief and possibly even tactile and other sensory experiences involving a cat that we are ordinarily socialized into from childhood on.[7] For example, it does not know that a cat can be a pet or that it is a mammal. There are whole cultures surrounding cats and different cultures understand cats differently. Moreover, such cultures may be hard to reduce to training a neural network.

Thus, training an AI agent to even partly share our conceptual world remains an open question. It is difficult to know whether today's neural networks are up to the task or additional models of the kind I have outlined here will be required.[8] If full-fledged humanlike concepts like *bald* and *democracy* turn out to be unattainable for an AI agent, then there is no hope for it to acquire our kind of language. On the other hand, if even a single cluster of concepts could somehow be transferred to it, then thousands more would become accessible because it is easy to repeat any success with a computer. This, then, is part of the challenge in getting AI agents to develop a flexible intelligence of the kind we possess.

How does ChatGPT fare in the face of such obstacles? As the reader will undoubtedly have noticed, the whole discussion turns on the subtle but frustrating question of what understanding is. Certainly, ChatGPT is able to churn out reasonable responses to various vague questions:

> Me: Is Hungary democratic?
>
> ChatGPT: Yes, Hungary is a democratic country, but it has faced criticism in recent years for changes to its electoral system, media laws, and curbs on the independence of the judiciary that some have argued undermine its democratic character.
>
> Me: Can you handle vague words?
>
> ChatGPT: As a language model, I can handle vague words to some extent by using the context of the input and my training data to make educated guesses about the intended meaning. However, vagueness can make it difficult to understand the intended meaning, so my answer may not be as accurate or specific as it could be.
>
> For example, if a word such as "it" is used in a sentence, I would have to use context clues to infer what "it" is referring to. If there is not

---

7. Hubert Dreyfus (2012) has long argued for this kind of perspective based on insights from Heidegger, Merleau-Ponty, and Bourdieu.

8. The "knowledge approach" to concepts discussed by Murphy (2004, chap. 3) is also especially relevant here.

enough context or the input is too vague, I may be unable to provide a specific or accurate answer.

It's also worth noting that my understanding of the meaning of certain words or phrases may not always align with the intended meaning of the speaker or writer, and that my training data may not include all the nuances of certain words or phrases.

Again, this is impressive, but our judgment of its performance ought to turn on whether its answers are simply *patterns* it has generated *without* any actual connection to the world it is *about* or are similar to what an expert on Hungary or vagueness might say based on a partial *understanding* of the relevant subject matter. There appears to be a great divide on this matter with some claiming (as ChatGPT itself seems to) that the language model does understand meanings and others claiming it does not, and yet still others claiming the issue of understanding is irrelevant as long as its behavior is more or less appropriate to the queries posed. Clearly, an understanding of understanding is required and this is what I will begin to address in the next section and more fully later.[9]

As we have also seen, vagueness partly produces a moral world. Even if an AI agent could be inducted into our communities by giving it our more or less shared conceptual world, would a driverless car or a chatbot endowed with such knowledge be a moral agent? I will return to this question when we discuss my accounts of how language acquires meaning and situated AI.

## 4.5  Can Computers Think?

Related to this discussion is the often-asked question, "Can computers think?" This has been widely debated in AI and cognitive science and philosophy. Alan Turing, perhaps the founding figure of computer science, himself considered it.[10] The question has resurfaced recently owing to the growing ubiquity of AI in daily life based primarily on various ways of deploying neural networks and the massive availability of data.

---

9. See Sections 7.6 and 11.4.
10. Turing (1950, 1996).

The key to answering the question is knowing how to approach it. The main thing to notice is that not only is "think" vague, it is also ambiguous. We use the word in a bewildering variety of ways depending on the context. How can we possibly answer such a question without first determining what meaning we should attach to it?

There are three principal ways to disambiguate "think" as illuminatingly discussed by the philosopher Jack Copeland.[11] One is the experiential or phenomenological sense which ascribes thought only to those beings that are conscious.[12] By "conscious" I mean having an inner qualitative feel that accompanies experiences. This seems to be the wrong type of restriction for two reasons. The first is that human beings do a lot of nonconscious thinking—for instance, when we communicate with each other. We are seldom fully conscious of all the planning and comprehension that goes on when we utter and interpret sentences. The second reason is of a conceptual sort: it seems arbitrary to yoke thinking to consciousness. Why should it be necessary for something that thinks to be conscious?

Another sense is biological: assuming only beings with our biochemistry are capable of thought. But an alien from outer space could convince us it could think and have a completely different neurophysiology. So this distinction will also not do.

The last meaning of "think" is the commonsense one that involves the ability to "form plans, analyze situations, deliberate, reason, exploit analogies, revise beliefs in the light of experience, weigh up conflicting interests, formulate hypotheses and match them against evidence, make reasonable decisions on the basis of imperfect information, and so forth."[13]

Crucially, this ability is not just tied to external actions but also to the internal processes that cause the external actions. Otherwise it may be possible to demonstrate it behaviorally in a relatively narrow domain—such as playing chess using brute-force search, as IBM's program Deep Blue did in the mid-1990s—that would not add up to thinking because the actions were not executed in the right way. We recognize one another as thinking beings because we know our internal processes are similar. Of course, this is not an unassailable argument

---

11. Copeland (1993, chap. 3).

12. Block (2002) seems to hold this view.

13. Copeland (1993, p. 55). Perhaps this view was first stated explicitly by Hobbes (1997, chaps. 1–10) in the seventeenth century.

for the requirement of relevant internal processes, just something that makes it plausible.

Can one say more about the nature of these internal processes in an abstract way that does not arbitrarily restrict them to our biology? This is a highly controversial topic with weighty opinions on all sides.[14] In my view, the agent involved must be at least minimally aware of its environment, its situatedness, so that it "knows" it is reasoning about the world and acting in it.[15] Another way of putting this is to say that it must have not only a semantics but also a minimal awareness of its semantics—of its connection with its embedding world.[16] This is a meta-level constraint that makes plain the role of meaning in AI. A chimpanzee clearly satisfies the constraint and an ant does not but what about a crow? What about a Roomba robot vacuum cleaner that responds to the room it is vacuuming? What does "minimal awareness of its environment" mean? It need not involve being conscious, but it is difficult to give a precise criterion even though it is evident that these considerations link up with those involved in getting an AI agent to share our conceptual world.

Despite this imprecision, we can say that any agent—whether a person, another animal, or complex machine—that can do the range of things in this third sense of "think" in the right way can be said to think. The ability to represent with clarity and flexibility—and to represent such representations—plays a crucial role in executing this strategic power. Computation of a certain sort is the key and the difference between persons and many other animals and most machines is the relative complexity and kind of calculations involved.

The flexibility and complexity and kind of computation required make this last concept vague. Thinking in this sense is an essentially contested concept. As we have seen, vague concepts involve clear cases, borderline cases, and cases where the concept clearly does not apply. So we should expect all three sorts of cases to arise in our application of this concept to a potential candidate for

---

14. See, for example, Searle (1980). A related recent study is Burkart et al. (2017).

15. I don't mean it must know in a literal sense as knowledge involves having beliefs caused in a certain way and beliefs involve having a certain type of digitally represented information, something that not all simpler agents may be able to have even though they may be capable of thinking. See Chapter 5 and also Dretske (1981, p. 86).

16. This is broadly called "apperception" and has been considered by many philosophers from Descartes to Sartre. See especially Danto (1979, chap. 2) and Rosenberg (1981). It is also called "metacognition" in psychology and AI. It is pervasive in Indian epistemology.

thinking. Moreover, where we draw the line will to an extent be arbitrary and depend on the community's exemplars. AI researchers tend to set the bar relatively low and humanists tend to set the bar relatively high.

The AI that is all around us is often called *narrow* as each AI agent does somewhat narrow tasks—such as playing Go or Jeopardy or responding to varied prompts as ChatGPT does—although even these harbor many complexities. The neural networks involved do partially represent the embedding world in which they have to act in a way that earlier syntactic symbol-processing systems did not. Do they have a minimal awareness of it? This is where the vagueness hinders a clear resolution. My own prejudice is to say that current AI agents do not think, but there is nothing to rule out this possibility in the future—whether or not they are conscious and whether or not they have our biology.

Even so, narrow AI is quite impressive and will profoundly transform the economy and society. To shift the focus momentarily to the related question of intelligence,[17] few people seem to believe that AI currently has methods that will allow it to achieve general intelligence, let alone ultra-intelligence that surpasses human intelligence. But what if many narrow agents were combined into a more flexible and meta-level agent that possessed real strategic power?

## 4.6 The Story So Far

This first part of the book focused, in an intertwined way, on what meaning is generally, on its instantiation in language together with the pervasive difficulties of ambiguity and vagueness, and on the resulting challenges for AI. I introduced some intricacies surrounding language not only to get a better feel for what is involved in building a general intelligence but also because language is analogous to other social institutions, and the latter are also ambiguous and vague, and pose many similar obstacles to a scientific understanding.

In the next part, I will approach the problem of context and develop the two mathematical frameworks—situation theory and situated game theory—that will move the plot forward toward our ultimate quest for a partial utopia.

---

17. Chollet (2019). My view of intelligence demands more: see the discussion of persons in Section 9.3.

# PART II

## SITUATIONS AND GAMES

# CHAPTER FIVE

# The Ubiquity of Context

The novelist David Foster Wallace once narrated the following story in a commencement speech: "There are these two young fish swimming along and they happen to meet an older fish swimming the other way, who nods at them and says, 'Morning, boys. How's the water?' And the two young fish swim on for a bit, and then eventually one of them looks over at the other and goes, 'What the hell is water?'" Wallace added, "The immediate point of the fish story is that the most obvious, ubiquitous, important realities are often the ones that are the hardest to see and talk about."[1]

Not only our more-or-less shared world but also the smaller situations we inhabit are, like this ambient water, often invisible but always inescapable. Situations or contexts accompany all individual entities, whether they are inanimate or animate, whether they are planets and stars, or forks and knives, or fishes and humans, or books and civilizations. They also accompany other types of entities such as properties of things like Fred being *bald* or a country being *democratic*, as well as relations between things like a planet *circling* a star, a fork *complementing* a knife, a goldfish being *smaller* than a human, or a book *belonging* to modern times. One of the countless ways in which we become aware of these surrounding situations is through simple actions like saying "It is four p.m." on, say, October 18, 2023, in New York and conveying to an addressee that it is four p.m. on that particular day in New York even though the sentence contains no explicit mention of this relatively sparse context that we might call a discourse or utterance situation.[2]

---

1. David Foster Wallace commencement speech to graduating class at Kenyon College, 2005.
2. These insights come not only from Buddhism (e.g., Garfield 1995, pp. 87–94) and the more recent continental tradition of Hegel (1977) and especially Husserl (1913/1967, pp. 68–71) and Heidegger (1927/1962, Division One), as well as Sartre (1963), Merleau-Ponty (1962, pref.), and Gadamer (see Malpas 2018), but also from the ecological psychology of J. J. Gibson (1986/2015) and Michael Turvey (2019), and especially from the situated analytic framework

All living things are generally involved in some practical activity. Ann and Bob could be working or resting or talking or looking or thinking. What makes these actions practical is their being directed to some end. As Ann traverses her day, she has a diffuse feeling of being in a world she generally ignores unless something causes her to attend to it. If she dwells on this vaguely sensed whole, she will notice smaller situations of which she is also a part, such as the discourse situation in which she is telling Bob a joke.

Husserl expresses this sense of an embedding world thus:[3]

> In this way, when consciously awake, I find myself at all times, and without my ever being able to change this, set in relation to a world which, through its constant changes, remains one and ever the same. It is continually "present" for me, and I myself am a member of it. Therefore this world is not there for me as a mere *world of facts and affairs*, but, with the same immediacy, as a *world of values, a world of goods, a practical world*. Without further effort on my part I find the things before me furnished not only with the qualities that befit their positive nature, but with value-characters such as beautiful or ugly, agreeable or disagreeable, pleasant or unpleasant, and so forth.[4] Things in their immediacy stand there as objects to be used, the "table" with its "books," the "glass to drink from," the "vase," the "piano," and so forth. These values and practicalities, they too belong to *the constitution of the "actually present" objects as such*, irrespective of my turning or not turning to consider them or indeed any other objects. The same considerations apply of course just as well to the men and beasts in my surroundings as to "mere things." They are my "friends" or my "foes," my "servants" or "superiors," "strangers" or "relatives," and so forth.

---

of Barwise and Perry (1983). I use their diverse insights in my own way, especially as they belong to different traditions and have seldom been brought together as I am doing here.

3. Husserl (1913/1967, pp. 70–71).

4. Here, "positive" means *empirical* or *factual* and "value-characters" means *properties involving values*. Fred's being bald is a "positive" property and his baldness being disagreeable is a "value-character" and both are *immediately* encountered even though only the former property belongs primarily to Fred.

In some sense, this is the fundamental condition we find ourselves in: oriented to a world of objects occurring as constituents of facts and values and goal-directed activity in one or more situations.[5] We could even call it 'the human condition' described in the barest of ways. It occurs in two possible modes—analog and digital—that are often present in combination.

## 5.1 Analog and Digital

These common terms are usually identified with what is continuous and discrete, with things that take place along a continuum and those that happen in chunks, the archetype being the bits 0 and 1 that form the basis of a digital computer. The philosopher Fred Dretske introduced a generalization of this distinction that he applied to all kinds of representations.[6]

If Ann asks Bob, "How full is the glass?", he could either show her the glass or say, "It is half full." The first response reveals not just that the glass is half full but discloses in addition the size and shape of the glass, what liquid it has in it, and also that it is half empty. This is called an analog representation of the information because it contains more specific information than Ann requested. The second response conveys solely what was asked, nothing more and nothing less. It is a digital representation.

We extract a fair bit of digital information from our surroundings but a great deal is omitted. During this conversion, there is always a *loss* of information because not all that is taken in is digitized, and language can handle only the digitized part. When we want to describe seemingly ineffable aspects of our thoughts—like the glimmer of an idea—we have to digitize some of our analog information. That is why *articulating* our ideas and experiences is seldom easy. Such a gap between word and world, possibly responsible for some of our sense of alienation, becomes most evident in the arts.

Music, dance, and painting are broadly analog whereas literature is broadly digital, but all art is able to enlist both modes via suggestion and implied

---

5. Heidegger (1927/1962, p. 368), too, says: "In saying 'I', I have in view the entity which in each case I am as an 'I-am-in-a-world'. Kant did not see the phenomenon of the world...." Also, Heidegger (1927/1962, Division One).

6. Dretske (1981, p. 177). See also Goodman (1976).

meanings.[7] When we try to capture our experience of dance in words, we sense correctly that we are losing a lot of information. That is why we say a picture is worth a thousand words.

One can see how the digital/analog distinction generalizes the discrete/continuous distinction, because a continuous representation is always analog but not vice versa, and a discrete representation is always digital but not vice versa. That is, the former more general distinction can be applied to more representations than the latter less general distinction.

A simple way to think about the two modes is that in analog representations the information represented is available only implicitly whereas in digital representations it is explicit and articulated.

## 5.2 Ways of Being

When Ann and Bob are talking, their awareness of their dialogue situation may be largely implicit. To the extent it is, it is analog. To the extent it is explicit, it is digital. As should be obvious, much of our awareness is usually mixed: partly implicit and partly explicit. Often, when we are focused on something like telling a joke, the content of the joke is fairly explicit in our minds whereas the precise way we will do the telling remains relatively implicit. That is, the ends of our practical activities are generally more explicit than the means by which we might bring them about.[8]

These mixed ways of being are fundamental and they occur in all our dealings with the world, both in our everyday interactions and in the establishing of the entities that underlie them which we tend to take for granted.

---

7. But see Goodman (1976) who has a more complicated view of the matter.

8. This is similar to but also different from the way in which Heidegger (1927/1962, Division One, chaps. 3 and 5) conceives of activity via his notions of "ready-to-hand" and "present-at-hand." In particular, he seems not to allow mixed modes, although I think they are the most common. When hammering a nail, we focus on the nail more than on the hammer, an activity that combines both modes.

## 5.3 What Does the World Have in It?

I have started with the world in which we find ourselves. As I observed at the outset, there are other words that describe similar encompassing wholes: contexts, situations, conditions, ecological niches, frames, fields, systems, environments, and backgrounds. Readers from different fields will recognize the relevant terms from their own domains.

As we go about our daily activities, we carve up reality and create smaller wholes like the dialogue situation in which Ann and Bob talk to each other. We have seen that such situations contain individuals and their properties and relations to other individuals. They generally contain items that are a part of reality but can also contain things—like ghosts, goblins, and gods—that are not real. Carving up reality means individuating the entities in it and making them distinct objects of our perception and action. Individuation is digital.

Not only are there individuals, properties, and relations but there are also composite entities, such as individuals *having* properties and *standing in* relations to other individuals. There is not only the individual object *fork* and its property *steel* but there is also the compounded entity *fork having the property steel*. Likewise, there is the relational object *fork complementing knife* which has two individual objects *fork* and *knife* together with the relation of *complementing* between them. In other words, we cannot see the fork without also seeing its steel and we automatically think of holding a fork in one hand and a knife in the other and think of the two as complementary.

Complexes like *fork having the property steel* and *fork complementing knife* are called *states of affairs*. When we carve up reality, we first individuate or discriminate situations, then states of affairs, and then the individuals, properties, and relations that constitute them. So we may start with a "holistic" situation at a dinner table, then notice the two states of affairs it contains as *fork having the property steel* and *fork complementing knife*, and further notice the individuals *fork* and *knife*, the property *steel*, and the relation *complementing*.

When a state of affairs reflects reality, it is called a *fact*. So *the earth circling the sun* is a fact, whereas *there being a ghost in the cabinet* is not. Or, if you wish, going back to the example of the California fires, *global warming causing the fires* is very likely a fact whereas *poor forest management resulting in the fires* is probably not. The notions of states of affairs and facts may be a bit hard to grasp at first but once understood it becomes evident that they are all around us and that we deal with them all the time.

Some social theorists like to say all facts are "socially produced" or "socially constructed." This sort of language makes it seem that the existence of all facts is up to us, but this is clearly wrong. Otherwise, we could simply stop believing in gravity and jump off a tall building without any consequences. What it is correct to say is that facts are socially *individuated, noticed,* or *acknowledged* by us. When this happens, we can include them in our reasoning about the world and our actions in it. But if we fail to individuate or notice a fact, that does not make it disappear. The process of science is precisely discovering more and more facts as part of a larger structure.

However, the words and concepts with which we choose to name and identify facts may not be neutral and may reveal only some of their facets. To take an everyday example, two different names were used for the planet Venus, the morning star and the evening star, until it was discovered they were the same object. The two names point to different properties of Venus. In the same way, the British named the 1857 Indian uprising against the British East India Company the Indian Mutiny, whereas some nationalistic Indians call it the First War of Independence. These two different identifications offer different subjective perspectives on the *same* objective event just as happens in Akira Kurosawa's film *Rashomon* and in the ancient Indian story of the six blind men and the elephant.

If you are in Montreal and I am in New York, you will say Boston is to your south and I will say it is to my north, but it is easy to grasp that this is an objective fact seen from two subjective points of view, each of which is also a fact. A half-filled glass may be described as half full or half empty but it cannot be described as one-third full, which tells us that there are objective facts independent of us even when we describe them subjectively. Likewise, the 1857 Indian uprising cannot be described as a celebration of Indian independence in 1947.

When Shakespeare's Juliet says that a rose by any other name would smell as sweet, she is clear-eyed and does not confuse Romeo's family name with who he is as a human being, but most of us filter reality through how it is described in words. We tend to confuse language and reality, words and things. In *The Making of a Scientist*, the physicist Richard Feynman says, "I learned very early the difference between knowing the name of something and knowing something."[9]

But this is not to say no facts are socially constructed. If someone correctly conveys it is Thursday, then that is a fact relative to a certain calendar, which is

---

9. Feynman (2001, p. 14).

partly a social construct. Many social facts are like this, whether we are speaking about the outcome of an election or a sporting event or whatever. Such states of affairs are facts only relative to some social construct and if the social construct were not to have existed, neither would the corresponding facts. A social construct like a calendar or an election or a sporting event is just a set of socially created states of affairs that are often themselves social facts. That is, something like an election is a collection of social facts.

The cultural theorist Edward Said sums up these subtleties well in the context of the West's representations of the East called "Orientalism": "In the first place, it would be wrong to conclude that the Orient was *essentially* an idea, or a creation with no corresponding reality. . . . There were—and are—cultures and nations whose location is in the East, and their lives, histories, and customs have a brute reality obviously greater than anything that could be said about them in the West. About that fact this study of Orientalism has very little to contribute, except to acknowledge it tacitly."[10] In other words, Said clearly distinguishes between the Orient as (a partly socially constructed) object and as represented by the West.

To get back to our main theme, collections of states of affairs—some of which may be facts—form contexts or situations, parts of the world we occupy as agents and move about in. A situation may contain the earth circling the sun, a person on earth sitting at a desk writing a book, and a darting goldfish in a fish tank. Notice how the situation contains various individual objects attached to various properties and relations, each of which is inside a state of affairs. And the three states of affairs are all inside the situation.

There is a simple way to display the states of affairs present in some situation $s$. For example, we may write:

- $s$ supports the earth circling the sun.
- $s$ supports a person on earth sitting at a desk writing a book.
- $s$ supports a darting goldfish in a fish tank.

This need not be an exhaustive listing of the states of affairs in $s$. Just as we replaced a phrase like "the situation" with the letter $s$, we can also replace the other entities with corresponding symbols to obtain a more compact way

---

10. Said (1979, p. 5). As he goes on to say, his interest is not in the correspondence or otherwise between Orientalism and the Orient but rather in the internal consistency of Orientalism's ideas about the Orient.

of expressing such relationships among individuals, properties, relations, states of affairs, and situations. Such symbolization eventually leads to the mathematical framework I described as situation theory, but I will continue to use plain English as it is easier to read.

All of these entities—individuals, properties, relations, states of affairs, and situations—are present in our awareness in mixed ways, partly analog and partly digital, partly implicit and partly explicit. The world we are in is itself simply a large situation and we, as well as other entities, are all situated beings.

There are two more types of entity in the world that are absolutely crucial. One is the special connection or relation between situations I called *meaning*. In carving up reality, one of the key things agents do is discover or create these connections between two or more entities such as, say, smoke and fire or an utterance and its content. We say that smoke means fire and, likewise, that an utterance of "There is a fire" in suitable circumstances means there is a fire in some situation. Reality is full of such connections or meanings. Indeed, science, broadly construed, is the attempt to comprehend them and, in this sense, it can be said to be *the search for meaning*.

As we have seen, a situation can be a large or small thing. It can contain a great number of goings-on or it can contain one or two. When Ann and Bob are talking, there is an infinite background of facts and other contextual elements that they draw upon in their conversation including the actual structure of their interaction. Generally, when people or other living things interact, part of the structure inside the (dialogue) situation is a *game*, something we will take up in the next chapter. As far as I know, treating games as parts of the world rather than as abstract models or representations of specific situations of interest as most game theorists do is a new way of approaching them and offers many advantages.

Thus, the world, itself a situation, has in it individuals, properties, relations, states of affairs, games, situations, connections between situations we call meanings, and a few other things we need not bother with (e.g., types, parameters, and similar entities of a logical nature). All of these entities in the world make up what is called an *ontology* or, alternatively, an *informational space*.

## 5.4 Information

I have used the word "information" occasionally and we often refer to our times as an information age. There is even a celebrated quantitative theory of information developed by Claude Shannon[11] that considers the *amount* of information transmitted in a message. But what exactly is information in a qualitative sense? It is the basic stuff of reality we partly individuate. It is the individuals, properties, relations, states of affairs, games, situations, and connections. All of these entities taken together are information, and contexts may be considered the bearers of information as well. An informational *space* is all the information together with its structure (e.g., that a fact belongs to a situation or that one fact implies another).

Even something as large and complex as a civilization is just information. People sometimes balk at such a vast reduction to "mere" nature because they fear that our exalted feelings and the very spirit of humanity will disappear. But when water is reduced to hydrogen and oxygen and their chemical bonds, it does not disappear. On the contrary, not only does it remain but we understand it better, and this enables us to do things with it that were not possible before. The same applies to civilization.

Information forms the substrate for meaning, which is, as we have seen, a connection between two (or more) situated items of information. Intuitively and informally, meaning is structure. Science is the attempt to grasp structure and that is why I call it the search for meaning.

## 5.5 Natural and Artificial Meanings

The vast domain of connections or meanings can be roughly divided into natural and artificial, those independent of humans and those dependent on them. Smoke meaning fire is a natural connection and an utterance of "There is a fire" meaning there is a fire in some situation is an artificial connection. One of the challenges of science is to reduce such artificial connections to natural ones.

Natural meanings are studied mainly in the physical and life sciences. Some artificial connections like the one above involve *symbol systems* that enable a

---

11. Shannon and Weaver (1949).

person to represent one thing with another—recall the connection between two situated items of information—and convey this to another person. A traffic light may *tell* a driver to stop or to go; a photograph may *depict* a sunrise or sunset; a song may *evoke* joy or sorrow; a wave of the hand may *signal* a greeting or a goodbye; a building lobby may *express* warmth or coolness. All these elements and more are representational or artificially meaningful and form parts of different symbol systems.

Representation does not simply exist in the world; it requires a complicated type of agency.[12] *People* create symbols and the world is full of many symbol systems. Indeed, these systems form a central part of civilizations in addition to other systems, such as the technological, economic, and political systems of a country or region which are both manmade and meaningful but are not symbol systems.

It appears that a symbolic consciousness emerged from primates and the great apes a few hundred thousand years ago with the Neanderthals, or possibly much earlier with *Homo erectus*, although this has yet to be confirmed.[13] Before this, the world must have been a much-impoverished place because there were no symbol systems and so no *symbolic* ways to communicate. One can imagine the vast advance made in progressing from pre-symbolic civilizations to symbolic ones because we do not even call the former "civilizations." And this also helps us to appreciate the key role played by symbolic communication in creating civilization.

The traffic system—not just traffic lights but also the whole system of traffic rules—is a relatively simple symbol system because it has little ambiguity or vagueness. One of the most complex symbol systems is verbal language. Other fairly complex symbol systems are the visual and gestural systems, each of which has many subsystems—such as visual art and dance, to mention just two. I will be looking at the meanings of images and actions later.

Semantics, which ought to be the study of symbol systems generally, has often come to be more narrowly identified with the study of linguistic meaning. Its main problem is to understand how language acquires meaning. How is it that an utterance, whether spoken or written, carries one or more meanings from a speaker to an addressee? Because language has so many varied devices, such as

---

12. I discuss this in some detail in all my books and especially in Parikh (2019), giving definitions of various related concepts.

13. Deacon (1997), Tomasello (2010).

## Chapter Five: The Ubiquity of Context

nouns and verbs and tone and emphasis, to convey meaning, this turns out to be a very large question made up of many subquestions.

Some readers may feel this question is either obvious—because they converse effortlessly with their fellow human beings—or irredeemably academic—because only scholars might care to know the details of an answer. A simple way to deflect the first objection is to ask if they could explain whether and how an artificial agent like a computer might be made to carry out a conversation; the second objection requires a little patience to see how deeply enmeshed we are in meaning and how important it is for not just our individual lives but equally for society and civilization.

I mentioned earlier how context is made visible through simple sentences like "It is four p.m." uttered at some particular time and place. In fact, all sentences require context for their interpretation, even something mathematical like "Two plus two equals four," owing to the ubiquity of ambiguity and vagueness.[14] Since context accompanies all entities, it also accompanies utterances, and it is the utterance situation that partly enables the disambiguation of ambiguous and vague sentences. Unfortunately, as context remains poorly understood in almost all the relevant fields, utterance comprehension and related issues like understanding action in the social sciences remain equally mysterious.

After I have described what games are in the next chapter, I will sketch in the following part of the book how Communication Games inside utterance situations help us with such comprehension. Later, I will show how society-wide Language Games lead to the emergence of conventional meanings in the first place. Communication Games and Language Games will clarify how linguistic meaning is both an individual and social thing. And they will give us more formal insights into how many jokes work and why political speech is often extreme. Lastly, these relatively precise insights can then be carried over to other fuzzier domains such as image comprehension and even the meanings of actions and objects.

---

14. In this mathematical sentence, the numerical base with respect to which the numbers are to be added is left implicit. If they are taken with respect to base three, then the result would not be four but eleven. So before we can say what it means and whether it is true or false, we need to know this contextual information to disambiguate it. Another interpretation of the sentence relative to a different context might be *two (drops) plus two (drops) equals four (drops)* where the drops are implicitly intended via free enrichment, which I mentioned in Section 3.1, leading to a possibly false assertion because the addition may result in just one large drop, not four.

## 5.6  Context and Calculability

Ambiguity, vagueness, and especially context make the life sciences, social sciences, humanities, arts, and AI difficult to "calculate" or "compute."

In the physical sciences, contexts typically occur in the form of relatively precise conditions such as those that are responsible for a solar eclipse or the curvature of spacetime. The ingenuity lies in isolating the phenomenon and identifying the conditions but even this can be a real challenge in areas like predicting the weather or anticipating earthquakes where things are not clearcut. Of course, this is not to say that physics and chemistry are easy—the structures in these sciences are inordinately complex as we know from relativity and quantum theory and the study of phase transitions.

But often infinitely many and weakly structured facts inside a background situation pose quite different sorts of difficulties: in diagnosing and curing illness with certainty, enacting a sound economic or social policy, or making machines do even simple things like open a door or sit in a chair, let alone participate in an open-ended, unscripted conversation. Even a single utterance can have an infinitely complex meaning.

In the realm of technology, current data-driven approaches in AI, such as deep learning and reinforcement learning, have cleverly circumvented the problem of meaning by replacing causal and informational connections with correlations between one type of data and another and so have managed to make significant advances. However, such approaches, too, will sooner or later have to face the fact that we live in a meaningful world. Many feel humanity is special and irreducible, and context cannot be mastered, and so full-fledged AI is impossible. Others choose not to give context its due and continue to approach things either in the purely abstract way of the physical sciences or through the concrete correlations of deep learning as it has achieved such remarkable successes. Let us first deepen our understanding of meaning and place ourselves in a better position to arrive at a more nuanced solution to this conundrum.

The physical sciences are tightly structured and the life sciences, social sciences, humanities, arts, and AI are loosely structured. Whether the meanings in these domains are described as the connections between conditions and consequences or contexts and contents, it is these very meanings that will need to be transformed to realize possible partial utopias.

## 5.7  Context and Partiality

Apart from the role situations play in meaning, another profound consequence of the situatedness of entities, their occurrence in multiple contexts, is that our understanding of things is almost always partial. The path from Aristotelian physics to Newtonian physics and then to Einsteinian physics can be seen as one of a widening context of inquiry. Indeed, every object, even an ordinary one like a chair or table, has an infinite number of properties and relations with other objects. No understanding or theory can encompass all of them; science is a progressive and potentially endless endeavor.

Situations are themselves partial objects because they are just a small part of the world. Partiality itself may be seen as a generalization of this property that we attribute to situations. It applies to many things and perhaps all that is common to different attributions is that it is "not whole," "not total."

When we act, we typically do so based on imperfect knowledge. In game theory, this lack of knowledge is usually translated into uncertainty about each of several possible situations. But, in fact, we seldom if ever know the full range of possibilities. So, choice of any kind is always based on partiality. In addition, when we consider an action, we do so based on only a few of its properties. We cannot include all of them in our deliberation. In other words, we use partiality as a tool or *principle* to eliminate some properties—as well as some possibilities when there are too many—to make it easier to choose.[15] So choice is also partial in this sense even though when we act, we perform full actions. This is part of the reason why it is difficult to anticipate all the consequences of an action. For example, when Ann has to decide whether to carry an umbrella, she simply looks at how likely rain is and not at any of the other possibilities that may occur. And she considers the action of carrying an umbrella just by its property of protecting against rain, not any of its other infinitely many properties. It could well happen that it turns out to be an overly bright day and the umbrella provides relief from the sun, a serendipitous consequence that was not part of her decision-making.

---

15. This use of partiality is a little like the idea of *satisficing* introduced by Simon (1956) to explain the behavior of decision makers in situations where optimal solutions cannot be easily computed. It may be called *partializing* the action or choices. There is also a connection here with Frank H. Knight's (1921/2009) distinction between risk and uncertainty.

Lastly, actions are related to ethical systems and perhaps no ethical system should be expected to solve all ethical problems.[16]

What is the larger significance of partiality?[17] In a nutshell, it suggests that we approach our individual and collective endeavors not as totalizing projects but as partial efforts that build partial meanings and partial utopias. I will say more about this in the final chapter but here is Salman Rushdie on partiality:

---

16. For those familiar with Gödel's incompleteness results, themselves an illustration of partiality in logical systems, it is as if there is an analogue in ethics as well. (Gödel's incompleteness theorems are two seminal theorems in mathematical logic that show the inherent limits of every formal axiomatic system capable of modeling basic arithmetic.)

17. Poststructuralist thought (e.g., the later Barthes, Foucault, and Derrida) often deals with fragments, perspectives, discontinuities, displacements, and other such partial objects. For those who know it, its core idea is rather different from the notion of partiality mentioned here because poststructuralism, as its name indicates, relies on structuralism's hermetic structures and then makes its transgressive moves. This is most clearly evident in Derrida (1978) and Foucault (1980). But such moves, whether via Foucauldian genealogy or Derridean deconstruction, would convince only those—like the structuralists themselves—who believe in such total and brittle structures. Most others—even the encyclopedic Hegel—simply would not accept such sharply identified totalities, and then the entire poststructuralist procedure of breaking or going outside systems collapses. Most social or conceptual systems can, in fact, accommodate, co-opt, and even domesticate, or, when necessary, smoothly expand, adapt, and even change. And they are all partial. Indeed, it is more correct to see partiality everywhere and imagine partial objects and partial understandings as existing among other partial objects and other partial understandings. There are practically no complete wholes in a strict sense because everything is situated in partial contexts and also because such wholes usually result in antinomies and paradoxes or have fundamental limits as shown by Gödel, Church, and Turing. The fact is that poststructuralism is a marriage of Cartesian rationalism with a romanticism gone awry.

Indeed, it may be possible to see a fundamental flaw in much twentieth-century French thought. Descartes's dualism of mind and body led to a series of binary structures starting with Saussure's signifier and signified in linguistics, which influenced the anthropologist Lévi-Strauss and other structuralists' varied binary "oppositions," and which has finally led to quite extravagant Nietzschean twists and plays on the same binary structures, whether by imaginative thinkers like Foucault or Derrida or others. Unfortunately, like Hegel's dialectical "triadism" (see Maybee 2016), this "dyadism" is too Procrustean a bed (or episteme, to use Foucault's (1966/2002) own terminology against him), because the world is too rich, diverse, and variable to be captured by any single way of carving out distinctions and individuating reality.

Famously, Hegel (1977) said the whole is the true and Adorno (1951/1996, p. 50) said the whole is the false. In my view, the whole is neither the true nor the false: it is the indeterminate.

But human beings do not perceive things whole; we are not gods but wounded creatures, cracked lenses, capable only of fractured perceptions. Partial beings, in all the senses of that phrase. Meaning is a shaky edifice we build out of scraps, dogmas, childhood injuries, newspaper articles, chance remarks, old films, small victories, people hated, people loved; perhaps it is because our sense of what is the case is constructed from such inadequate materials that we defend it so fiercely, even to the death.[18]

I turn next to a somewhat different topic alluded to in the first chapter that is also relevant to our concern with contexts.

## 5.8 Internal Contexts, Concepts, and Reduction

We can now dispel some of the mystery of why our consciousness feels so different from nature. I suggested that part of the reason why we recoil from physicalism has to do with the internal contexts within our minds. Indeed, we can even appreciate why we tend to resist reductionism in general.

We know that we have mental concepts that represent collections of things in the world. The concept of water stores various experiences of water as well as linking up with other concepts such as wetness and water's ability to slake our thirst. And so we have various bits of information we share with each other, such as about how the rainwater made us wet, how water quenches our thirst, and so on.

Then we learn the special fact that water is $H_2O$. We might have already had some acquaintance with hydrogen and oxygen and the way they bond and might have studied some of their properties. Among other things, we do not in any way immediately associate wetness or the taste of water with $H_2O$. So while we find ourselves comfortable saying water is wet, we initially find it odd to say that $H_2O$ is wet, even though by the very identity we have learned between water and $H_2O$, it must be true.[19] Even later, once we have fully absorbed the idea of the reduction of water to $H_2O$, we continue to find the ascription of

---

18. Rushdie (1991, p. 12).
19. I am deliberately ignoring the fact that $H_2O$ can also occur as steam or ice.

certain properties—like wetness—a little strange because our concepts of water and $H_2O$ remain different despite the thing they represent being the same.

Although this is just a conjecture, this strangeness, this dissonance, seems to lie at the heart of our opposition to reductionism. If a scientist tells us that we are little more than swirling atoms and their interrelations, we find it puzzling and disturbing because the properties we normally associate with persons on the one hand and with atoms (and the forces that relate them) on the other are quite different. People have capacities and needs, they have values and feelings, they are active and social beings. Atoms and fields seem to have no such properties. So how could the former possibly be identical to the latter? With water and $H_2O$, the reduction is straightforward and easy to grasp, yet we still find aspects of it peculiar. With people and elementary particles, it is unlikely that an actual reduction will be within our scientific reach any time soon (if ever), and so the identity requires a prodigious feat of imagination, and this is why we object to it even more strongly. The key to the mystery is that two concepts can be different even when the thing they represent is the same.

Consciousness, too, is similar. It must be explainable via brain and other bodily processes because there are no other plausible accounts available, and yet, because a sip of a good wine or the longing for a loved one seem to have such different experiential properties, our minds seem quite separate from nature. Our internal contexts or situations contain our concepts for these apparently disparate things, these concepts play completely different roles in our lives, and so imagining one to be reducible to the other seems absurd.

In a famous paper *What Is It Like to Be a Bat?*, the philosopher Thomas Nagel argued that we cannot know what it is like to be another person or an animal with consciousness such as a bat because this is a subjective experience and all the reductions of current science are to objective things, such as $H_2O$ or atoms and fields.[20] Indeed, he says that even if we knew all of a bat's neurophysiology, something within our scientific reach, we could not know what it is *like* to be a bat, to experience a bat's consciousness or experience. And the same inaccessibility applies to other persons. This is undoubtedly a powerful and elegant argument against standard "objective" reductionism.

---

20. Nagel (1974).

## Chapter Five: The Ubiquity of Context

"I mean, I've got the costume and I've got the gadgets but I just can't shake the feeling that I'll never know what it's like to be a bat."

To φ or not to φ

© Tanya Kostochka 2015

Figure 5.1  What Is It Like to Be a Bat?

Nagel's paper has led to many reactions and I can only offer my own view here. I believe he uses the commonsense contrast between "subjective" and "objective" to make his point. But there is no reason—in this instance—to think that a subjective experience cannot also be objective. Our ability to actually feel what another person feels or what a bat feels has natural limits, but this does not automatically imply that consciousness cannot ultimately be neurophysiological, although Nagel seems to make this unwarranted leap. Both items or states of affairs—the subjectivity of others' experiences and their objective reducibility—could simultaneously be true.

To put it differently, just because we cannot feel what others feel does not mean their feelings are necessarily different from ours in essential ways: they could be *objectively* the same. That is, other persons' experiences of a pin prick may be importantly similar, making allowances for different thresholds of pain and so on. Their more complex feelings, such as the longing for a loved one, may be unique because of their unique lived histories that are sedimented in their brains and bodies. Unless we can somehow occupy or inhabit their bodies, we can never experience their experiences because each body is unique. But this fact is neither here nor there; it is, in a sense, orthogonal to the question of their objective reducibility.

In yet other words, objectivity doesn't entail access to others' experiences, and Nagel's argument is about access. So, even if he's right that access is unobtainable, nothing follows from that fact about objectivity and/or reducibility.

Toward the end of his paper, Nagel says almost what I am suggesting:

> Very little work has been done on the basic question (from which mention of the brain can be entirely omitted) whether any sense can be made of experiences' having an objective character at all. Does it make sense, in other words, to ask what my experiences are *really* like, as opposed to how they appear to me? We cannot genuinely understand the hypothesis that their nature is captured in a physical description unless we understand the more fundamental idea that they *have* an objective nature (or that objective processes can have a subjective nature).

To conclude, I have offered a partial way to understand the mystery of reduction and why we resist it, whether it has to do with our minds and consciousness or our civilizations. The reason for this slight detour is to make plausible the grounding of our vision of the world in physical nature and patterns in physical nature, in inanimate stuff and things made out of inanimate stuff, as I said in the first chapter. Actually carrying out these reductions is obviously an altogether different and inordinately difficult task.

We return now to our theme of things in the world and, in particular, to games.

# CHAPTER SIX

# What Is a Game?

The situated agents who people the world are finite in their capacities, have a range of concerns, and constantly face choices their environments and capacities make available. When concerns are articulated digitally, they become *goals*. All agents have a complex and shifting hierarchy of concerns and goals, from survival at the top that is almost always present to particular ones below, such as a desire[1] for ice cream in some situation. An agent's concerns or goals can be equivalently expressed as *preferences* between situations, for example one in which they are eating ice cream and another in which they are not.

In addition to our concerns and goals, we have access to perceptual information that is transformed into cognitive information in a single partially *constructive* process as we act in the world. Our sensory/perceptual awareness of situations tends to be analog and our partial cognitive grasp of them digital.[2]

The choices afforded by a situation, together with an agent's beliefs and preferences, form a situated choice problem for the agent. When the situated choice problem involves solely the agent, it is a situated decision problem; when it involves other agents, it is a situated game. To avoid having to say "decision problem or game" each time I refer to an agent's choice problem, I will use "game" to cover both situations.

---

1. I use "goal," "desire," "wish," "purpose," and other synonyms interchangeably to relieve the tedium of repetition.

2. Most classical Indian philosophies also held that "perception must be of two kinds, each corresponding to a stage of its unfolding: at first a nonconceptual, nonlinguistic taking-in of whatever is presented to the senses, and then a conceptual, linguistic, predicative cognition in which the entities presented to the senses are knit together as qualifier and qualified." See Mohanty (2007, p. 31).

Arguably, aesthetic impressionism, whether visual (e.g., Claude Monet) or verbal (e.g., Anton Chekhov), may even be defined as attempting to render the first analog stage of perception owing to its painterly manner of depiction.

Just as we are always embedded in situations, we are also always embedded in the games that occur within them. A situated game consists of four things: an embedding situation, agents, choices for each agent, and payoffs (or preferences) for each combination of choices. Being (partly) rational, agents do the best they can, given how the other agents may choose, and such a jointly optimal (i.e., best response to one another) choice for each agent is called an equilibrium. This is a complex idea, and I will illustrate it through a simple example.

Games, too, can be analog or digital, implicit or explicit, just like the situations they are in. Ann and Bob may not be aware they are playing a conversational game when they talk to each other in a dialogue situation.

## 6.1 A Simple Example

Suppose Ann and Bob are trying to meet in Manhattan but are unable to communicate with each other first. Assume they could meet either at Grand Central Station, which is closer to both of them, or at Penn Station, which is farther away. If they go to different stations, neither benefits. Such a situation can be captured by the matrix in Figure 6.1.

|               | Grand Central | Penn Station |
|---------------|---------------|--------------|
| Grand Central | (2, 2)        | (0, 0)       |
| Penn Station  | (0, 0)        | (1, 1)       |

Figure 6.1  A Coordination Game $G$

This picture depicts a game $G$. Ann has the two choices indicated in the two rows, either to go to Grand Central or to Penn Station, and Bob has the same two choices indicated in the two columns. Their respective payoffs—which encode their preferences—are mentioned in the four cells of the matrix, the first number being Ann's payoff and the second being Bob's in each cell. If both agents go to Grand Central they get a payoff of 2 units because it is closer to them, if they both go to Penn Station they get 1 unit because it is farther away, and if they end up at different stations they get 0 because they fail to meet.[3] Both Ann and

---

3. Notice how payoffs are a different way of recording relational preferences because $2 > 1 > 0$.

Bob are at least partly rational and so prefer more payoff units to less, but each of them can only select their own action even though the outcome depends on what they both do. Incidentally, this is exactly the situation with communication, where the outcome depends on both the speaker and the addressee, and it is, indeed, the same with most other interactions between people as well.

Both agents have to choose a course of action based on what the other agent will choose. This particular game is called a coordination game because the agents have compatible payoffs and there is no conflict, that is, they do not value the same outcome differently.

By varying the payoffs, it is possible to generate a range of games even in this simple two-agent, two-choice setting. For example, if Ann had been closer to Grand Central and Bob to Penn Station then the game would look as shown in Figure 6.2.

|  | Grand Central | Penn Station |
| --- | --- | --- |
| Grand Central | (2, 1) | (0, 0) |
| Penn Station | (0, 0) | (1, 2) |

Figure 6.2 A Mixed-Motive Game $G'$

In the game $G'$, if both go to Grand Central, Ann gets a payoff of 2 units as before but Bob gets only 1 unit as he is farther away, whereas if both go to Penn Station, the payoffs are reversed. This reflects the fact that Ann prefers Grand Central and Bob Penn Station. Of course, they both prefer to meet so if they choose different stations, they both get 0 as in the earlier coordination game $G$. These numbers neatly account for all the different preferences they have in the situation including the fact that it contains a mix of conflict and coordination. Ann would gravitate to Grand Central and Bob to Penn Station but both would want to meet.

The payoffs and choices available to Ann and Bob depend partly on objective factors—like Grand Central being closer than Penn Station to both in $G$ but not in $G'$—and partly on subjective, agent-based factors—like both preferring shorter distances.[4] A game is thus a partly objective, partly subjective structure. It is the surrounding situation that provides the details that make up the game.

---

4. In more complex situations involving emotions like surprise, confidence, gratitude, disappointment, and embarrassment, the payoffs can also depend on what each agent thinks other

In general, there can be more than two agents and more than two choices of action for each agent and all kinds of payoff numbers. $G$ and $G'$ are among the simplest nontrivial games where interesting interactive phenomena occur. It should be apparent that game theory can provide a flexible tool for describing interactions between people in society.[5]

## 6.2  Solving Games

Once a game like $G$ is set up, the next step is to see how rational agents wanting to choose the best action would act given that the other agents want to do the same. The resulting jointly optimal strategies are called the solution to the game. Studying the solution process formally involves a number of definitions of terms like "strategy," "equilibrium," and the like as well as somewhat subtle analyses, so

---

agents believe, and on what each agent thinks they believe others believe, and so on. See Geanakoplos, Pearce, and Stacchetti (1989).

5. For an example with more conflict, consider a different situation where Ann and Bob are having a quarrel and their options are to concede to the other or not to concede.

|  | concede | don't concede |
|---|---|---|
| concede | (2, 2) | (-3, 3) |
| don't concede | (3, -3) | (-2, -2) |

I have deliberately chosen these payoffs to illustrate the famous Prisoner's Dilemma game. (The name of this game comes from a different scenario involving two prisoners but the two situations are structurally the same.) If they both concede, they both benefit with a positive payoff of 2. But Ann would like best not to concede with Bob conceding and this is reflected in her getting 3 with Bob getting -3 as this is his worst outcome. These payoffs are shown in the lower left cell. The situation is reversed in the upper right cell with Bob not conceding and Ann conceding. And if neither concedes, then they are both stuck with a negative outcome which is valued at -2 for both. In other words, both agents prefer not to concede to conceding if the other concedes because they get 3 instead of 2, but in so choosing they lose their chance to get the maximum joint benefit from the situation of 2 and both end up with -2 instead, the lower right cell of the matrix. Incidentally, the Prisoner's Dilemma game can describe even an arms race between two countries: just replace the concede and don't concede options with disarm and arm.

I request you to simply accept that most simple games can be solved and their solutions are *equilibria* of one kind or another.[6]

There is a great deal more to the games needed to understand meaning and communication let alone society, but this is as far as we will go. For our purposes, it suffices to know what games are in a basic sense—a structure of situations, agents, choices, and payoffs—and that they can be solved by equilibria to a greater or lesser degree. I will use this sketch as a platform from which to informally launch further ideas.

## 6.3 Situated Games

So far, what I have said about games is fairly standard. Now I introduce a new and possibly controversial element. As we have seen, games are themselves

---

6. For those interested in a basic account, one key idea is that jointly optimal actions should be such that no agent will want to deviate from them unilaterally. In $G$, if Ann were to choose Grand Central then it is optimal for Bob to choose the same, and vice versa. If Ann were to choose Penn Station, then it is optimal for Bob to choose the same, and vice versa. In other words, both (Grand Central, Grand Central) = (GC, GC) and (Penn Station, Penn Station) = (PS, PS) are pairs of actions that neither agent will want to deviate from unilaterally. They possess a kind of stability. On the other hand, both (GC, PS) and (PS, GC) are, in this sense, precarious pairs of choices because both agents will want to shift their strategy. Each can do better by a unilateral change to a different action. For example, with (GC, PS) Ann would benefit by shifting to Penn Station because she would then receive 1 instead of 0 and, likewise, Bob would benefit by shifting to Grand Central because he would then receive 2 instead of 0, assuming the two agents do not both shift simultaneously. If any single agent can do better by a unilateral change to a different strategy, then the initial pair would not be selected as jointly optimal. A pair of strategies that is immune to any such unilateral deviation by any agent is called a Nash equilibrium.

(GC, GC) and (PS, PS) are Nash equilibria and such solutions exist in many games but they are often not unique. This requires ways to eliminate certain equilibria that are counterintuitive from a commonsense viewpoint. In $G$, both agents would be better off selecting (GC, GC) rather than (PS, PS) because they would both receive higher payoffs, (2, 2) rather than (1, 1). Such Nash equilibria that make at least one player better off without making any other player worse off are called Pareto-Nash equilibria.

Some excellent textbooks on game theory are Watson (2002), Hargreaves-Heap and Varoufakis (2004), Osborne and Rubinstein (1994), and Myerson (1991).

situated. Why are these embedding situations relevant? For this, take a second look at Figure 6.2.

The payoffs in $G'$ were derived by making the implicit assumption that both Ann and Bob were atomistic agents concerned only with their own outcomes and payoffs. This is in fact the standard assumption in game theory. So, Ann might choose Grand Central and Bob Penn Station resulting in their not meeting. What this game captures is just the outcomes, the overt behaviors, that result from their choices, not how they came to value these outcomes by the payoffs shown. What if we wanted to include this information as well?

Consider a different scenario where Bob feels generous toward Ann and so is happy to go to Grand Central which she prefers.[7] Then he might alter his valuation of Grand Central to 2 units and Penn Station to 1 unit to match Ann's valuations. This would convert $G'$ back to the coordination game $G$ and both would meet at Grand Central as before.

However, the information about Bob's generosity is nowhere represented as the game matrix describes just the outcomes or behaviors and resulting payoffs. The game theorist may respond that the payoffs are now different from those in $G'$ and the difference in payoffs reflects the difference in underlying motivations—selfish behavior in $G'$ and Bob's generous behavior in $G$.

But the first time we considered $G$ *both* Ann and Bob were closer to Grand Central, whereas in the present scenario Bob is further away but acts magnanimously. In the latter, both Bob's distance from Grand Central and the underlying *reason* for Bob's behavior, the *way* his choice is made, are different.

To represent such differences that lead to the behaviors and thence to the payoffs in the matrix, we resort to the embedding situations. It is the surrounding situation that contains the facts about how the agents regard themselves and their counterparts, and so why they wish to act one way or another.[8]

We saw in the previous chapter how to display the information in a situation, so we can write:

- $s$ supports the coordination game $G$.
- $s$ supports both Ann and Bob being closer to Grand Central.

---

7. Building on Geanakoplos, Pearce, and Stacchetti (1989) cited in Section 6.1, Rabin (1993) incorporates issues of fairness in game theory. This has led to a large literature (e.g., Nelson 2001) on how game theory can include social considerations of reciprocity, fairness, and equity.

8. This phenomenon is called intensionality. Standard game theory is extensional but situated games are intensional. See Parikh (2010, appendix A) for more details.

- *s* supports Ann and Bob being atomistic agents concerned only with their own outcomes and payoffs.

And with the second version of the situated game $G$, we would write:

- *s* supports the coordination game $G$.
- *s* supports Bob being further away from Grand Central.
- *s* supports Bob being generous toward Ann.

Now, the embedding situations are different even though the games are identical. Thus, to fully understand an interaction between two or more agents, games by themselves are not enough, and we need to look to the situations they are inside. The game theorist may respond that the situational information can be incorporated into an expanded game thereby dispensing with the ambient situation. This is true but it makes the game more complex to solve for Ann and Bob. And there may still be other relevant information left out that would either require an even more complex game or an embedding situation. Thus, there is always a trade-off between what to represent explicitly within the game and what to leave outside in the surrounding situation, and various considerations, including those involving complexity, allow us to conclude that there will always be a need for situating games.[9]

---

9. A consequence of game theorists trying to solve games and resolve the problems raised by multiple equilibria through so-called refinements *without* recourse to the ambient situation is that they don't avail of all the information present in real-life contexts. Moreover, the same narrowly understood game may have different solutions in, say, an economic context and a political context and a cultural context. So, it seems multiply wrong to ignore the situation that contains the game.

As discussed in Parikh (2010, appendix A) an analogy can be drawn between situated games and situated sentences, allowing one to conclude that trying to solve/interpret either games or sentences without their accompanying situations will never work for *all* games or sentences as can be seen, for instance, in the enormous difficulties faced by game theorists or in the failures of ChatGPT and similar systems which work only with the linguistic context as they have no access to the situational context.

## 6.4 Situated Games and Conversation

Another element that is not well understood in the study of games is the role that conversation can often play in them. When conversation is mentioned, its benefit is usually confined to the selection of an equilibrium as there are usually multiple equilibria in a game, and ensuring that both parties choose the same one can be simplified if communication is possible. In the coordination game $G$ in Figure 6.1, communication was not possible and so the two agents had to make their choices on their own. But if it had been, as it usually is via cell phones today, then it would be easier for Ann and Bob to coordinate where to meet.

The value of communication and, indeed, extended conversation, in the playing of a game is in fact immense in all its aspects, not just in equilibrium selection.[10] Conversation can also influence the available actions, the payoffs or preferences, and even the number of agents in a game.

In the mixed-motive game $G'$ in Figure 6.2, Ann might remind Bob that the last time they met at Penn Station so why not consider Grand Central this time? This might lead Bob to change his payoffs to be similar to Ann's and thereby convert the game to a coordination game like $G$. Such persuasion is the real stuff of most of the games we play in everyday and not-so-everyday life. It involves what is popularly called *framing*, which refers to how one tries to influence someone via communication. Bob could also respond by suggesting a third location instead, thereby enlarging the pool of available choices. Communication can be especially useful when the game involves significant conflict because in such situations, especially when the stakes are high as in politics, a mediator, that is, a third agent, can sometimes help defuse the tensions as well.[11]

We have seen how all three things that make up a game—the number of agents, the available actions, and the payoffs or preferences—can be altered via conversation. A little reflection reveals that the possibilities for such changes are enormous. I will return to this later but as society is made up of situated games,

---

10. Of course, as I will show in Chapter 7, communication itself involves a multitude of games because it is a social interaction like the others.

11. Yamey (2021) argues that a zero-sum game involving the global distribution of vaccines among rich and poor nations during the COVID-19 pandemic can be potentially converted to something close to a positive-sum coordination game via international discussion and cooperation. In other words, game theory suggests that donating doses can help nations of *all* income levels.

there is great scope to alter the many adversarial games that exist in society via communication. Jürgen Habermas's suggestion that societies tend toward ideal speech situations undistorted by power or deception that help societies evolve toward greater freedom and fulfillment can be seen in this light.[12]

Where should such conversations that lie outside the game proper be located? By now the reader can probably answer this: in the embedding situation, of course. There is thus yet another key role for situated games to play. So we can write, as before:

- $s$ supports the game in question.
- $s$ supports a conversation about this game.
- $s$ supports a possible new game that results.

It may happen that the situation $s$ itself changes to a new situation $s'$ as a result of the conversation, in which case we would write:

- $s$ supports the game in question.
- $s$ supports a conversation about this game.
- $s'$ supports a possible new game that results.

Based on their interests, the agents can define $s$ and $s'$ in as broad or narrow a way as they like.

## 6.5 Situated Games and Common Knowledge

I have deliberately left out a crucial but somewhat technical part of all that is involved in a situated game: common knowledge. It involves what the two or more agents in a game need to share about the game in order to play it. If Ann and Bob do not share that they are both considering Grand Central Station and Penn Station, they will be unable to play the game properly. The same applies to their shared knowledge of each other's payoffs. And, of course, each agent must know who else is in the game. That is, both agents must have shared knowledge of the game's whole structure.

---

12. Habermas (1979). For those interested, see Bohman and Rehg (2017) for how Habermas has more recently replaced ideal speech situations with the pragmatic presuppositions of discourse that function as "*standards* for a self-correcting learning process." See also Section 8.5 for further discussion.

The nature of this sharing is a bit complicated. It is simplest to present it first and then discuss it a little. The intuitive idea is not just that Ann and Bob both know the game's structure but that they also have access to the knowledge that they know it, and access to the further knowledge that they know that they know it, and so on ad infinitum. Situation theory allows us to express this nested availability of knowledge in a particularly compact way. All we need to say is that Ann and Bob have common knowledge of a game situated in $s$ just when

- $s$ supports the game in question.
- $s$ supports Ann knows $s$.
- $s$ supports Bob knows $s$.

Ann knows $s$ just means that she knows everything in $s$. So this description of common knowledge has a certain harmless circularity—because $s$ contains Ann knows $s$ and Bob knows $s$—which is unavoidable. We need not worry more about the details,[13] but we will see that this notion is central not only to the games we play but also occasionally to larger structures in society and civilization.

As its definition indicates, the common knowledge that agents have of a game is located in its embedding situation.

## 6.6 Situated Games and Power

We have now seen how changing the embedding situations, agents, actions, and payoffs allows us to generate a wide range of games. In this section, I introduce the idea of power in a new and preliminary way and then will develop it more fully in the last part of the book.

It should be apparent that there is a complex relationship among all the payoff numbers in a game. They have a complex structure that partly derives from their position in the payoff matrix and partly from the rational way in which the agents make their choices. At a preliminary and local level, power is just this complex structure. In some cases, especially when the distribution of payoffs is symmetric as in the games $G$ and $G'$, the agents will be evenly matched and have the same power. But in other cases, the relevant matrix could make one agent

---

13. They can be found in Parikh (2019, sec. 2.2.2).

more powerful than the other agent. However, just by looking at a game, it may not always be clear which agent has the upper hand if any, and this reflects the complexities of many real-life situations.

So it is the game that creates the local power structure. As I said earlier,[14] the payoffs and choices available to Ann and Bob depend partly on objective factors—like Grand Central being closer than Penn Station to both—and partly on subjective, agent-based factors—like both preferring shorter distances. A game is thus a partly objective, partly subjective structure. It is the surrounding situation that provides the details that make up the game. Sartre looks at historical situations and Foucault especially introduces their relation to power through the metaphor of war.[15] But the connection of (local) power with situated games makes the idea clear and precise without sacrificing its complexity.

One caveat is that in many ordinary games—like jointly choosing a location— each agent is usually able to opt out of playing the game without incurring any cost. In such cases, there is no uneven power between the agents because they only voluntarily choose to participate, even if the game or its power structure is very unfavorable to them. Whenever such an option to pass on a game is available, it is always located in the embedding situation.

Such a notion of power can help us understand many different situations such as a business negotiation or trade talks between countries or even an anti-colonial liberation struggle, all cases where an opt-out alternative may not exist. When common knowledge of a game does not obtain, the power structure may be quite difficult to grasp. As we have also seen, talking about a game can help the agents to change the game and the relations of power it induces.

I will return to these themes later in the context of society.

## 6.7 Rationality, Irrationality, and Existence

It may seem that I have portrayed human beings as rather one-dimensional creatures driven entirely by cold calculation rather than their passions or values. There are two aspects to this concern.

---

14. Section 6.1.

15. Sartre (1963), Foucault (1997/2003).

In the eighteenth and nineteenth centuries, payoffs were directly linked by social theorists first to monetary rewards and then to the actual pleasure or pain resulting from different choices people might make.[16] From these linkages, it might appear that we are always narrowly driven by whatever yields greater money or pleasure. While there is some truth in this observation across the animal kingdom,[17] the matter is often more complex: one may choose to listen to a sad song because it is more beautiful, one may prefer a more difficult but morally better path because it is the right thing to do, and one may opt for a more complex viewpoint because it is true.

In the twentieth century this close connection between payoffs and money or pleasure was generalized and payoff numbers were simply to be understood as representing our abstract preferences *independent* of their particular content or relation to our feelings. This makes the optimization of payoffs more or less tautological: it can potentially describe the remotest corners of our experience and the actions of even the most passionate of individuals such as Kierkegaard, Dostoyevsky, Nietzsche, Kafka, and other existentialists and absurdists. It does this precisely by abstracting from the content or passion and focusing on the form. As humanists, our interest is often in this content and not in its formal structure, but when we want to explain our choice of actions in the world, we have to resort to the latter.

In other words, old-style utilitarian rationality, often derided as a shopkeeper's mentality by Nietzsche and others, was generalized or sublated[18] by what I think of as a new-style *existential* rationality: a more or less inescapable form of behavior rooted in the situated choices we constantly face as we go about our lives. Both utilitarian rationality and existential rationality are often labeled "economic" as they originated primarily in economic theorizing.

Optimization, whether explicit or implicit, conscious or unconscious, still shapes this more general existential form, and it is this feature especially that romantics object to as it seems to make "instrumental," goal-directed calculation ubiquitous. Romantics believe even the form of some behavior is beyond rational capture. Such form mimics its irrational content and is itself unruly. They are certainly right that there can be genuinely irrational behavior that may not be rule-governed, but it is also true that many seemingly irrational behaviors can be

---

16. Bernoulli (1738/1954), Mill (1863).
17. Glimcher (2004).
18. "Sublate" means *assimilate a smaller or lesser entity into a larger or greater one.*

understood rationally at a formal level: as Polonius says in Shakespeare's *Hamlet*, "Though this be madness, yet there is method in 't."

Despite the relative ubiquity of existential rationality, it is nevertheless too restrictive a form of behavior to capture the full range of humanity's actions. As those familiar with choice theory will know, the seminal work of Maurice Allais, Herbert Simon, Daniel Kahneman and Amos Tversky, and Richard Thaler and Cass Sunstein has demonstrated the inadequacy of using rational models of decision-making in many situations by establishing that people can be *systematically* irrational—a category in between existential rationality and existential irrationality.[19] The consequences of this behavioral revolution have yet to crystallize despite much experimental research[20] and many popular books[21] on the subject. The broad consensus is that most departures from existential or economic rationality are systematic and predictable via a number of new principles of irrational behavior (e.g., framing) and that this predictability makes them different from full-fledged irrationality.

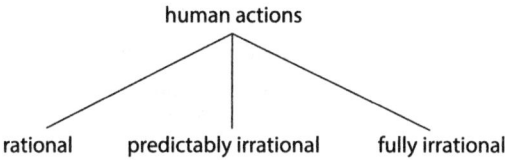

Figure 6.3  Classification of Human Actions

This use of "rational" and "irrational" is completely different from both colloquial uses and other philosophical uses, such as those of Kierkegaard, William James, and Sigmund Freud, among others. If Fred enjoys skydiving every weekend, some may deem him irrational in a colloquial sense because they think he is endangering his life too much, but if he has carefully weighed the pleasure he derives from the activity against its risks, then in an economic or existential sense his choice would be rational. The other philosophical senses relate only indirectly to my distinction in Figure 6.3. They originate in different models of the mind and have different applications.

---

19. Allais (1953), Simon (1955, 1956), Kahnemann and Tversky (1979), Kahnemann, Slovic, and Tversky (1982), Thaler and Sunstein (2008).
20. For example, Camerer (2003), Vlaev et al. (2011).
21. For example, Ariely (2008), Kahneman (2011).

My single term for rational and predictably irrational actions is "partial rationality." Game theory involves choices addressed by partial rationality and I will consider it in greater detail in the coming pages.[22]

## 6.8 Situated Games and Heidegger

I now discuss an entirely unexpected connection that may upset game theorists as well as Heideggerians. Whatever its merits, it shows at least the desirability of seeing through the obscurantist and incantatory way many approach Heidegger's use of language to what it might mean.

Recall from the opening paragraphs of this chapter that a situated game consists of four things: an embedding situation, agents, choices for each agent, and payoffs for each combination of choices. Being (partly) rational, agents do the best they can given how the other agents may choose, and such a jointly optimal choice for each agent is called an equilibrium. Recall also that just as we are always embedded in situations, we are also always embedded in the games that occur inside them. This conception of situated games turns out to be compatible with Heidegger's famous notion of "Being-in-the-world," if both are viewed in the right way.

Game theorists typically use games as models in somewhat abstract and isolated ways to examine phenomena of interest to them, whether they involve the oligopolistic structure of many industries, voting behavior in different democratic settings, the behavior of nonhuman organisms in their ecological niches, or other "social" phenomena. My own view of games is broader and ontological: just as situations are ubiquitous as contexts for all the entities in the world, so are situated games for all kinds of agents.[23] In particular, human agents are always in one or more situated games all the time, whether Ann is talking to Bob or is considering how to design a chair or how to vote or even just make up her mind about taking an umbrella with her depending on how dark the clouds look. Keep in mind that I am using the term "game" to cover both multi-person and single-person choice situations. Much of the time these games remain implicit

---

22. Also see Parikh and Parikh (2018) for an application of partial rationality to architecture and social well-being.
23. There is some evidence for this in Glimcher (2004).

and human beings play them without quite realizing what they are doing. Occasionally, when involved in some important decision more explicitly—whether to rent or buy an apartment, for example—the available choices and their preferences and beliefs get articulated more clearly and are transformed from relatively analog to relatively digital representations. For a game theorist, such situated games become fully digital and are often even stripped of their embedding situations, which remain as implicit and unarticulated penumbra of the games in their minds.

For Heidegger, a person is a Being-in-the-world who acts in and interacts with the world or surrounding environment through what he calls *care*—which could be understood as *interested* action. In other words, a person is a *situated* being as I have said before or, equivalently, a Being-in-the-world, and care is the person's fundamental *relation* to the embedding situation or world.

Two of Heidegger's basic distinctions are (1) Being/individual and (2) ready-to-hand/present-at-hand.

As Michael Wheeler says, "The question of the meaning of Being is concerned with what it is that makes beings intelligible as beings, and whatever that factor (Being) is, it is seemingly not itself simply another being among beings."[24] In my view, this background factor that makes beings (i.e., individuals) available as beings is their individuation or discrimination by persons in society together with the fundamental nature of reality that makes this possible.

*Ready-to-hand* refers to things encountered by the agent through care or interest and *present-at-hand* refers to things encountered disinterestedly. For example, a brick may be considered in a *care*ful or interested way by a bricklayer or civil engineer or architect but disinterestedly by a scientist studying the composition of bricks or, say, their hardness or strength or extension.[25] A related type of care applies to interactions with other people in the situation as opposed to things. Such care or interest may be positive, negative, or indifferent, by which I mean that it may be oriented for or against them or may be indifferent to them.[26]

---

24. Wheeler (2018).
25. Heidegger (1927/1962, p. 124) explicitly discusses such properties in his section on Descartes.
26. Heidegger (1927/1962, pp. 439–440) says: "When we are with one another in public, our everyday concern does not encounter just equipment and work; it likewise encounters what is 'given' along with these: 'affairs', undertakings, incidents, mishaps. The 'world' belongs to everyday trade and traffic as the soil from which they grow and the arena where they are displayed.

This "Heideggerian" picture of situated agents dovetails nicely with the situated game-theoretic view. The preferences of agents are nothing but their interests or care. More precisely, preferences and payoffs describe the *form* of our interests. Heidegger also looks at the choices an agent faces in terms of their *possibilities* for being one way or another.[27] And the wider situation of the game is just the world of the agents. This is why I called the partial rationality of agents *existential* because Heidegger uses this term to describe the Being of agents, and their partial rationality is surely one such feature. Indeed, situated games and how they are played can be seen as a further specification of a person's fundamental being, in particular, of the structure of their world, what Heidegger calls their world's *worldhood*.[28]

Such a connection between situated games and Heidegger also suggests a different way of looking at his distinction between ready-to-hand and present-at-hand. As I just said, the latter comes to the fore when a person attends to something in their environment in a disinterested way, the way the archetypal dispassionate scientist supposedly might. However, we can argue that there is almost never any disinterested action. Everything is more or less pursued through our interests or care, that is, through our preferences or payoffs. The scientist studying the composition of a brick has different interests from the scientist studying its hardness or strength or extension, and both have different interests from the bricklayer and civil engineer and architect, all of whose interests also differ from each other's. So there are just different and more or less concrete or abstract and more or less narrow or wide interests or cares that human beings have. In other words, everything is ready-to-hand and there is nothing present-at-hand in an absolute sense. Even an impartial and neutral umpire's situated disinterestedness is a higher-level interest circumscribed by the situation they are in. Heidegger wavers between allowing completely disinterested behavior and most actions being partially rational as I take them to be.[29]

---

When we are with one another in public, the Others are encountered in activity of such a kind that one is 'in the swim' with it 'oneself'. One is acquainted with it, discusses it, encourages it, combats it, retains it, and forgets it, but one always does so primarily with regard to what is getting done and what is 'going to come of it'."

27. Heidegger (1927/1962, sec. 31).

28. Heidegger (1927/1962, Division One, chap. 3).

29. Heidegger (1927/1962, p. 177) says: "By looking at the world theoretically, we have already dimmed it down to the uniformity of what is purely present-at-hand, though admittedly this

There is a lot more that could be said in this exploration of a possible parallelism between two very different traditions of thought. Part of my purpose throughout is to suggest a way these traditions can be seamlessly conjoined via the study of situated choice and action. This is important because these two broad traditions emerged largely from the Enlightenment and Romanticism, two defining and divergent periods in modernity responsible for some of the polarization in our times—crudely put, between reason and emotion, fact and feeling—and if a way can be found to bring them closer together, it might help to heal our split self-understandings and self-interpretations.

## 6.9  Situated Games and Complexity

I will be using situated games to understand communication and the meanings of linguistic and visual utterances and also to understand the structure of society. Before I do this, it is important to be aware of two potential challenges for game theory.

First, many social situations can be quite complex and so the games carved out to grasp their essences are best used in an abstract way where one focuses on relatively few choices and corresponding payoffs. This is, in any case, how people with limited capacities involved in such games represent them.

The games I have looked at in this chapter considered two choices for each agent. More choices can certainly be included but the simplicity of the models then naturally diminishes and the insights they provide into the dynamics of a situation suffer. Differently put, a certain skill in modeling is required where the right level of partiality and abstraction is deployed so that the results obtained are maximally useful. Indeed, this is the task we all face as we talk to and interact with each other. Those who are able to see into the essence of an interaction more adroitly may be able to play the game better. The exercise of this

---

uniformity comprises a new abundance of things which can be discovered by simply characterizing them. Yet even the purest ... [theory] has not left all moods behind it; even when we look theoretically at what is just present-at-hand, it does not show itself purely as it looks unless this [theory] lets it come towards us in a tranquil tarrying alongside.... Any cognitive determining has its existential-ontological Constitution in the state-of-mind of Being-in-the-world; but pointing this out is not to be confused with attempting to surrender science ontically to 'feeling'." Here, "ontological" just means *related to Being* and "ontic" just means *related to entities*.

ability is colloquially called *strategy*. Let us call this difficulty the representational challenge.

Second, in my description of various games, I said the choices and preferences or payoffs resulted partly from objective factors and partly from subjective factors. However, this was an oversimplification. Even subjective factors may be socially influenced by the larger society in which a game is embedded. An agent's preference for chocolate ice cream over vanilla ice cream or, more consequentially, for democracy over authoritarianism can be the result of their prior socialization. And the choices made in such situations can in turn affect social outcomes—through a purchase of chocolate ice cream or a vote for a democratically inclined candidate, for instance. This apparent circularity of individual action affecting society and society affecting individual action poses formidable difficulties for social theory. It is generally tackled purely descriptively with the precise mechanism underlying this circularity left unexplained. I will address it in the next two parts of the book but I point out here that this circularity challenge interacts with the one above of representational complexity, and it may allow only a partial solution.

To summarize this chapter, I introduced the idea of situated games that are made up of situations supporting games proper. The relevant games proper consist of two or more agents, choices of action for each agent, and payoffs for each combination of choices. This tripartite structure can be compactly represented visually in a matrix. The situated games are solved by certain equilibrium concepts that tell us how the agents are likely to play the game, that is, what actions they are likely to choose. It is the partial rationality of agents that guides their choices and behavior.

## 6.10 The Story Further Along

This second part, somewhat more abstract and complex than the first, involved the tools—situations and games—we need to tackle the ubiquitous problems of context and action that form the bedrock of language and society as interlaced with the web of meaning.

The explicitness of situations as opposed to vague talk of contexts, and the concreteness of games—their choices and payoffs—as opposed to vague talk of interactions between people, provide additional detail, indeed additional constraints and connections, that is, *meanings*, that a mere verbal description cannot. Think of how much more the concepts of supply and demand and their equilibrium add to our understanding compared to saying that people produce goods and services that other people buy.

In some cases, these two tools may even suggest ways we can *act* in the world to *change* a social situation because games model what we choose to do. By understanding the games we are engaged in, we can bring about social change and transform social reality.

We now move onward to grasp verbal communication in a thorough way that grounds our approach to the structure of a widening arc of systems and social institutions. Along the way, I will continue to discuss AI, ending with my own suggestions for a situated AI before proceeding to the finale.

# PART III

# MEANING AND MODERNITY

# CHAPTER SEVEN

# How We Communicate

So far, I have discussed what meaning is in general, what makes linguistic meaning difficult to understand (the presence of ambiguity, vagueness, and context), some connections between language and AI and language and politics, and, finally, what games are and how they permeate our social lives. I now turn to communication—where many of these themes come together. Practically all contributors to language have considered communication in one way or another. I will restrict myself to my own approach.

The reason for my extended attention to language and communication is twofold: without them, no society or civilization is possible, and second, their detailed study provides a concrete insight into the nature of society because they mirror other social institutions and, indeed, society at large.

## 7.1 The Key Ideas

### 7.1.1 Fixed and Variable

Every social institution including language involves some parts that are relatively fixed and others that vary from situation to situation. This is the general distinction between structure and agency in the social sciences, or what, in the case of language, Saussure[1] first identified as *langue* and *parole* or, as I refer to it, language and communication.

For our purposes here, I will be ignoring the role of syntax and phonetics in (spoken) communication; the relatively fixed part of language I will consider is what I have called conventional meaning. Only words have conventional

---

1. Saussure (1960). See also Barthes (1968).

meanings and all agents represent them in their heads as concepts.[2] In this chapter, I will take conventional meanings as fixed; in the next chapter, I will show how they, too, result from communication in society.

The relatively variable parts of language are the intended meanings—also called referential meanings—we attempt to convey to our addressees in particular utterance situations. An ambiguous word like "bank" with two or more conventional meanings can be "exploited" to convey *a certain type of financial institution* in a particular utterance like "Why do you rob banks?" to which Willie Sutton apparently replied, "Because that is where the money is," a clear case where the conventionally ambiguous word "bank" was correctly disambiguated to its intended referential meaning. (By the way, this old joke also involves a switch in meanings from a stress on "rob" to a stress on "banks.") There are also unintended meanings that are part of the whole meaning of the utterance and discourse but they are not part of the communication which is understood as the conveying of intended meanings by a speaker to an addressee.

Thus, conventional meanings and referential meanings are the relatively fixed and relatively variable parts of communication. As I will show in this chapter and the next, there is a quasi-circularity between these two kinds of meaning and therefore between (a part of) language and communication. This kind of circularity between institutional structure and agency where each influences the other—that is, where relatively fixed meanings influence relatively variable meanings and vice versa—is, in fact, the rule rather than the exception, as we will see. This is part of the reason why social institutions are hard to understand and why they sometimes appear immutable.

### 7.1.2 Parts and Wholes

Suppose Ann and Bob are chatting about a local election and Ann says, "Fred ran." Assume they both know two Freds, Fred Smith and Fred Jones—the former a local politician who has campaigned for political office and the latter a runner who frequents sporting events. These ambient facts make the utterance highly ambiguous because "Fred" could refer (via its conventional meaning) to either of the two Freds and "ran" could refer (again via its conventional meaning)

---

2. I ignore some subtleties here. See Putnam (1975), Parikh (2010, p. 291), Parikh (2019, sec. 26.2).

to either *stood for election* or *participated in a race*.³ Given the context of their conversation being about the local election, the odds are greater that Ann means to convey *Fred Smith stood for election*. How does Bob figure out what she intends?

The two parts of the utterance "Fred" and "ran" are interdependent. If the first refers to Fred Smith the politician, then it is more likely that the second refers to *stood for election*. And vice versa. Each reinforces the other probabilistically, and the utterance situation also reinforces this pair of interpretations. But the other two possible referents, *Fred Jones* and *participated in a race*, also reinforce each other probabilistically although the utterance situation pushes away from them.

Thus, even in this exceedingly simple utterance, it is possible to see a complex probabilistic dynamics of one part of the utterance or system influencing another part and vice versa. And the role of the utterance situation or context brings in the influence of the ambient information and the whole direct (and indirect) meaning of the utterance. This interplay of parts and whole is central to the production and comprehension of meaning at multiple levels: conventional meaning and referential meaning, word and sentence, sentence and discourse (or text), discourse (or text) and context, and speaker and addressee.

It turns out that this interaction between parts and whole can be perfectly captured by games between Ann and Bob corresponding to "Fred" and to "ran" and to the whole sentence "Fred ran," and its resolution—Ann's intended meaning—is then given by the equilibrium of this set of games. The new feature of these games is that they are interdependent and they can be multiplied to represent the interactions between the parts "Fred" and "ran" and the whole "Fred ran." The entire complex of games involved in communication is called a Communication Game. When Ann and Bob converse, it is a Communication Game that emerges between them and that they solve to convey meanings to each other and understand each other.

This is all there is to inferring intended meanings from scratch, at least in my theoretical framework, which I call Equilibrium Semantics. I say "from scratch" because almost nothing beyond the partial rationality of Ann and Bob is assumed. Naturally, I haven't gone into the details.⁴

---

3. Note that "race" is ambiguous between a sporting event and an electoral event here but I will use it throughout to mean the former.

4. I believe this is a richer framework closer to actual human behavior than offered by so-called reinforcement learning in AI. See Sutton and Barto (2018).

It is a Communication Game—or some equivalent formalism—that an artificial agent needs to play to engage in genuine communication where ambiguity, vagueness, context, and other difficulties are handled adequately. In my view, it should form the heart of the subfields of AI called natural language understanding and generation.

The interactive tension, the push and pull of probabilistic influences in a Communication Game, is a mathematical generalization of two principles Frege outlined a century ago, the compositionality principle and the context principle. The first said the meaning of the whole sentence results from the meanings of the parts, and the second said the meanings of the parts result from the meaning of the whole sentence. Subsequent scholarship has noted this tension but has had relatively little to offer to deal with it.[5] Communication Games fully resolve the conflict between them by clearly representing the competing forces and finding an equilibrium among them.

Indeed, what seems not to have been noticed before, Frege's principles can be seen as two halves of an instance—between word and sentence—of a broader but vaguer insight into deciphering meaning called the *hermeneutic circle*, perhaps first identified in the West by Schleiermacher, Dilthey, and others.[6] The hermeneutic circle refers to the kinds of interdependencies I mentioned above at multiple levels: conventional meaning and referential meaning, word and sentence, sentence and text, text and context, and speaker and addressee. It is because of such interdependencies that reading a text twice or hearing a piece of music twice enables one to grasp it much better. Those who pursue hermeneutics typically approach the task in a fuzzy and descriptive rather than clear and analytic way as I am recommending. And again, it is the idea of equilibrium that cuts through the Gordian knot of circularity at all these multiple levels.

---

5. See Dummett (1996, pp. 4–5). There are different ways of interpreting especially the context principle as pointed out by Matilal and Sen (1988). Indeed, they also show that there were quite remarkable debates in classical Indian philosophy of a similar sort from roughly the fifth century CE to the seventeenth. Their key proponents espoused "sentence holism" (similar to the context principle) and what is called "designation before connection" (similar to compositionality) and "connected designation" (intermediate between the two principles). These discussions went on for centuries.

6. Modern hermeneutics is a primarily continental approach to the science of interpretation. See Bleicher (1980) and also Mantzavinos (2016) and Malpas (2018). See Keating (2018) for a little about classical Indian hermeneutics.

Finally, such circularities occur not only in language and communication but also in other social institutions and in society as a whole.[7] In fact, it is a fairly general problem that affects many systems, not just social ones. As the writer Paul Auster has said, "In the same way, the world is not the sum of all the things that are in it. It is the infinitely complex network of connections among them. As in the meanings of words, things take on meaning only in relationship to each other."[8]

## 7.1.3 Networks

The first key idea had to do with the relatively fixed and relatively variable parts of communication called conventional meaning and referential meaning. When conventional meaning is held fixed in a single utterance situation, communication involves exploiting it to convey referential meanings. The third key idea completes the circle—mentioned under the second key idea of parts and whole—between conventional meaning and referential meaning by showing how the two co-determine each other.

Recall that conventional meanings are concepts that are more or less shared across society. They affect not just the conversation between Ann and Bob about a local election but all the conversations taking place in society. They are a part of language itself.

Communication Games help us figure out what our interlocutors are conveying. (Indeed, they even enable what we say and how we say it given our goals and intentions.) They assume the existence of conventional meanings in language and yield referential meanings. But how do words get their conventional meanings in the first place? Where do they come from?

The answer must be that they also come from communication, just as with referential meanings. When Ann and Bob engage in conversation, they not only exchange referential meanings but also reinforce or modify conventional meanings, that is, *create* conventional meanings. When we talk to each other, we are typically aware only of the referential meanings we transmit, but we are also

---

7. Aron (1965/1981, p. 15).
8. Auster (2007, p. 160).

playing a small part in creating language itself, sometimes by changing a conventional meaning, but more often by maintaining it.[9]

Such changes usually take a long time to develop fully. The conventional meanings of a single word like "dog" result from countless conversations and countless conversations are affected by these conventional meanings in a diachronic way. And it is through these very encounters that they also *change*, as becomes evident if one traces the word's evolution from the Old and Middle English "docga" and "dogge" to its modern form and meanings.

To understand how conventional meanings emerge and are maintained or change, we have to consider not just the one utterance situation between Ann and Bob but multiple interlocking conversations across society. Just as the ideas of interdependence between games and products of games were required to grasp the interactions of parts and wholes, here it is the idea of a network of Communication Games that enables us to apprehend how conventional meanings and referential meanings reciprocally influence each other and evolve from what I call a *meaningful* equilibrium. Such a network of Communication Games is called a Language Game, a term I have borrowed from Wittgenstein but use in my own way. I call the study of Communication Games micro-semantics and the study of Language Games macro-semantics based on a rough analogy with microeconomics and macroeconomics.

The same kinds of mechanisms apply to various social institutions, whether it is something small like greeting someone with a conventional namaste or something large like the global economy. Indeed, my inspiration for this network model of macro-semantics is a large analogy between the social institution of linguistic communication and a market economy, which is similarly ongoing and circular both with respect to the equation of supply and demand within a single market as well as within the wider interactions among different markets. Comparing the idea of meaningful equilibrium above with the idea of general economic equilibrium,[10] utterance situations are like markets, words are like commodities, conventional meanings are like the prices of commodities, and

---

9. Wittgenstein (1953/1968) famously compared words with tools. While he is right about referential meanings, the analogy breaks down when considering how conventional meanings emerge and change. Hammers have separate processes of manufacture and use. With words, the same process of communication is involved.

10. See Arrow and Debreu (1954).

referential meanings are like the quantities of commodities bought or sold. Just as prices and quantities emerge from a general economic equilibrium, so conventional meanings and referential meanings emerge from a meaningful equilibrium. Language change is roughly similar to the way in which the prices of goods in a market economy change. And just as a price system spares us the trouble of bargaining every time we buy or sell goods, so conventional meanings (and grammar and standardization of the communicative devices we use—the spellings of words, for instance) ease our effort.

I will discuss Language Games in the next chapter. Suffice it to say here that these three ideas together allow one to answer in a precise way perhaps the most fundamental question of semantics: how language acquires meaning.[11]

## 7.2 Communication and Jokes

Recall from the earlier discussion of jokes that a switch from a common to a rare meaning was found to be a necessary condition for a discourse to be a joke. In light of the framework above, we can now say that the switch in interpretation is really a switch from one equilibrium to another. Reconsider the first joke I mentioned:

> "Every ten minutes a man gets mugged in New York. Tonight we are going to interview him."

The first sentence results in a Communication Game with the common meaning as its equilibrium and the whole discourse results in a larger Communication Game with the rarer meaning as its equilibrium. This requires extending Communication Games to two or more sentences, not to mention extending them to single sentences with many more words than "Fred ran." This requires some work, especially the extension to discourse, but it can be done by applying the idea of interdependent parts and whole to all the sentences in the discourse taken together. When there is a pun or double meaning, there will be two equilibria.

---

11. For a fully worked out account, see Parikh (2019).

These insights also allow us in principle to build part of an AI system that might fulfill one necessary condition for understanding jokes.[12]

## 7.3 Communication and Political Speech

Earlier, I also gave an informal argument for why many politicians—both good and bad—and, indeed, even the rest of us—are often driven to more extreme versions of our views to avoid unscrupulous others from exploiting what may be seen as weakness as opposed to nuance.

The example I considered was climate change as the primary explanation for the fires in California. If an ethical politician were to say, "Very likely, climate change is primarily responsible for the fires," their statement is likely to be distorted by an unethical opponent and even turned into its opposite. So they could be driven to say, "Certainly, climate change is primarily responsible for the fires" or just "Climate change is primarily responsible for the fires," much stronger statements that may not be warranted by the available evidence.

Indeed, most situations in political life are plagued by unavoidable uncertainty and ambiguity and complexity, and so, especially when the stakes are high as they tend to be in politics, greater honesty and a nuanced language of probabilities should be encouraged in the public sphere. But, apart from the greater difficulty in understanding such statements of likelihood, because politicians have their eyes on reelection and related extraneous matters, they generally succumb to extreme speech.

Now that I have outlined a simple model of Communication Games involving how a single utterance is understood, one can envisage how slightly more complex models might be constructed that capture dialogue and anticipated responses to one's utterances. The key insight is that the possible responses of addressees are taken into account in speakers' plans and influence what they choose to say. In political speech, speakers are more likely to opt for more extreme utterances because their addressees may misrepresent their statements and the stakes are high. It isn't necessary to pursue the details here as it is more

---

12. Some aspects of this are discussed in Parikh (2019, chaps. 7–8).

important for our purposes to get a flavor of it than a full taste.[13] Other dimensions of political communication in the public sphere can also be understood in similar ways.

## 7.4 Utterance Meaning and Discourse Meaning

To return to our main topic of communication in general, I reproduce Figure 3.6 as Figure 7.1 to remind you of the overall picture of meaning I had provided earlier.

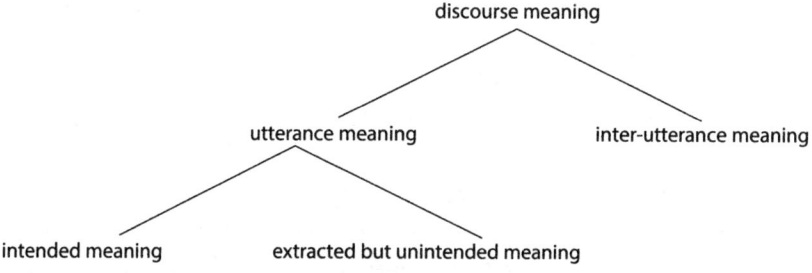

Figure 7.1   Classification of Discourse Meaning

I have discussed how direct intended meanings of utterances like "Fred ran" could be derived using my framework of Equilibrium Semantics. This method can be extended to indirect intended meanings. Both types of intended meaning together make up what is communicated in an utterance and are accounted for by Communication Games.

For extracted but unintended meanings that fall outside the domain of communication, fewer such definite inference procedures are available, as such meanings are usually extracted from an utterance via quite varied techniques. Some of these are amenable to handling by situation theory but others may need to be simply described in words.

---

13. A general model can be found in Parikh (2001, chap. 8) and especially in Parikh (2019, chap. 7). Reception Theory, developed by the cultural theorist Stuart Hall (1980), can be modified and added to my model to account for communication via various mass media. It would need to be modified because Hall builds on literary theorists Roland Barthes's and Umberto Eco's semiotic theories, which leave much to be desired.

## 7.5 Referential Meaning

I have clarified that conventional meanings are concepts, situated mental representations more or less in our heads. However, the precise status of referential meanings, which include all intended meanings, has been left implicit.

First, the possible direct referential meanings of a word like "Fred" or "ran" come from its conventional meanings. This can be pictured thus:

$$\text{word} \xrightarrow{u} \text{conventional meanings} \xrightarrow{u} \text{referential meanings}$$

A word leads to its possible conventional meanings, each of which results in one or more referential meanings relative to the utterance situation $u$. If conventional meanings are held fixed, the framework allows us to disambiguate the possible referential meanings via Communication Games, and if the conventional meanings vary, the framework allows us to disambiguate both the conventional and referential meanings via Language Games. And this is done for the whole utterance, not just for a single word. In this way, all linguistic meaning can be seen as a connection between utterances and (semantic) contents. This fits in with the general understanding of meaning as a connection between situated entities.

Second, referential meanings, the semantic contents of an utterance, are also just situated states of affairs. For the example at hand—Ann saying "Fred ran" to Bob in $u$—the disambiguated referential meaning is the state of affairs *Fred Smith stood for election* which is situated as follows:

- $s$ supports Fred Smith stood for election.

As there are both direct and indirect intended meanings, there are usually many states of affairs that result from an utterance. And especially with indirect meanings, they often appear probabilistically in $s$. Such a complex—a situation supporting multiple states of affairs probabilistically—is called a proposition. Utterances can thus be said to express propositions,[14] although when communication is partial there can be more than one proposition involved.

Implicit in this view of referential meanings and propositions is a sharp distinction between utterances and their contents. This separation is questioned

---

14. Indeed, the notion of an utterance is not just linguistic: as I said in Section 5.5, a traffic light may *tell* a driver to stop or to go; a photograph may *depict* a sunrise or sunset; a song may *evoke* joy or sorrow; a wave of the hand may *signal* a greeting or a goodbye; a building lobby may *express* warmth or coolness—all these are also instances of utterances expressing propositions.

by the philosopher Charles Taylor who points out that when language is used to express our feelings, it makes them clearer and more defined, and hence transforms them.[15] Thus, utterances about our emotions are *not* sharply distinct from them. That is, the distinction between utterances and their contents breaks down in certain cases.

It has been a basic assumption of referential semantics since Frege that the referents of words are wholly independent of them. This is true of objects like forks and knives but not of many emotions. In other words, depending on what they are about, utterances can partly affect the propositions they express. Despite this partial influence, propositions do not become linguistic entities themselves. Indeed, the key concept of reference still applies to all words.[16] In some cases the states of affairs represented will be independent of the uttered words and in other cases they will be partly modified by them.

## 7.6 What Is Understanding?

So far, I have said that (linguistic) communication involves conveying propositions from the speaker to the addressee. However, we all know intuitively that communication is more than this. Happy or sad news may affect the addressee differently, possibly even creating palpable bodily effects. Thus, communication not only involves relaying propositional content but also has nonpropositional *effects*; while the former is cognitive, the latter can involve the whole person. Based on this broader idea of communication, we can now say that linguistic understanding involves grasping both its aspects, its propositional content as well as its effects.

In my view, to grasp a proposition is not only to represent it in one's head but also to know how it hooks up with the physical and social world, just as I said that in order to be said to think, an AI agent must not only have a semantics— a connection between representation and world—but also be aware of its semantics. Thus, thinking and understanding seem to obey the same meta-level constraint. Even if an AI agent could disambiguate the various examples of

---

15. Taylor (1977/1999).

16. Taylor (1981/1999, p. 101) himself accepts this. See also Parikh (2019, chap. 6).

ambiguity I have discussed, that would only get it to have a semantics. To also be aware of its semantics is a further step that may or may not be within its reach.

As we have seen, ChatGPT succeeds partly with the challenges of ambiguity, vagueness, and context. Its key idea of *self-attention*—roughly, the overall correlation of a word in a sentence with other words in the same sentence—results in its representing the world in a partial way:

> As side benefit, self-attention could yield more interpretable models. ... Not only do individual attention heads[17] clearly learn to perform different tasks, many appear to exhibit behavior related to the syntactic and semantic structure of the sentences.[18]

Notice that in Section 7.1.2 the framework of Equilibrium Semantics also considers the connections between "Fred" and "ran" in a way similar to self-attention. In my view, self-attention comes close to exploiting the full *linguistic* contexts of all the words in a sentence but doesn't accomplish this as fully as Equilibrium Semantics does. But it has the possible advantage of repeated multiple layers of a "deep" neural network, whereas Equilibrium Semantics involves a one-shot process.

In any case, ChatGPT has no recourse to the *situational* context and so cannot handle certain simple types of prompts at all:

> Me: It is four p.m.
>
> ChatGPT: I'm sorry, I am an AI language model and do not have the capability to keep track of time. Is there anything else I can assist you with?

So, in terms of the first level of one part of understanding—having a semantics—its abilities are partial. It does not exploit the sentential context fully and it has no way to get at the situational context. However, it should be added that it does incorporate human feedback via so-called *reinforcement learning* and this can give it indirect partial access to some aspects of the situational context.[19] As far

---

17. Each attention head computes a different correlation, which may be related to the syntax or semantics of the sentence.
18. Vaswani et al. (2017, sec. 4); see Vaswani et al. (2017, pp. 13–15) as well.
19. Ouyang et al. (2022).

as the second level goes—having an awareness of its semantics—it could be said to be entirely absent although, as I said earlier, the vagueness of this criterion hinders a clear resolution.

Some further clarity may be achieved by turning to the schema for conventional and referential meanings from the previous section:

$$\text{word} \xrightarrow{u} \text{conventional meanings} \xrightarrow{u} \text{referential meanings}$$

Should an awareness of the semantics, that is, understanding, be identified purely with the referential meanings of an utterance or do its conventional meanings also play a part? That is, is understanding purely denotational or is it also connotational?

In a perceptive essay, the computer scientist Christopher Manning says:

> The dominant approach to describing meaning, in not only linguistics and philosophy of language but also for programming languages, is a *denotational semantics* approach or a *theory of reference*: the meaning of a word, phrase, or sentence is the set of objects or situations in the world that it describes (or a mathematical abstraction thereof). This contrasts with the simple *distributional semantics* (or *use theory of meaning*) of modern empirical work in NLP [natural language processing] whereby the meaning of a word is simply a description of the contexts in which it appears. Some have suggested that the latter is not a theory of semantics at all but just a regurgitation of distributional or syntactic facts. I would disagree. Meaning is not all or nothing; in many circumstances, we partially appreciate the meaning of a linguistic form. I suggest that meaning arises from understanding the network of connections between a linguistic form and other things, whether they be objects in the world or other linguistic forms. For example, if I have held an Indian *shehnai*, then I have a reasonable idea of the meaning of the word, but I would have a richer meaning if I had also heard one being played. Going in the other direction, if I have never seen, felt, or heard a *shehnai*, but someone tells me that *it's like a traditional Indian oboe*, then the word has some meaning for me: it has connections to India, to wind instruments that use reeds, and to playing music.[20]

---

20. Manning (2022, p. 134).

While awareness of purely conventional meanings or connotations (i.e., meanings related to but not quite the same as what Manning calls "distributional semantics," the linguistic contexts of words) also counts, and should enter our concept of understanding, we would have to acknowledge that a language model like ChatGPT does *not* acquire even this connotational understanding because a conventional meaning, as I said earlier, is a *concept*, and concepts are inextricably linked to the world: they are *not* just linguistic forms like "traditional Indian oboe" which is all that ChatGPT has access to. Manning says that when he is told that a *shehnai* is like a traditional Indian oboe, he acquires a connection to India and to wind instruments; this is only because *he understands the relevant comparison*, unlike ChatGPT. In other words, ChatGPT would acquire a connection only to the word "India," not to the corresponding country itself as Manning does.

The information ChatGPT amasses through self-attention is partly syntactic and partly semantic but is nevertheless encoded purely formally. This form is roughly isomorphic to the (syntactic and semantic) content and so it learns—indirectly and abstractly—to partially represent the world. The formal structure of the phrase "traditional Indian oboe" is roughly similar to the structure of its content. Another way to think about it is to imagine what one would learn if one looked at a dictionary of a foreign language one didn't know at all (e.g., a Japanese or Arabic dictionary for a typical English reader). Thus, Manning is right that understanding is not merely denotational but is wrong that it is also distributional because the latter just mimics the content; instead, its content is syntactic or grammatical, and also connotational and denotational or, as I prefer to put it, conventional and referential.

The tricky thing here is that there are two distinctions in play: syntax/semantics and form/content. As shown in Figure 7.2, the former distinction can be represented both purely formally (as it is in us and in ChatGPT) or purely by its content (as it is only in us).

|  | syntax | semantics |
| --- | --- | --- |
| form | Humans/ChatGPT | Humans/ChatGPT |
| content | Humans | Humans |

Figure 7.2   Two Crosscutting Distinctions

The second part of understanding—to grasp the effects of an utterance—is more difficult to define but perhaps one can say it is just to experience a relevant feeling or at least to simulate it. For those familiar with it, so-called sentiment analysis in AI is able to partially identify a sentiment or feeling, usually in a coarse-grained way as positive or negative, but is not yet able to simulate it. It is difficult to say what is involved in such a task as we understand our own feelings rather poorly.

So, in conclusion, it could be said that ChatGPT exhibits only part of what is required to understand an utterance. Moreover, what is left out is likely to involve radically different approaches than those currently used in ChatGPT.

> Me: Can you understand an utterance?
>
> ChatGPT: As a language model, I am able to understand the meaning of an utterance to some extent. My understanding is based on my training data, which includes a wide range of text from various sources such as books, articles, and websites, as well as my ability to use context clues and make inferences.
>
> However, my understanding is not perfect, and there may be cases where my understanding of an utterance is not accurate or complete. Factors such as ambiguity, vagueness, or a lack of context can make it difficult for me to understand the meaning of an utterance. Additionally, my understanding of certain idioms or colloquial expressions may not align with the intended meaning or real-world usage.
>
> As a language model, my main goal is to respond to the inputs given with coherent and relevant information. And I strive to understand the intent of the user based on the given inputs and provide a response that is as informative and accurate as possible.

The other issue that has arisen in the debates that have followed the release of ChatGPT is whether understanding is essential for an intelligent language model. The definition of understanding I have provided itself explains why it is necessary for participating in society in an intelligent way. Without a connection to the world, without reference and meaning, without an awareness of semantics and feelings, all of which comes with understanding, humanlike intelligent behavior is not possible.

Can equipping an AI agent with the mathematics of Equilibrium Semantics help with grasping the propositional content of an utterance? Prima facie, it might be argued that if *we* understand linguistic meaning via something like

Equilibrium Semantics or its equivalent, then so could AI agents endowed with such mathematics. But this question needs more careful discussion, which I will save for the last part of the book.

## 7.7 Some Consequences of the Framework

We can now remark on some of the broader consequences of Equilibrium Semantics although, strictly speaking, we must wait until we can unfix conventional meanings and develop Language Games in the next chapter.

All these games together allow us to define communication, that is, give its necessary and sufficient conditions in simpler terms. Rather than say as some do that communication always occurs or never occurs,[21] one can offer a more nuanced observation of the conditions under which it takes place. This makes it clear that communication is often partial.

I started the discussion of language by saying that it was not easy to define simple-sounding notions like word meaning and reference even though anyone can look up a dictionary to find the meaning of a word or simply utter "this table" to refer to a table. We now know that word meaning is nothing but conventional meaning and, just as the many different Communication Games in society give us the many different referential meanings conveyed, Language Games give us more or less shared conventional meanings. Reference is just referential meaning so this problem, too, gets solved.

Such notions—communication, referential meaning, conventional meaning—are semantic, and the main upshot of being able to define them in terms of games is that this makes possible a reduction of the semantic to the psychological and social because games involve only our psychological attributes—mainly our beliefs and preferences—and the social relations between speakers and addressees in addition to objective factors.[22] So it is a part of the process of science of reducing complex things to simpler things because our psychological and social attributes may in turn be reducible to physical things.

---

21. Derrida (1988) comes to mind. For a critique and deconstruction of deconstruction, see Parikh (2017).
22. I say more about this in Section 8.4.

I had also raised various other questions about linguistic meaning earlier:[23] How do spoken sounds carry one or more meanings from speaker to addressee? How do the words uttered get their individual meanings in the first place? How are these individual meanings put together to create a meaningful whole? I think these questions have now been partially addressed (in Section 7.1) and will be more fully addressed by the end of the next chapter on Language Games. I had also said in Section 2.1 that I would proceed from surface phenomena to deeper concepts and this is exactly what we have done.

Since early human civilization people have often wondered about the mystery of language, how just by emitting sounds we are able to convey meanings and influence one another and learn about our fellow humans' beliefs, desires, hopes, joys, and sorrows, and Equilibrium Semantics could be a part of the answer. If something as elusive as linguistic meaning can be shown to fit in with the rest of the causal physical universe, then some of this enduring mystery will have been solved.

I have also described how Frege's two principles are generalized and the tension between them resolved by Communication Games. A further generalization follows because Frege also assumed that semantics mirrors syntax—that is, the grammatical structure influences the meaning structure in a unidirectional way. But Communication Games show that syntax and semantics—and, indeed, phonetics—reflect one another in what may be seen as yet another aspect of the hermeneutic circle with none of them having priority. In other words, just as the possible referential meanings of "Fred" affect and are affected by the possible referential meanings of "ran," so the syntax and phonetics of the parts and whole are also thrown into the mix, and each bit of information affects and is affected by the others. It is the equilibrium concept that handles all these moving parts, the probabilistic dynamics, and that is why the framework is called Equilibrium Semantics.

Further, I have shown how Frege's principles are just an instance of the so-called hermeneutic circle, and that the several levels of the hermeneutic circle—conventional meaning and referential meaning, word and sentence, sentence and text (or discourse), text and context, and speaker and addressee, not to mention syntax and semantics, and intended and unintended meaning—can all be incorporated into the situated game-theoretic analysis.

---

23. Section 2.1.

As I have said, the problem of meaning—what it is, how it is conveyed, and how it relates to reality and knowledge and belief—has occupied humanity for over three thousand years through multiple types of inquiry, chief among these being philosophy and linguistics but also the social sciences broadly considered. Meaning has been seen in analytic thought as *reference* (Frege, Russell, early Wittgenstein) and as *use* (later Wittgenstein, Austin, Grice), and in romantic and continental thought as *expression* (Herder, Humboldt, Hegel) and as *difference* (Saussure, Jakobson, Barthes, Derrida). Equilibrium Semantics offers a new paradigm: meaning as *equilibrium* which synthesizes especially the ideas of reference and use in a novel way but also goes beyond them.

A new subspecies of meaning as use has emerged through deep learning as developed by Google, OpenAI, and similar companies but its connection to the *problem* of meaning and especially understanding appears to be at best partial and at worst entirely absent, although this remains controversial.

Lastly, the framework gives us a material feel for how communication occurs, for its nuts and bolts, and when we consider broader issues of society and civilization in later chapters, we will be in a position to pin down and ground the argument because we will know whereof we speak. For example, a great deal has been said about communication in the public sphere but without a solid grasp of what communication actually is and what its possibilities and limits are. Our approach will be relatively concrete rather than abstract and that will, I hope, make it less speculative and more scientific. Later, we will see that other social institutions and society itself are structurally similar to language and embody the key ideas of fixed and variable, parts and whole, and networks, and so a relatively greater concreteness should be available to us for those considerations as well. I have tried to walk the middle path between the Scylla of a sweeping and overly abstract idealism and the Charybdis of a narrow and overly concrete materialism. As the architect Mies van der Rohe rightly observed, god is in the detail.

# CHAPTER EIGHT

# Language at Large

As we saw in the last chapter, a key assumption of micro-semantics is that the conventional meanings of words[1] are fixed and given and are exploited by speakers and addressees in communicating referential meanings. This makes it possible to give a fairly complete account of communication and meaning at an abstracted, micro level. But this leaves unfinished the explanation of how semiosis gets off the ground, how language—that is, sounds or written marks—acquires meaning in the first place. Conventional meaning itself must emerge through communication because there is nothing else, no other possible source. To understand this origination, it becomes necessary to shift from a single utterance to society-wide conversations, from micro-semantics to macro-semantics.

## 8.1 How Conventional Meanings Emerge

In macro-semantics, the assumption that conventional meaning is fixed and *externally* given is relaxed. Now, imagine conversations going on in a large number of utterance situations across society with each agent participating in multiple exchanges either as speaker or addressee. Initially, the conventional meanings of words are not fixed but emerge *internally* through the conversations by converging to relatively fixed and stable properties or concepts, just as the prices of different goods in a market economy converge to relatively fixed and stable numerical values. The precise mechanisms through which a meaningful equilibrium[2] and a general economic equilibrium emerge are naturally different but

---

1. In Equilibrium Semantics, only words have conventional meanings. Longer expressions such as phrases and whole sentences do not. Idiomatic expressions (e.g., "kicked the bucket") and such multi-word expressions are treated differently.
2. See Section 7.1.3.

one can still say a kind of invisible hand operates in both. No single individual or group can control the outcomes although some may exert a disproportionate influence (e.g., Shakespeare in the case of language and a monopoly in the case of a market economy).

What then is the mechanism for language? The new idea is both simple and natural: all we require is that *whatever* the conventional meanings may eventually turn out to be, they be *consistent* across users: *the same agent will not use a word with different conventional meanings every time they speak or interpret.* That is, consistency implies that both parties to a conversation will use the same conventional meanings not only in the exchange at hand but in *all* their communications. For example, both Ann and Bob will use "bank" or "zoo" with the same conventional meanings—whatever these may initially be—not only when talking with each other but in all their conversations across society. As should be evident, this is a result of rationality because the cognitive cost of maintaining changing conventional meanings for the same word would be prohibitive. Consistency severely limits the range of conventional meanings a word can acquire and makes it possible to derive not only referential meanings via the relevant Communication Games but also conventional meanings for each of the words in the language. The society-wide collection of interlocking Communication Games, linked via this "Consistency Condition" on conventional meanings, is what I called a Language Game. There can be many different kinds of Language Games based on the variety of networks—connections between people via Communication Games—that are possible in society.

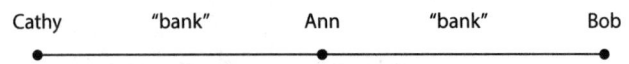

Figure 8.1   A Language Game with a Network of Two Communication Games

By employing the Consistency Condition across such Language Games, it is possible to show that the society converges to a meaningful equilibrium where each word gets connected with its corresponding conventional meanings.[3]

---

3. For a discussion of how this happens for a simple type of Language Game, see Parikh (2019, chap. 22). Incidentally, the double fact of identifying a finite number of possibilities for conventional meanings based on frequency of use and then identifying the equilibrium of the relevant finite game seems to solve the Wittgensteinian skeptical paradox (of plus and quus) as discussed by Kripke (1982).

When conventional meanings emerge through Language Games, the society of agents becomes a *linguistic* community. It is possible in principle to envisage multiple networks, as shown in Figure 8.2, encompassing the entire population of the planet that comprise many linguistic communities with some agents being members of more than one such community. As populations move about, coming closer or drawing apart either spatially or culturally, the links among them will change and so will their languages. Indeed, there is an entire politics of global language dynamics through history that can be studied, in principle, via Language Games.

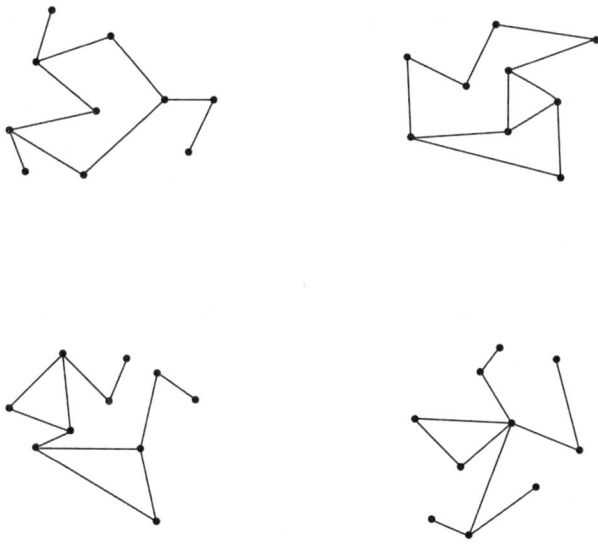

Figure 8.2  Language Games in Society

Gestures preceded verbal language in our evolution and it is likely that early humans both pointed at objects in their visual environment and uttered accompanying grunts. So, language could build on gesture and early attempts at verbal communication were probably overdetermined: the addressee could infer the correct verbal response also from what the speaker was pointing at. Of course, pointing and other gestures also involve solving games but here context and salience play some role in eliminating most possibilities. There is also an element of naturalism as opposed to conventionalism in gestural language—just as there is with visual language—that is absent in verbal language. Thus, semiosis uses quasi-naturalistic symbols to ascend to purely conventional symbols. So-called displaced reference—reference to objects that cannot be pointed to because they are not in the perceptually accessible environment—comes later, building upon a base of already acquired conventional meanings.

Combined with the observations in the previous chapter, this also shows how to complete the reduction of meaning, how both conventional meanings and referential meanings attach to utterances, assuming little more than the partial rationality of interacting finite agents. It requires first solving the problem of communication abstractly—micro-semantics—assuming conventional meaning is fixed, and then solving the problem of communication in its full societal setting—macro-semantics—allowing conventional meaning to vary.

Thus, networks of local Communication Games that encompass all of society can generate global meaningful equilibria. This new result is extremely important as it can be applied to a wide variety of networks across society that are formally similar to but substantively different from Language Games. Such equilibria, both static and dynamic, pervade all of society.

## 8.2 How Conventional Meanings Change

Not only do relatively fixed conventional meanings emerge through communication as meaningful equilibria, they also evolve over the centuries.[4] Such semantic change is part of the wider changes that occur in all aspects of language.[5]

The conventional meanings of a single word like "dog" stabilize over countless conversations and countless conversations exploit these relatively stable conventional meanings. But it is through these very exchanges that they also slowly transform, as can be seen from how the Old and Middle English "docga" and "dogge" meaning *large and powerful dog* changed into the word's current broader meaning encompassing *all* dogs.

Usually when Ann says something to Bob, she will merely reinforce standard ways of speaking (or writing). Occasionally, something is altered. For example, a single word may involve a broadened meaning as with "dog." Bob then has to understand the utterance despite the alteration by using the available

---

4. Sometimes, language change occurs quite rapidly as we have seen in our age of ubiquitous texting.

5. See Crowley and Bowern (2010) for an introduction to what is called historical linguistics.

utterance situation and linguistic context. If he is successful, the relevant change gets established between Ann and Bob and can potentially be repeated between them. Such a change may then also be transmitted to Cathy and others by either Ann or Bob via similar utterances and may thereby spread through the linguistic community and become a change in the language. This process of an initial change becoming established between two people—the communicative aspect—and then being disseminated through society—the propagative aspect—can be modeled by a Communication Game and a version of a Language Game.[6]

There are two seemingly contradictory properties of such changes in meaning. One is that it is quite difficult for a single person to bring about such a change intentionally. It is an improbable, even conservative, process that is highly dependent on the circumstances because at each step of its propagation a chain in the network can be broken by an uncooperative participant. Second, meanings do nevertheless keep changing despite these difficulties because there are a lot of participants in the relevant Language Games and each participant contributes to possible changes intentionally or unintentionally. These two facts are important not just for understanding the dynamics of language but, indeed, for the evolution of all social institutions as we will see.

Overall, then, uttering sentences serves at least two functions: the first, generally conscious and intended, is to communicate something, and the second, generally unconscious and unintended, is to either reinforce or change aspects of language. This makes us all co-creators of language, from its origins to its dynamics over history. However, these dynamics reflect the larger sociopolitical context of global society, and inequalities of power and influence are as rife in language as in other social institutions, as can be seen from how colonialism affected languages across the world over the course of modernity.[7]

## 8.3 Convention

Why do we call conventional meanings conventional? What are conventions—like greeting someone with a namaste or, far more important, practicing reciprocity or, in other words, treating others as you would like to be treated yourself, a social norm

---

6. For the details, see Parikh (2019, chap. 24).

7. Some of Bourdieu's (2003) essays deal with such issues but within a different framework.

found in almost all societies around the world from the dawn of human history—and how do they emerge? In a nutshell, conventions (or social norms) are to actions what conventional meanings are to words and utterances: they are a *language of actions* that powerfully shapes society and partly makes it what it is.

The philosopher David Lewis has said there are three basic requirements for a regular practice among members of a population to be a convention: the regular practice itself, a system of mutual expectations about it, and a system of preferences involving it. On top of this, he demands that these three requirements be common knowledge in the population.[8]

Imagine that Ann meets a stranger in such a population. How should she greet them? Should she extend her hand for a handshake? Should she do a namaste? Her choice will depend on the situation and the clues available to her. She will estimate the likelihood that the stranger is party to either convention and proceed. If she guesses correctly, she will succeed, and if her guess is incorrect, her action may be inappropriate, and she may have to revise it. Likewise, when approaching a stranger on the streets in New York, should one speak in English or in one of the myriad other languages spoken in the city? One estimates probabilities based on the concrete situation and acts. Similar examples suggest that Lewis's requirement of common knowledge may be too strong. Moreover, many conventions (e.g., a namaste) are instantiated locally (e.g., between two people). Lewis modeled convention with a single large game played by all the members simultaneously. This represents an extreme case, and his implicit use of a single game is a special case of a network of games. This becomes dramatically clear when seen in the context of Language Games because conversations are also carried out locally and not with the whole population present.

My approach to convention, which removes these restrictions of common knowledge and a single large game played by the whole population, is as follows. For me, a regular practice among members of a population is a convention only when they are part of a network of games involving the practice. Instead of common knowledge, there are individual guesses whether or not someone is part of the network. An analogue of the Consistency Condition is also required.[9]

---

8. Lewis (1969, p. 58). The regular practice must also be one of at least two equilibria in the game.

9. See Section 8.1. For a formal definition, see Parikh (2019, chap. 23). Language Games are also seldom common knowledge among the participants. The analogue of the Consistency Condition is realized through mutual expectations in the formal definition.

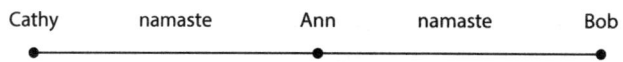

Figure 8.3   A Network Game with Two Local Games

Ann may hold her palms together in a namaste (the regular practice mentioned above) to Bob in one situation and to Cathy in another situation. And Bob and Cathy may correctly interpret the gesture as a greeting. The Consistency Condition restricts Ann to using a namaste in both situations. Under such conditions, and also in much larger networks across society, it can be shown that the convention emerges as a network equilibrium just as a conventional meaning emerged as a meaningful equilibrium in a large Language Game.[10]

It is important to realize that such a network equilibrium is a *meaning* in the broader sense of meaning I have identified: it represents a *connection* among myriad different situated games, each involving the interpretation of a namaste as a greeting. That is, the convention or network equilibrium is connected to and, therefore, is the meaning of all the local situated games taken together.

Stop and reflect just how many of our actions are conventional or normative in this sense and are therefore meaningful in our broader sense, especially when we interact with one another. It should now be clearer why I initially wrote[11] that it is such connections between contexts that make all the difference in both our physical and social worlds: all life depends on them. Indeed, they *constitute* our civilizations. However, there is still some distance that remains for us to arrive at society as a whole.

Not only this, but such conventions also change in society through an alteration made by someone in a particular situation—the initial communicative aspect—followed by its later spread through society—the subsequent propagative aspect. For example, the precise way in which a namaste is carried out—accompanied by a bow or not—could change as a result of other changes in society.

---

10. There is a more precise analogy to be drawn between a namaste and its use in a particular situation to convey a particular greeting to someone and a conventional meaning and its exploitation in an utterance situation to convey a particular referential meaning to an interlocutor. In one case, it is performed by holding one's palms together, and in the other, by uttering a word.

11. Section 1.3.

As this network definition of a convention is a generalization of a Language Game, we can immediately see why the meaning that results from a meaningful equilibrium is *conventional*. For language, the regular practice mentioned above is just the pairing of a word with a concept or property. In other words, conventional meanings are conventions and that is why they are so named.

Thus, conventions or social norms such as greeting someone with a namaste and treating others as you would like to be treated are like conventional meanings. Essentially, they depend on a global network of local games and emerge and change in roughly the same way. And so they can be understood in terms of and reduced to the individual people who observe them and to their interrelations.

## 8.4 The Social Nature of Language and Convention

As I said at the start of the book, rather than being a psychological construct, language is a social institution, a consequence of our sharing—more or less—conventional meanings and other aspects of language. We are now in a position to understand this sociality in a deeper way and this will eventually help us understand society itself.

First, recall the coordination game $G$ in which Ann and Bob are trying to meet in Manhattan without being able to communicate with each other first. They can meet either at Grand Central Station, which is closer to both of them, or at Penn Station, which is farther away. If they go to different stations, neither benefits. This situation is captured by a matrix[12] and it is the ambient situation that provides the details that make up the game. Further, such games can be solved by finding appropriate equilibria.

I said earlier that a game is a partly objective, partly subjective structure. This is because things like Ann's and Bob's physical distance from Grand Central are objective facts and things like their preferences are subjective facts. More accurately, however, a game is a partly objective, partly subjective, and *partly intersubjective* structure. The intersubjectivity has to do with the way the available choices and the resulting payoffs *interact*. It can thus be said that a game is a *social* structure in part. That is, it is not just Ann and Bob and their individual properties that make up the game but also the *relations* between them. This is obvious

---

12. See Figure 6.1.

once it is pointed out but it is important to see it clearly. At the same time, however, it should be noticed that there is nothing *irreducibly* social about the game. Its social nature emerges through its individual elements and their interrelations, that is all, although it is its sociality agents become aware of first and only then begin to distinguish its parts. Moreover, the solution to the coordination game, its equilibrium, is also social as it results from the actions of both agents. Thus, a situated game and its equilibrium are both social entities. Indeed, as we saw in the previous section, the equilibrium is the social *meaning* of the situated game as it is a product of the game.

By analogy with this reasoning, one can see that Communication Games—the subject of micro-semantics—and their equilibria—referential meanings—are also social. And Language Games—the subject of macro-semantics—and their meaningful equilibria—conventional meanings—are not only social but, indeed, societal, as they encompass the entire population of society. It is in this sense that we can now fully justify calling language a *social* institution.

And by a further analogy with Language Games, we can conclude that all conventions, not just conventional meanings, are also social institutions.

## 8.5 The Public Sphere

A key social institution or *system* of modern societies is the so-called public sphere, a part of civil society separate from the private sphere of the family. As Habermas, the key thinker about it, says, "By 'the public sphere' we mean first of all a realm of our social life in which something approaching public opinion can be formed. Access is guaranteed to all citizens. A portion of the public sphere comes into being in every conversation in which private individuals assemble to form a public body."[13] It is situated in all the physical and virtual spaces where public discussions take place. Language, especially verbal language, more than action, is its true medium. In contemporary life, it is often mediated by technology-based institutions in one form or another, either the mass media like the newspapers and television, or the digital social media where a wider public participates directly. A healthy public sphere is a necessary condition for democracy.

---

13. Habermas (1974, p. 49).

It is divided into a political public sphere, a literary public sphere, and so on, in each of which somewhat different but related matters are discussed. One can also envisage finer subdivisions where particular issues such as environmental policy, energy policy, and medical policy are discussed, largely by experts but in the public domain where all can learn of the different proposals being debated. Such conversations then influence both the state and various economic agents such as firms and their employees, not to mention consumers at large.

Public discussion of matters concerning life and death and the world we live in goes back, in fact, to ancient times, perhaps most notably in ancient India—given the many schools of Indian philosophy; in ancient China—within the Confucian, Taoist, and other traditions; and in ancient Greece—starting with the Pre-Socratics, all in the context of the fledgling institutional structures that existed then and the interactions among them across civilizations.[14] In modern times, the importance of public discussion was implicit in the liberal tradition and in the evolving institutions of capitalism and modernity. Immanuel Kant and John Stuart Mill made it explicit and pivotal to social and political life.[15]

Habermas describes the different attributes of the public sphere during the late medieval period, early liberal capitalism, and twentieth-century "welfare state mass democracy."[16] In particular, contemporary capitalism is characterized by a conflictual and competitive public sphere that can sometimes become violent, as I noted in the Introduction.

I first summarize Habermas's communicative approach and then offer a thorough critique. The centrality of meaning and language in public life now becomes apparent in a more concrete way. Throughout, it should be evident how much our solid grasp of Communication Games and Language Games, not to mention the three key difficulties they address—ambiguity, vagueness, and context—gives us the confidence and the tools to assess one of the more important social theories available today.

To ground his social description of the public sphere, Habermas needs to show how *public* opinion, that is, a kind of consensus, is possible, at least potentially, as that is what is involved in the very definition of the public sphere. He does this through a complex notion of *communicative* action, which he

---

14. See Deutsch and Bontekoe (2007) and Guthrie (1950/1993), for example. See Bailyn (1967/1992). See also McEvilley (2002), Sen (2005), Ganeri (2009), and Vajpeyi (2012).
15. Kant (1784/2001), Mill (1859/1956).
16. Habermas (1974); see also Habermas (1996, chap. 8).

distinguishes sharply from the *rational* action I have been employing. Simplifying greatly, communicative action involves the use of language oriented to mutual understanding.[17] He claims that such uses of language involve norms that have the potential to lead people who may initially disagree about some matter to eventual agreement. This happens, in his view, because they give reasons for their opinions to one another and, presumably, convince their interlocutors that their reasons are better. If the giving of reasons fails to elicit agreement, they may resort to "rational action" that he conceives as instrumental and even "selfish." Thus, a consensus of sorts is reached either via the giving of reasons to one another, which is truth-seeking, or via bargaining and compromise, which is narrowly goal-seeking or utilitarian.

I do not think the situation is so straightforward and believe that Habermas is seriously mistaken in his foundational account of communication. To start with, his view of rational action is too narrow. As I showed earlier, the motivations that game-based rational agency can capture are vast: rational action can be "existential," that is, capable of capturing any preference, rather than merely utilitarian, that is, narrowly selfish. If one accepts this, then Habermas's distinction between communicative and rational action breaks down. There simply are *no* norms in communication that point the interlocutors toward agreement. It could be argued that eventual agreement and consensus can be realized via rational action in my existential sense of the term. But this, too, leads to insuperable difficulties.

First, how do you show your opponent that your reasons are better? When discussing facts there are usually empirical tests that can reveal who is right.[18] But when preferences and values are involved, and there is nothing blatantly illogical in anyone's argument, there is no easy answer. Arguably, one could run a simulation on a computer in principle to see whose prediction is right: is a free market system better or is a welfare state system better or is a socialist system better for human freedom and flourishing? But such an experiment would not get off the ground because all kinds of assumptions would need to be made, assumptions that would themselves be highly contestable. A free market supporter may feel human flourishing lies in an individual egoism, a welfare state supporter in a kind of syncretism, and a socialist in a leftist communitarianism. And these descriptions are themselves caricatures of the complexities involved

---

17. See Habermas (1996, chap. 1) and Habermas (1976/1998, 1988/1998).
18. This is what gives Peirce's view of eventual consensus in natural science some force.

in more sophisticated conceptions of the good life.[19] Of course, some progress toward a kind of consensus is possible at a local level, say in town hall meetings where the stakes may be smaller, and this is a significant part of why Habermas's conception is attractive despite its shortcomings.

Second, it has become increasingly clear through findings in behavioral economics that people can be systematically *irrational* in their conversational behavior.[20] It is best to quote journalist Joe Keohane's piece from the *Boston Globe* in 2010 at some length.[21]

> Facts don't necessarily have the power to change our minds. In fact, quite the opposite. In a series of studies in 2005 and 2006, researchers at the University of Michigan found that when misinformed people, particularly political partisans, were exposed to corrected facts in news stories, they rarely changed their minds. In fact, they often became even more strongly set in their beliefs. Facts, they found, were not curing misinformation. Like an underpowered antibiotic, facts could actually make misinformation even stronger.
>
> This bodes ill for a democracy, because most voters—the people making decisions about how the country runs—aren't blank slates. They already have beliefs, and a set of facts lodged in their minds. The problem is that sometimes the things they think they know are objectively, provably false. And in the presence of the correct information, such people react very, very differently than the merely uninformed. Instead of changing their minds to reflect the correct information, they can entrench themselves even deeper.
>
> ⋮
>
> What's going on? How can we have things so wrong, and be so sure that we're right? Part of the answer lies in the way our brains are wired. Generally, people tend to seek consistency. There is a substantial body of psychological research showing that people tend to interpret information with an eye toward reinforcing their preexisting views. If we believe something about the world, we are more

---

19. See Hausman et al. (2017).
20. Section 6.7.
21. At http://archive.boston.com/news/science/articles/2010/07/11/how_facts_backfire/.

likely to passively accept as truth any information that confirms our beliefs, and actively dismiss information that doesn't. This is known as "motivated reasoning." Whether or not the consistent information is accurate, we might accept it as fact, as confirmation of our beliefs. This makes us more confident in said beliefs, and even less likely to entertain facts that contradict them.

Third, many distortions can occur, say between two people discussing politics in a café via an extended Communication Game or between a news source and an audience via an extended Language Game. There can be outright falsehoods uttered knowingly or extreme speech as we have seen (e.g., fake news or even propaganda); the interlocutors can *frame* the topic differently (e.g., as a mutiny or a war of independence); the topic can be subtly or unsubtly changed without a proper resolution (e.g., when a difficulty is raised for a particular viewpoint); ambiguities in interpretation or even word meaning can be exploited (e.g., the many examples already discussed); only a favorable part of a position may be selected for discussion, thereby sidestepping its real weaknesses (e.g., in defending a controversial new law); the meaning of a word itself can be changed (e.g., "secularism" or "socialism" can be redefined via the switching of equilibria as with jokes); and so on.

This list is far from exhaustive, and politicians and journalists are skilled at such maneuvers that thwart the goal of mutual understanding. All of these and other stratagems result in the meaning of a statement or fact or event being altered by connecting it to something else. Mill and Habermas assume something like the rules of formal debate, where a conversation in the public sphere proceeds through responding to each point made, but this is seldom the case, especially in contemporary times. Indeed, the political public sphere can even sometimes appear like the theater of the absurd! If opinion formation at the local level can be manipulated, what hope is there that the *public* opinion that emerges at the global level will accurately reflect both the truth and the real aspirations of human beings?

Fourth, there is the large issue of power imbalances in society. While Habermas is certainly aware of this, he is not able to address it adequately because he relies on a highly abstract version of systems theory as a model of society. In particular, the systems he posits, influenced by the sociologists Talcott Parsons and Niklas Luhmann, are not reducible to the individuals that comprise them and their interrelations. This leads to a *functionalist* sociology where all the systems and subsystems of society magically act and respond as they are more or less required to. The connection with flesh-and-blood people embedded in their concrete histories is lost. To be fair, Habermas does also use the notion of a network and people coordinating their plans through such networks, but because he disparages rational action and game theory, this remains a vague and metaphorical idea.

For me, the public sphere is a more or less complex *network game* across society—of the kind that generalizes Language Games—made up of local conversational games between two or more parties that could be individual persons or groups. Depending on one's interest, one can make such a model as concrete or as abstract as one wishes. But at bottom there are simply individuals and groups talking to one another, possibly via a technological medium like a newspaper rather than face-to-face, and jointly creating public opinion as an equilibrium just as people create language as an equilibrium via Language Games made up of interlocking Communication Games. What does such a model tell us?

As one example, consider the concept of *hegemony* introduced by the political theorist Antonio Gramsci. Hegemony is the dominance of one group or country over another but Gramsci inflected it to mean primarily the dominance of a system of ideas promoted by special interests as the interests of everyone.[22] The special interests are generally able to secure the spontaneous consent of others owing to the "prestige (and consequent confidence)" which the dominant group or person enjoys because of their position and function in society.[23]

Such ideological hegemony operates at the local conversational level and emerges as public opinion at the global network level. However, Gramsci does not show how this spontaneous consent of the masses is achieved. On the other hand, the situated game-theoretic approach that underlies Communication

---

22. Gramsci (2014). For Gramsci, the special interests are class interests but the concept can be generalized. Another name for the generalized concept is "charisma."

23. Gramsci (2014, p. 12). Foucault's (1966/2002) notion of *episteme* and Herman and Chomsky's (1988/2002) notion of *manufacturing consent* orbit the same terrain although they apply at different levels of society, the former more widely than the public sphere and the latter more narrowly than the public sphere. Foucault's notion does not make room for human agency as it is pitched at a rather abstract level. Connolly (1993), whom I mentioned briefly in Section 4.3, applies the idea of vague and essentially contested concepts to politics and sees conceptual change as necessary for political change. Finally, Bourdieu (2003) has interesting things to say about language and power but I believe his *theory of practice* falls short of linking language to action as situated game theory is able to do, and manages only to link it to *dispositions*, which are best thought of as *constraints* on action.

Games and Language Games and more general network games just needs to represent the available strategies and payoffs appropriately. To keep things simple, assume Ann is a charismatic leader and Bob is in awe of her. Then a schematic game that might capture their interaction might be as shown in Figure 8.4.

|                 | Ann's interest | common interest |
|-----------------|----------------|-----------------|
| Ann's interest  | (2, 2)         | (0, 0)          |
| common interest | (0, 0)         | (1, 1)          |

Figure 8.4  A Hegemony Game

I have shown the Hegemony Game as a simple coordination game with self-explanatory generic actions that can be further specified in particular situations. I have assumed that neither Ann nor Bob wants a conflict of interest and so they both get zero units when they choose different actions. If they both choose what is in their common interest, which is also Bob's interest, they both get positive payoffs of one unit each. If, however, they both choose Ann's interest, then Ann certainly gets what she wants, but Bob, too, gets a bonus from following his charismatic leader and being associated with her despite some loss from having his "immediate" or "real" interest overridden, and so they both get the highest payoff of two units. This is a case of *hegemony* because Ann's interest *appears* to Bob as his *own* interest: he is simply following his own desires.

To be sure, I have made certain simplifying assumptions (that belong to the embedding situation $s$ for the situated Hegemony Game) about the underlying costs and benefits that result in the payoffs. These can be exchanged for more realistic or more realistic assumptions and also varied to illustrate different circumstances. The main insight to be gleaned is that such simple models *clarify* the essence of what is going on when a hegemonic special interest prevails in a local conversational game and emerges in the network game at large. Ann can persuade Bob and Cathy and other followers to abandon their "real" interests and follow hers, and her own interest may itself reflect a larger group interest by which she is influenced.

As an aside, I point out once again how easy it is to maintain the underlying structure of a game while reimagining the actions and the underlying motivations for the payoffs. This shows how the "same" game—the coordination game $G$ in this instance—can capture different situations simply by reinterpreting who the agents are, what their choices are, and how their payoffs arise from the ambient situation.

I have said that it is the game that creates the local power structure, and added that when the game is a coordination game, the agents are evenly matched and have the same power. This is the case with the Hegemony Game in Figure 8.4. But it is clear that Ann has more power than Bob in this situation. How are we to explain this discrepancy?

Notice that Ann has not coerced Bob to suit her interests. He has done it on account of his own desire to acknowledge her leadership and to be associated with her. In other words, the source of Ann's power over Bob lies at a deeper level, in how his motivations are formed. Recall what I observed when I discussed the complexity of games:[24] an agent's preference for chocolate ice cream over vanilla ice cream or, more consequentially, for democracy over authoritarianism can be the result of their prior socialization. It is Bob's—and Ann's, for that matter—prior socialization that shapes their preferences in the situation at hand. Indeed, the public sphere itself plays a major role in this preference formation. I will address this larger and seemingly circular aspect of power later but suffice it to say here that the Hegemony Game captures only the *local* power structure. For a full understanding of power, we certainly need to look at the larger society in which such games are played.

To round out the discussion of power in the public sphere, the "spontaneous consent of the masses" is realized first in the Hegemony Game and then as an equilibrium of the global network game that builds upon the interlocking local games. If the circumstances are right, a demagogue can sway the masses one way or another without the use of force and prevent the formation of emancipatory group desires, although in real life a threat of violence often accompanies such hegemony. Such hegemonic behavior may explain how authoritarians can be democratically elected.

This completes my account of the difficulties for mutual understanding at the local level of Communication Games and the formation of public opinion at the global level of Language Games. I have focused on some of the *internal* difficulties as they bedevil Habermas's "communicative action" itself. However, there are many obvious *external* obstacles as well, such as various inequalities in education and preparation and opportunity for dialogue among the public at large. This has been exacerbated by the large-scale fragmentation of the media

---

24. Section 6.9.

landscape, especially owing to the online availability of news and opinion, which has intensified polarization and the spread of misinformation and has made the very existence of a public sphere highly questionable.[25]

Despite all these problems, I believe Habermas is on the right track and the public sphere is a cornerstone for a *deliberative* democracy.[26] He is often dismissed as defending a communicative version of an old-fashioned liberalism but I cannot see how a post-liberal democracy can exist without deliberation and the influence of public opinion. If other foundational aspects of society evolve in ways that create a greater harmonization of interests among the public—taking class, race (or caste), gender, religion, and other divisive institutions into account—then that is one way through which a less conflictual public sphere can emerge. It will certainly be imperfect but, as we noted at the start of this section, a healthy public sphere is a necessary condition for democracy and, indeed, for a partial utopia.

---

25. See the insightful report by Fukuyama et al. (2021) where they discuss the economic, social, and political harms that result from the enormous concentration of power among the world's technology platforms like Meta, Google, Twitter (now X), and Amazon. In addition to various proposals to combat this, such as antitrust regulation, they offer the possible remedy of "middleware": "By mediating the relationship between users and the platforms, middleware can cater to the preferences of individual consumers while providing significant resistance to unilateral actions by the dominant players" (p. 32). And "middleware's primary benefit is that it dilutes the enormous control that dominant platforms have in organizing the news and opinion that consumers see" (p. 34). They also quote Jack Dorsey, former CEO and co-founder of Twitter, thus: "We need to open up and be transparent around how our algorithms work and how they're used, and maybe even enable people to choose their own algorithms to rank the content or to create their own algorithms, to rank it. To be that open, I think, would be pretty incredible. So that we can all come to better solutions, because it affects society in such large ways" (August 8, 2020; p. 30). One possible pitfall is that the middleware can itself become a platform and thereby limit consumer choice.

26. Habermas (1996, chaps. 7–8). For a perceptive critique, see Raymond Geuss (2019). His sharpest point seems to be the problem of radical indeterminacy and radical translation that Quine (1960) raises for communication. But this is a red herring: it is not necessary to accept Quine's conclusions about radical indeterminacy because the individuation of entities and, therefore, a *shared* world can also be derived from Language Games *in principle*. Thus, there is no fundamental reason why successful communication cannot exist. See Parikh (2010, sec. 7.6).

## 8.6 Language Games and Artificial Intelligence

As I argued earlier, it is a real challenge to get a robot to share our concepts and our world, concepts such as *bald* or *democratic* or even *cat*. Now, with the help of the idea of Language Games, we can see more clearly why. It would be necessary for an artificial agent to participate in local Communication Games and, through them, in the larger Language Games across society in order to acquire the conventional meanings and referential meanings that emerge through their meaningful equilibria. At least this is one way to tackle the problem of understanding language, which is also presupposed in so many other tasks for AI.

Indeed, it is possible to think of artificial agents like Amazon's Alexa in precisely this way. There are presumably thousands of Alexa copies in people's homes and offices and they keep learning aspects of language by participating in conversations with humans and simply eavesdropping. Of course, Alexa isn't really playing Communication Games, as that isn't the model implemented in her, but it can nevertheless be thought of as cruder participation in many conversations and, therefore, in a crude Language Game. Most advantageously, unlike people, she has multiple copies and each copy shares its learning with the others. This allows rapid global learning—just as happens with other artificial agents such as Apple's Siri, driverless cars, ChatGPT, and even Google's and Microsoft's search engines as well as others. At the moment, their algorithms are not as smart as required for true language acquisition, but such a possibility nevertheless exists.

The same considerations apply to *actions* in general as well as conventions and norms in society. There are again local games and global network games that could potentially be played, enabling robots to share our world in deeper ways. At present, the progress is slow, as there are many other difficult considerations robots simultaneously face that we take for granted, things like how to pick up a glass without crushing it or how to open a door with an unfamiliar doorknob. Most actions are physical and involve interactions with the material world. Our bodies evolved over millennia and our hands and feet and sensory apparatus are exquisitely tuned to the external world. For robots that have to be flexible and deal with it as we do, in a multitude of tasks, some of which they may never have encountered before, rather than merely do a fixed set of tasks repetitively as many factory robots do today, calls for real breakthroughs in a kind of commonsense physics of the natural world. Situated decision and game theory can help immensely here too, I believe, as some of the same issues of ambiguity, vagueness, and context stymie these efforts. In this sense and others, it is crucial to realize that all such issues AI faces are merely different facets of *meaning*.

I also asked earlier whether an AI agent could learn to be a moral agent. As we have already seen in our discussion of vagueness and as I will also show later, our values arise ultimately from our preferences and judgments in our situated and lived individual and social histories—trivially, is Fred bald or not, and, more importantly, is modern civilization democratic or not and, if so, then to what degree—and are, in this sense, part of the natural world. So, there is no obstacle *in principle* to AI becoming moral but it remains, despite all the progress in machine learning, a tall order.

# CHAPTER NINE

# Images, Actions, and Objects

So far, we have used the framework of situated games to understand how meaning is expressed through language and especially how the difficulties of ambiguity, vagueness, and context are handled. We have also begun to broaden the scope of meaning by applying this understanding to social conventions and institutions like the public sphere. And the promise of and possibly insurmountable obstacles to a full artificial intelligence have accompanied our investigation.

In this chapter, I will consider three different ways to go beyond language. One is toward other symbol systems. I will show how static and moving images can be grasped by Equilibrium Semantics and I will look at both ordinary pictures as well as those that occur in art. My account will be relatively brief as my purpose is twofold: to show how meaning emerges in other symbol systems, including various art forms, and to demonstrate that the same theoretical ideas can yield equally rich insights for them as well.

The second extension is to the meanings of actions. This is a broad category as it includes symbol systems and in certain ways can even be conceived as constitutive of society. I will look at not only ordinary actions, such as picking up a glass of water, but also at actions that function as utterances. To illustrate the latter, I will show how a common action involving one country amassing troops on the border of an adjacent country—an action in the realm of international relations—might be approached. This is another step toward a wider social theory. In the opening pages of the book, I raised the question of the mysterious *Waiting for Godot*, and for want of a better place for this iconic existential play, I discuss it under the category of action as all its dimensions and devices are ultimately the result of actions of one kind or another belonging to one medium or another.

Lastly, I explore the largest category: the meanings of objects. By "object" I mean any entity treated as an individual—whether it is an individual, property, relation, state of affairs, game, situation, connection between situations, or whatever else that makes up our shared informational space. Objects form the largest category because all entities can be treated as individuals. For example, *kindness* is an object because the property of being kind is treated as an individual. I will focus initially on four different types of objects—rocks, toasters, cats, and persons that exemplify things as such, artifacts, animals, and we ourselves. I will then briefly discuss an encompassing and somewhat abstract object—modernity—to see how some of its meanings might be intuited.

## 9.1 Images

Images are generally representations of objects in the sense mentioned above although they are often hard to individuate. If a picture shows Ann and Bob talking to each other, is it one image or two? The matter is highly contextual and also depends on our purposes. Picasso's painting *Guernica* may be thought of as made up of many related images. Representational pictures generally may be thought of as consisting of one or more images, however they are individuated.

Pictures are enormously complex to analyze partly because they are often analog in form and do not have a clear-cut, externally specifiable syntax.[1] This makes them even more ambiguous and vague than ordinary language. Even the processes of identifying the images in a picture at a basic level—recognizing the picture of a cat as a cat, as we have seen—let alone inferring its further meanings, can be extremely difficult. And in visual art there are all kinds of additional challenges as nonrepresentational elements can be mixed in with representational elements, not to mention the presence of deliberate ambiguity and vagueness and unfamiliar representational conventions. My interest here will simply be in what might be called its high-level interpretation assuming the low-level interpretation is given.

What a low-level interpretation provides is the imagistic equivalent of words in an utterance or discourse. Indeed, a picture can be taken to be like a discourse or text containing multiple utterances. I will use the ideas of fixed and variable, parts and wholes, and networks to develop a theory of how pictures might be interpreted and understood.

---

1. See Goodman (1976).

### 9.1.1 Pictures

Look at the visual joke in Figure 9.1. In the given context, the photograph can be divided into two parts, the familiar scene of a somewhat empty arrival lounge at an airport terminal and the man in the foreground carrying a placard with the name "Godot."

Figure 9.1  A Visual Joke

How does the picture get interpreted and how does the joke work? Just as there were two words or parts in the sentence "Fred ran" so there are two images or parts in the photograph. And just as the words were interdependent and led to interdependent lexical games, which when solved yielded the meaning of the utterance, so the images are interdependent and lead to analogous "image games," which when solved yield the meaning of the whole picture. It is as simple or as complex as that. The details are, in fact, complex but it should begin to become clear why I have belabored the case of language as much as I have. Once this latter model is grasped, the models for other symbol systems drop out by analogy.[2] At least as far as ordinary pictures go. For visual art, more is required.

---

2. However, one has to be careful not to look for the same "devices" in different media as words and images and gestures are all different from each other. See, for example, Bordwell (1985,

| common meaning | chauffeur waiting to pick up someone |
| --- | --- |
| rare meaning | since Godot never comes, the wait is endless |

Table 9.1  Common and Rare Meanings in a Visual Joke

Before we turn to visual art, let us spend a minute on how the joke works. The common meaning that we expect to see is an ordinary name on the placard. Instead, we find "Godot" with the amusing prospect of an endless wait.[3] Remember that both components—the switch in equilibrium and the amusing outcome—are necessary for the joke to work.

At least three things happen when we attempt to interpret most kinds of art. First, both form and meaning become important, that is, the content of an artwork includes both formal and representational aspects. Form is the same as what I also call syntactic content and the representational meaning is part of the full semantic content.[4] So both syntactic and semantic content matter in art.

I did not make explicit when discussing Communication Games that interpreting an utterance of "Fred ran" requires not only semantic games but also syntactic games. These two types of games together give us both the equilibrium meaning (or semantics) and the equilibrium parse (or syntax) of an utterance. Earlier, our interest was in ordinary communication and so we cared mainly about the equilibrium meaning and we ignored the equilibrium parse. But when we are reacting to art of most kinds—including literature and visual art—the equilibrium parse or syntax or form is also significant. *Both* syntax and semantics or form and meaning become part of the content of an artwork. *Both* are communicated or at least inferred by the addressee.

---

chap. 2). Moreover, all these devices exhibit similar semantic and syntactic features involving ambiguity and vagueness as discussed in Chapters 3 and 4 in some detail.

3. The somewhat empty arrival lounge indicates the chauffeur has already been waiting a while. In a more detailed analysis, there would also be a game corresponding to this.

4. The representational meaning is the same as what I have earlier called the referential meaning, the former term being more commonly used in (visual) art. Notice also that I am using "content" in a broader way than is usual. Lastly, I am using "form" here as part of the content— differently from the way I used it in Section 7.6. The reason for this is that in the context of AI and the context of art these terms are used somewhat differently. In general, there are two distinctions, syntax/semantics and form/content, and they overlap in different ways in different contexts.

# Chapter Nine: Images, Actions, and Objects

Figure 9.2  Paul Cézanne, *The Card Players*, 1890-92, The Metropolitan Museum of Art Collection

Look at Figure 9.2 for instance. The image in the book lacks color[5] but it is clear that both form (color, shape, texture, and especially composition) and representational content (the narrative of the card game played by rural laborers in a tavern or room) affect us, with the former possibly even dominating the latter.[6] Further indirect and implied meanings, both intended and unintended, that make up the whole discourse meaning such as, for example, the social space the peasants occupy and, indeed, a conjured *world* can also be inferred. By using both syntactic and semantic games as well as extended methods involving implied forms and meanings, it is possible to attempt to *derive* such contents from partial rationality just as I did with verbal language rather than relying on impressionistic and nonconscious reasoning.[7] To be sure, as discussed below, as aspects of form and meaning become hazier, they shade off into suggestion and we are no longer in the realm of communication and shared understandings, but rather in the fluid world of imagination and other transformations of thought.

This brings us to the second new feature when we consider art as opposed to ordinary depiction: the interrelated ubiquity of ambiguity and vagueness and

---

5. For the color image, see https://www.metmuseum.org/art/collection/search/435868. I refer to the color of the image twice so the interested reader can follow the link if they would like to see the image in color.
6. I have drawn some of these details from Harvey (2015).
7. See especially the chapter on distance in Parikh (2019, pt. IV).

indeterminate contexts. While all the human and nonhuman images (e.g., the table and other objects) are readily recognizable without specialized art-historical knowledge,[8] a closer look reveals that especially the colors but also other aspects of form are hazily painted, indicating a certain vagueness of depiction that generates syntactic and semantic games that yield even more probabilistic contents than happens with ordinary utterances such as "Fred ran" or the visual joke above. These probabilistic contents are the way various ambiguities in form and meaning are represented, just as with puns where the probabilities are likely to be distributed fifty-fifty between two interpretations. In other words, the ambiguities that are present in ordinary communication are further intensified in art for aesthetic reasons.

This is underscored by the fact that unlike ordinary utterances such as "Fred ran" where the utterance situation is reasonably identifiable, artistic communication involves highly indeterminate and variable contexts that viewers and readers and critics bring to their interpretations of an artwork. As such contexts change and shift, so do the forms and meanings, as different aspects of the work get foregrounded. For example, one context may link Cézanne's painting to similar historical depictions of card games and compare and contrast them (e.g., none of the players seem to be winners or losers as in some traditional paintings) whereas another context may stress the vagueness of the upturned card on the table (e.g., is it a diamond or spade or neither?). This indeterminacy and variability of contexts thus makes all artworks ineluctably ambiguous almost by *definition*.

Lastly, as the film theorist David Bordwell[9] has pointed out in the context of motion pictures, artworks and even ordinary pictures always draw upon *both* external and internal conventions in their representations. External conventions can be either social or art-historical and internal conventions are generated through aspects of the form of the work. This is where the idea of fixed and variable and the idea of networks come in. Relative to a given situated viewing of an artwork at a particular point in time and place, the external conventions are relatively fixed. However, as time and place change, they also change. Conventions internal to a painting, especially if it breaks new ground, are generated on the fly and evoke its type and style (e.g., Post-Impressionism).

---

8. There is a large issue of conventionalism versus naturalism in visual depiction that arises here but I cannot go into it. See Goodman (1976) and Carroll (1999).

9. Bordwell (1985).

All three features—the relative importance of form, the interrelated nature of ambiguity, vagueness, and indeterminate contexts, and external and internal conventions—together create an overall lack of closure in the artwork and bring suggestion (as a weaker flow of information or content than strict communication which requires common knowledge between the artist and viewer) to the forefront. Especially around modernism and after, such *openness* has been almost a requirement for an object to be an acceptable artwork.

The foregoing is an extremely compressed account of pictures and much remains to be said about its detailed links with the situated games of Equilibrium Semantics. My effort here has simply been to make such a connection plausible using the ideas of fixed and variable, parts and wholes, and networks, and drawing upon the ubiquitous features of most uses of symbol systems, namely, ambiguity, vagueness, and context. Once such an account is spelled out, it is possible to extend it to "nonrepresentational" works by more or less identifying their form with their content.

It is important to mention that just like verbal communication, visual communication, too, involves both propositional contents as well as non-propositional *effects*. The latter are especially important in art and can sometimes completely outweigh an artwork's propositional contents. Arguably, the German Renaissance painter Matthias Grünewald's *Crucifixion* and the late nineteenth-century Norwegian artist Edvard Munch's iconic expressionist work *The Scream* are examples of such affective priority.

## 9.1.2 Motion Pictures

The shot in a motion picture is the rough equivalent of a static picture, at least for our purposes, even though it involves both time and space. It is like a verbal discourse, as pointed out at the start of this section. A motion picture then is a sequence of shots and so a sequence of discourses and therefore just a long discourse. Since we have just seen how static pictures can be analyzed by analogy with verbal discourses, it should be straightforward to extend the analysis to motion pictures. Essentially, there is a communication (or weaker information flow) where the "speaker" can be taken to be the whole team that makes the film and the addressee is the viewer.

As Bordwell[10] has pointed out, there are many *sui generis* devices in the medium of cinema (such as the camera, sound, editing, etc.) so the details of how interpretations are generated will be correspondingly different. However, at a high level, all we have is a complex collection of interdependent syntactic and semantic games to solve to derive the many contents and effects of a film.

As we know by now, even a single game can quickly become complex simply by virtue of having many actions. Certainly, an Equilibrium Semantics model of a motion picture will not be tractable, given the many interdependent games it will need to deploy. So a kind of zooming-in technique can be employed: either the whole film (or some part of it) can be analyzed at a relatively high level or one can zoom in to a lower, less abstract level to look more closely at a single or a few shots. The former would contain simple component games so that the long chain of interdependent games remains relatively simple, whereas the latter would allow more detail in the relevant component games that model a few shots.

Again, although I could go into more detail here, my purpose is simply to point out that a variety of symbol systems can be modeled using the same techniques. In the case of motion pictures, the same kinds of models will apply whether one is examining Hollywood or international films, or art films, or other types and styles of films where the formal aspects dominate the representational content, as happened in the case of visual art.[11]

It should now be apparent how much more is involved in understanding and responding to images than simply recognizing an image as a cat. The challenges for AI are formidable and they emphasize the need for AI agents that learn in a much broader sense than current machine learning envisages. Robots need to participate in appropriate counterparts and extensions of Language Games to handle the many complexities of pictures and motion pictures, not to mention other symbol systems.

---

10. Bordwell (1985).

11. See the related short analyses in Parikh (2018, 2023).

## 9.2 Actions

All utterances are actions but some actions also function as utterances. One might give someone something in order to communicate that one is generous. Indeed, this sort of communication pervades social life. One can offer a warranty on a product to signal the product's quality (economics), form an alliance with someone to indicate one's solidarity (political science), give a gift to someone to communicate one's status (anthropology), and push someone around to imply one's power (sociology).

In somewhat more detail, a salesperson can offer a warranty for a used car to signal its high quality. Here, they are offering two things, the warranty itself and some indirect indication of its quality. This kind of action is necessary in a context where mere talk is not likely to be believed. Likewise, one political party may form an alliance with another and thereby also signal its solidarity with that party. Here again, indirectness is necessary either because actual talk is cheap or because talk may be too costly—that depends on the context. Gift-giving is a well-known way to communicate one's status in the relevant community. It is not enough simply to proclaim one's status because, once again, talk is cheap. Lastly, a bully may push someone around partly just to show his power. Here he is again doing two things, actually pushing someone around and also conveying his power. All these examples are also, of course, context-dependent: they can communicate different contents in different situations. For example, gift-giving can convey generosity or status or both.[12]

As I have shown how linguistic and visual utterances can be modeled, the extension to actions functioning as utterances can be seen to follow more or less straightforwardly. The new feature in considering the meanings of actions is the nature of the physical action itself, even something as simple as picking up a glass of water to take a sip, whether or not it can also be taken as an utterance.

The most salient entities with which an action is connected are its intention and its result. These could be the same or different, as when there are unintended consequences of an action. There are other things actions are connected to as well but as their enabling intention or cause and ensuing result are the most salient, we can stipulate that these are to count as the meanings of an action. So when Ann picks up a glass of water, we can say it meant that she wanted to quench her

---

12. See Parikh (2001, 2019) and also Farrell and Rabin (1996).

thirst and it meant she quenched her thirst. The meanings of an action answer the question why someone did something and what resulted from it.

It should be immediately obvious that, in this sense, actions can be highly ambiguous because it is often difficult to tell why someone did something and also challenging to identify the consequences of an action. For the latter, there is generally a chain of intended and unintended consequences and so knowing what subset to pick out as the meaning can be highly contextual.

In addition to an action's intention and consequences, there is also a range of (largely unintended) situated meanings actions have depending on the situation within which they are interpreted. This is similar to the way in which a literary critic may bring a theoretical idea or some other contextual feature to bear on a text.[13] Ann casting a vote in an election can signify the background presence of a democratic system however tenuous the democracy might actually be.

### 9.2.1 International Relations

Consider an example from the field of international relations, which may be thought of as applied political science and sociology, not to mention economics. Imagine a situation where there are two neighboring countries, X and Y, and X begins massing troops near their common border. This is not at all an unfamiliar situation, even today, and one that can be quite ambiguous.

First, there is the physical action itself which could be an offensive or defensive move in the ongoing relations between X and Y. It could also be a response to internal developments in X (e.g., to divert attention from them). Which option it is depends upon the context. Such meanings, too, need to be discerned from various kinds of situated games, especially those involving conflict, by making them explicit and digital.

But beyond this level, there could also be a second level where the physical action functions as an utterance and conveys a meaning to the government of Y and possibly to other parties, such as the citizens of X and Y. This meaning could involve any of the possibly numerous contentious elements in the relations between X and Y. For example, the massing of the troops could serve as a warning—this would be a "force" of the utterance[14]—or intimate an intent,

---

13. See Section 3.2.
14. See Section 3.1.

depending on the concrete profiles of X and Y and their interactions. And it could be highly ambiguous and unclear.

There are innumerable such examples where an action's purpose is not restricted to its immediate characteristics or consequences but also includes a layer of implied meanings. And the apparatus of situated games applies to all of them in principle. Thus, its relevance for anthropology, sociology, political science, economics, and allied fields is not limited to the direct role of language and meaning in the emergence, evolution, and transformation of social institutions but also includes the entire realm of action itself. This is amply borne out by the wide use of game theory in the social sciences. My version of the theory would make the situations accompanying the relevant games explicit, thereby enriching the models of social contexts, a crucial part of social phenomena.[15]

Lastly, an expert in international relations can construct various contexts to provide a larger interpretation of such an action. For example, it may be viewed as a move within a wider set of regional conflicts or even relative to a world system, or it may just signify the sorry state of international affairs. However, it is important to guard against *arbitrarily* imposed meanings as they must satisfy the *broadly* causal nature of meaning. Otherwise, it is possible to end up with absurd and unwarranted conspiracy theories which may possess an internal coherence but no causal connection with actual actions and events.

### 9.2.2 Waiting for Godot

A great deal has been said and can be said about this baffling play.[16] Indeed, part of its allure is precisely the endless possibilities for interpretation that result from its minimalist form. To give an analogy, if someone utters the single word "table" with a specific intention, it will in most contexts fail to convey that intention to the hearer. If taken literally, it will convey something about tables to be sure[17] but the single word offers a feeble constraint on what is being said. Is it that the table is made of wood, is it that the table wobbles, or is it something else altogether? The range of possibilities can be narrowed by filling in the context, but even this

---

15. See, for example, Blumer (1969).

16. See Schechner (1988/2003, chap. 1) for some interesting remarks on time in the play. He also suggests relating performance more broadly to game theory. See also Eagleton (2008b, chap. 3).

17. Note that "table" is conventionally ambiguous between a piece of furniture and a systematic columnar display of information, but I have the former meaning in mind here.

will generally not lead to a unique intended meaning, because the single word "table" provides scant evidence for the interpreter. This, in turn, results in a much wider field of unintended meanings because intended meanings partly constrain unintended meanings, and if the former are relatively unrestricted, so will the latter be, proportionately. That is, an utterance of "table" offers too little information on which to base a meaning and this makes many more meanings possible, unmoored from the utterance though they may be. *Waiting for Godot* is similar and has the spareness of a modernist poem.

As I have already indicated some of the ways Equilibrium Semantics offers to derive intended and unintended meanings for a variety of symbol systems, I will focus here on how I see the larger overall meanings of *Waiting for Godot* without inferring them from its formal aspects. But it is important to keep in mind that such interpretations always need to be grounded in the action of the play as far as possible.

First, I see *Waiting for Godot* as broadly existential, that is, as dealing with the fundamental questions of existence such as the ultimate meaning of things. Its unique ploy, different from that of other existentialists such as Kierkegaard, Dostoyevsky, Nietzsche, Heidegger, Sartre, and Camus, is to adumbrate that such ultimate meaning never "comes," that it always eludes us. In other words, the mysterious character Godot stands for meaning itself and one could almost paraphrase the title as *Waiting for Meaning*. Needless to say, such a primary overall meaning does not rule out other coexisting secondary meanings such as the play's slapstick aspects. I think the existential meaning is a natural interpretation of the play and it must occur at some level to many if not most viewers—indeed, it occurred even to ChatGPT![18] I am deliberately stating it somewhat baldly and unsubtly because this whole book is about meaning, large and small.

The second overall meaning of the play I want to posit may be less common and is, in a sense, a generalization of the first. Could one say that *Waiting for Godot* signifies a key aspect of the *modern* human condition, that is, a key aspect of modernity itself? As I will argue soon, modernity, unlike past epochs, is radically *open*: many alternative futures are conceivable and possible in a way they weren't earlier. The play then is about waiting for this indefinable and inaccessible horizon, the ultimate open meaning of human history itself. This is not religious eschatology but rather one of many possible secular, finite, partial

---

18. See Section 3.4.

meanings—utopias or dystopias—given the profoundly ambiguous course of history up to this point.

Without going into details that would take us too far afield, one way to begin to justify such an interpretation is to point out that if Godot stands for meaning, then it must be a social rather than an individual meaning because the setting and action of the play involve ineluctably social elements which therefore evoke social and, indeed, historical meanings. Such options—whether the meaning is individual or social—can be represented as choices in an appropriate situated game just as earlier there was a choice between Fred Smith and Fred Jones: the weightiness of the former doesn't necessarily lead to any formal difference in its game-theoretic representation. In any case, a full derivation of such an interpretation from the situated games of Equilibrium Semantics would take some work as it would need to be related to the various actions and other elements of the play just as interpretations of verbal and visual language need to be related to the devices used in those media.

## 9.3 Objects

Objects, that is, entities treated as individuals, sometimes function as symbols but generally they are simply individuated as part of the causal structure uncovered by our actions in the world. So smoke can signal a meaning *symbolically* or can simply mean fire *naturally* depending on the situation in which it is viewed.

As there is no standard way to define the meanings of an object, we can stipulate that they are its many properties and relations. This has the consequence that objects become maximally meaningful because everything has an infinite number of properties and relations. But this overabundance is greatly reduced in practice because the contexts in which we view them are relatively limited by our goals and concerns. Smoke can also mean there is a cigarette smoker nearby but such contexts are increasingly uncommon.

I will first look at four subcategories of objects, and then turn to modernity, a large situation treated as an individual.

### 9.3.1 Rocks, Toasters, Cats, and Persons

Unlike entities that are not naturally individuated as individuals—such as properties—rocks, toasters, cats, persons, and other such entities naturally occur as individuals in our social worlds. Moreover, their individuation is often vague and so they do not always readily yield to the search for necessary and sufficient conditions without an element of stipulation. So their meanings get correspondingly bifurcated, although not sharply, into scientific and everyday ones.

A geologist may discover many scientific meanings for rocks, such as their relative hardness and chemical composition, which they progressively abstract from their everyday meanings, such as their amenability or otherwise to being climbed or being thrown. Even more basic is seeing a rock *as* a rock or as something else altogether.[19] It is again the situations in which they are apprehended that determine which meaning surfaces via the corresponding situated games. It is only when they are used as symbols and become part of a symbol system that Equilibrium Semantics applies to the derivation of their interpretations.

Toasters are tools that we create and so their capacity to toast becomes a privileged meaning. Heidegger offers an illuminating account of how our equipment fits into an entire network of purposes embedded within our worlds right from the start of our existence.[20] But toasters can also be used for novel ends as can all equipment: they can be used as a weight to hold something down, for example. So the central meaning of a tool is open-ended and depends radically on our imagination. Software engineers, especially, are aware of the endless repurposing of fragments of code. The biologist Susan Hockfield discusses how viruses composed of DNA or RNA inside a protein capsule can be used to build batteries.[21] Incidentally, the language of information, which provides a uniform way to access reality at different levels as we saw earlier, is widely used in more abstract domains such as biology and computer science but it is equally valid for simpler artifacts such as toasters as well as ordinary objects such as rocks. As we will soon see, this technological creativity—for good or ill—is in a way the heart of modernity.

Cats are, of course, complex biological creatures but also first appear, as Husserl and Heidegger would say, within our everyday worlds. The biological understanding comes later. There are whole cultures surrounding cats because they have been domesticated and become our pets. While rocks and toasters and cats all have an infinite number of properties and relations and therefore an infinite number of meanings, cats possess a greater density of *relevant* meanings

---

19. Heidegger (1927/1962, chap. V).
20. Heidegger (1927/1962, chap. III).
21. Hockfield (2019, chap. 2).

Chapter Nine: Images, Actions, and Objects

not only because of their greater complexity but also because of their deeper participation in our social worlds. We give them names like Panini[22] and Plato and connect with them in a wide variety of ways.

It is this greater density that would make it difficult for an AI agent to know what a cat is the way people do unless a way is found to socialize it by exposing it to cats in the many contexts we inhabit. It could be argued, however, that, say, a driverless car does not need such a detailed understanding of cats: all it has to do is to avoid running over one. But it can be countered that there are many so-called edge cases or borderline cases that require deeper and deeper embedding in our worlds. Such a dialectic may have no easy end. In any case, it seems clear that techniques beyond the standard ones like deep learning that are prevalent today will have to be invented. Once again, as noted earlier, it is the question of meaning that is the biggest obstacle to realizing a more general artificial intelligence.

Persons are the most complex objects of the four types we are considering. They are the most theorized and their interpretations are the most contested of all. I will confine my remarks to their central meanings. In my view, if one sticks to naturalism or physicalism, most interpretations can be eliminated as just plain false as they entail dualism of one sort or another. For example, most religious views—except perhaps certain nondual and materialist variants of Hinduism and Buddhism—can be eliminated because they posit immaterial souls as the essence of persons.

I will consider two contrasting views that offer the most promise, one the broadly Enlightenment view and the other the broadly Romantic view, updated to the present. Both start with the ordinary idea of persons as beings with certain capacities: "a person is an agent who has a sense of self, of his/her own life, who can evaluate it, and make choices about it," as Charles Taylor puts it.[23]

The first view treats all agents as entities that act on the basis of beliefs and desires, that is, that act generally in a "partially rational" way. There is no essential difference between animals (including persons) and complex machines. The ends of agents—their goals and concerns, their preferences and values—are taken as unproblematic. What distinguishes persons, therefore, is their ability to conceive and make more complex choices: their *strategic* power. The capacities listed above

---

22. One of the earliest linguists in the world and an intellectual giant who lived in India around the fifth century BCE.

23. Taylor (1981/1999, p. 103).

are seen in the context of this ability to plan. The power to represent with clarity plays a crucial role in executing this strategic power. Computation is the key and the difference between persons and other animals and machines is the relative complexity of the calculations involved. More broadly put, persons are primarily identified with their ability to *think*: as we saw earlier, this is the ability to "form plans, analyze situations, deliberate, reason, exploit analogies, revise beliefs in the light of experience, weigh up conflicting interests, formulate hypotheses and match them against evidence, make reasonable decisions on the basis of imperfect information, and so forth."[24] This is the dominant view in current scientific and philosophical writing about people.

The second view is a meta-view and a deeper view for that reason. It stems from Heidegger and, as Taylor puts it, conceives persons as beings for whom things matter in certain special ways, as subjects of *significance*. Things matter for all agents, but persons have qualitatively different concerns that are *sui generis*. In other words, the peculiar ends of persons come into focus. Thus, the difference between humans and other animals is not just their greater strategic abilities but also their unusual goals. This means consciousness consists not only in the power to represent but also in the power to constitute our concerns.[25] To express this unique latter power differently, persons are *self-interpreting* animals. They can interpret themselves in a variety of ways, not only as thinkers, by constituting their concerns differently. This self-interpretation is partly constrained by their bodies but also by the larger society in which people live: premodern times severely constrained the choices available to humankind. In general, though, both individual persons and whole societies can, within limits, reinvent themselves once this power of constituting our goals and concerns becomes widely understood.

Seen in a certain way, there is no great difference between the two views: both involve a partially rational agent setting goals and making choices. The first emphasizes the process, the second the meta-level content of interpretive possibilities. Unfortunately, in practice, they have had very different consequences as the Enlightenment and Romanticism and their aftermath show. What they share has been overlooked and contrasting self-interpretations have gotten cemented. This is why I tried to show that situated games, which are generally identified with the first view, and Heidegger, the originator of the second view,

---

24. Copeland (1993, p. 55).

25. There is a great deal more to be said about the nature of these concerns and the interested reader can refer to Taylor (1977/1999, 1981/1999) and Parikh (2019, chap. 6).

are closely connected: the preferences of agents are just their interests or, to use Heidegger's term, their care. This is what makes partial rationality *existential*.

For all these types of objects—rocks, toasters, cats, and persons—it should be borne in mind that they are always situated and that it is our situated preferences and values that guide the selection of meanings we ascribe to them. This is nicely illustrated by the following story. Two shoe salespeople were sent to a remote island to scope out the possibilities. One wrote back: "No possibilities here: no one wears shoes." The other wrote back: "Huge possibilities here: no one wears shoes." The situation each encountered was the same but the meanings they attached to it were diametrically opposed. These different framings show that there is often an element of creativity and value and choice that is present in the more complex meanings we elicit based on a bedrock of simpler factual meanings we share. This applies equally to our personal and societal self-interpretations.

## 9.3.2 Modernity

Being modern is a property that can attach to many different kinds of objects. *Modernity* is a large situation treated as an individual, roughly the way the object kindness is derived from the property of being kind.

I see modernity as a relatively abstract situation that emerged globally around 1500 CE in connection with the scientific revolution of the sixteenth and seventeenth centuries, brought about by figures such as Bacon, Galileo, Descartes, and Newton who built upon earlier worldwide scientific developments in the context of colonialism.[26] It became a somewhat encompassing

---

26. However, for alternative and, indeed, earlier developments of some aspects of the ideas of empiricism, calculus, and nongeocentric orbits, see Srinivas (2022). To quote from Mumford (2010), who is quoted therein: "Chapter 7 of Plofker's book is devoted to the crown jewel of Indian mathematics, the work of the Kerala school. Kerala is a narrow fertile strip between the mountains and the Arabian Sea along the southwest coast of India. Here, in a number of small villages, supported by the Maharaja of Calicut, an amazing dynasty of mathematicians and astronomers lived and thrived. A large proportion of their results were attributed by later writers to the founder of this school, Madhava of Sangamagrama, who lived from approximately 1350 to 1425. It seems fair to me to compare him with Newton and Leibniz. The high points of their mathematical work were the discoveries of the power series expansions of arctangent, sine, and cosine. By a marvelous and unique happenstance, there survives an informal exposition of these results with full derivations, written in Malayalam, the vernacular of Kerala, by Jyeṣṭhadeva perhaps about 1540. This book, the Gaṇita-Yukti-Bhāṣā, has only very recently been translated into English with an extensive commentary. As a result, this book gives a

situation with the resulting Enlightenment of the eighteenth century and especially the industrial capitalism of the middle to late nineteenth century.[27]

Modernity has been described in a bewilderingly large and even contradictory number of ways, as heralding progress via capitalism and democracy, as being open, as embodying individual autonomy, as alienating, as resulting in a loss of religious authority, as generating existential anxiety and rootlessness and anomie, as introducing and cementing new inequalities, and so on. I want to propose that all these meanings and others are consequences of more fundamental changes that are at least partially constitutive of modernity. To this end, I will approach modernity analytically in two new and complementary ways.

Common to both is how people act. Earlier, I introduced the idea of partial rationality which describes the *form* of our actions. In my view, all agents in all times and places are generally partially rational.[28] This way of acting presupposes a way of carving up reality, that is, it presupposes an informational space or ontology separate from language. I sketched one way of doing so in terms of individuals, properties, relations, and other entities in Section 5.3. I will call this way, relatively loosely understood, *informationally* or *ontologically* rational because it allows a certain efficacy in problem-solving and decision-making and action generally. Arguably, it is such an informational space or ontology that implicitly or explicitly undergirds science seen as the attempt to grasp structure or meaning. While everyone is almost always partially rational, not everyone is informationally rational; they only approximate the latter to a greater or lesser degree in one or another sphere of action. I will call a sphere of action *rationalized* when the actions in it are not only partially rational (which they almost always are) but also sufficiently informationally rational on a sufficiently large scale. Notice that this concept is deliberately vaguely specified.

So, for example, in my view, a necessary condition for an economic sphere to be capitalist is that it be rationalized. In other words, a sufficient number of people have to become sufficiently informationally rational in their economic actions. If one adds that the economic sphere involves firms maximizing *profits*

---

unique insight into Indian methods. Simply put, these are recursion, induction, and careful passage to the limit." See also Plofker (2009), Wagner (2019).

27. As background, the interested reader can consult Kim (2020), Bayly (2004), and Habermas (1990).

28. This view sides with the latter in the debate between the anthropologists Marshall Sahlins and Gananath Obeyesekere (1997).

(or some similar economic goal like maximizing shareholder or stakeholder value) then one gets both necessary and sufficient conditions and a possible *definition* of capitalism. One can also say such an economic system is *modern* when considering it more abstractly.

The first way of analyzing modernity is to divide society into partly overlapping economic, political, and cultural (or ideological) spheres of action and then to say that a necessary condition for it is that all three spheres be rationalized. Just as we added profit-seeking behavior in the economic sphere, we would need to add certain specific types of goals or, more broadly, constraints to the political and cultural spheres to develop both necessary and sufficient conditions and, therefore, a *definition* of modernity not to mention a definition of the modern state and modern culture as well. Needless to say, such constraints are likely to be challenging to specify, especially in the cultural sphere, and they are likely to be severely contested as well. For example, should a belief in god treated as an individual be counted as sufficiently informationally rational? If not, then most people today would have to be called premodern or insufficiently modern, at least within a certain area of action. And so on.

The second way of analyzing modernity is to divide society into a crosscutting collection of what might be called *traditions*.[29] For example, at the level of everyday life, the clothes we wear, the food we eat, and often even the thoughts we think are all nurtured or possibly stifled by the traditions that undergird them. They define us, both making our lives possible and simultaneously circumscribing our lives. They allow us to pose problems, whether in science, business, art, or everyday life, and solve them in one way or another. Thus, traditions can be thought of as providing more or less effective problem-solving capabilities to a culture and society. This may be an unusual way of thinking about traditions but it is extremely powerful because it conceives of traditions as potential tools for progress rather than as historical accidents that have to be preserved for their own sake. Traditions are embodied as "habits" in people, and habits are hard to break because they invariably become part of our self-definition.

We can now say that a necessary condition for modernity is that its traditions be rationalized. Additionally, with modernity, people figure out how to abstract themselves from their habitual embodiments and view things as relatively dispassionate problem-solvers and learners and, indeed, *self-interpreters*. To the extent that they learn to choose their traditions, a meta-level choice,

---

29. Traditions are regular practices as described in Section 8.3. So only some traditions are conventions, not all.

rather than be chosen by them, they become modern, assuming certain other constraints of the kind mentioned above are also satisfied.

Given this twofold understanding of modernity, each a different angle on or framing of the same situation, we can see that all existing societies are incompletely modern or partially premodern. While it seems possible to discern growing rationalization everywhere, the other conditions for modernity remain deeply uncertain, and so, modernity everywhere remains a radically open prospect and the increasingly powerful technologies we are developing in the twenty-first century remain radically ambiguous.

In this book's Introduction, I mentioned our increasingly authoritarian world. Part of the mystery is that large segments of the population seem to prefer authoritarian regimes. This gives the latter a certain legitimacy because many leaders are democratically elected. I think it is possible to elaborate the account of modernity I have sketched and argue that this has happened because these large segments of the population are in fact premodern: they either fail to be informationally rational or do not fulfill some other condition required for modernity. A consequence of the first is a relative inability to judge what is happening clearly and a consequence of the second is a reliance on premodern hierarchies, on outmoded traditions, of one sort or another.

In a democracy both the form and content of society are "democratic"; in fascism both the form and content are "authoritarian"; in the present situation, in many countries that have elections, the form is democratic but the content is relatively authoritarian—as judged by the contents of liberal democracies: for example, many of their norms have changed from modern formal equality back to premodern inequality resulting in various forms of majoritarianism without their being actual dictatorships. Those inclined to label current goings-on as "fascist" are likely to dismiss the formal democratic dispensation as merely nominal but this would be an error. On the other hand, those inclined to think of the current state of affairs as merely a series of temporary and inessential aberrations would err in the opposite direction. Both form and content matter to the identity of the situation: such societies may be better described as *authoritarian democracies*.[30]

This very possibility was, until recently, a relatively unnoticed property of modern democracies, unnoticed because it had been implicitly taken for granted that their embedding societies are also modern when, in fact, they may still be largely premodern, even in many advanced economies. Moreover, this substantive authoritarian

---

30. They have also been described as electoral autocracies.

trend emerging within a formal democratic machinery could be more stable than the liberal democracy of political science in the face of all kinds of internal and external forces brought about by modernization and globalization because the latter is far more constrained in its scope of actions than the former. This appears to be an inherent weakness of the democratic state and could even be a tendency toward an unsavory equilibrium. If this speculative thought turns out to be true, it could mean a more or less permanent alteration of our political life.

Thus, the advent of global modernity may not imply the kind of sharp break from the past envisaged by many Enlightenment thinkers and later observers not only in the social sciences but also in the arts. It remains *partial*.

## 9.4  In the Center of the Story

We are now in the heart of our story. Not only have we seen how the key institution of language works and how its fundamental problems might be addressed, we have also gotten deeply involved in its applications, both direct, such as the public sphere, and analogical, such as other symbol systems and modernity. Throughout, I have tried to show how the concepts and tools developed earlier bear on new systems and institutions as well as AI.

I remind you of the journey we are on by reproducing the map of the book in Figure B.

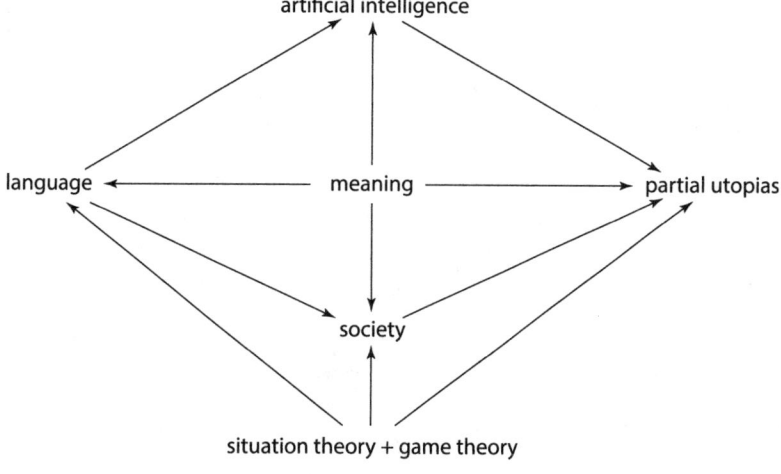

**Figure B   A Map of the Book**

# PART IV

## MEANING AND CIVILIZATION

CHAPTER TEN

# The Meta-Structure of Society

In this last part of the book, we move into a less strictly scientific and more loosely speculative—and analogical—space. The themes to be addressed are vast and, needless to say, I do not have the knowledge required for the task. They are also hugely contested issues.[1]

At a basic level, a society is made up of interactions between people. In other words, it is made up of situated games. The forms these games take are extremely diverse, ranging from single-person choice situations to potentially everyone on the planet participating in large global games. Not only this, a society includes many network games, and networks of networks, and so on, until everything is included. These network games are broadly analogous to and also include the Language Games I introduced earlier in the book. At bottom, however, there are simply agents choosing and performing actions—working or resting or talking or looking or thinking or some similar practical activity. In this sense, it is our actions that constitute society or, to put it differently, a society is a complex bundle of dynamic equilibria, that is, it is the ongoing collective *meaning* of all our actions.

The foregoing is an abstract picture of society, more a depiction of what might be called its "meta-structure" than its structure. I will unpack it a bit more

---

1. As background, the reader might want to consult Aron (1965/1981, 1967/1980), Parsons (1937/1968a, chaps. 2, 22), Parsons (1937/1968b, chaps. 23, 28), Goffman (1959, intro.), Blumer (1969, chap. 1), Bernstein (1976), Dallmayr and McCarthy (1978), Ordeshook (1986), Bruner (1990), Robbins and Aydede (2009), and Mesquita et al. (2010). See also Miller (2019) and especially Guala (2016, chaps. 1, 2) whose approach is game-theoretic. Many eminent economists and game theorists, starting with von Neumann and Morgenstern (1944/1947), Nash (1951), Arrow and Debreu (1954), Arrow (1974), Schelling (1960), Aumann (1976a, 1976b, 1985, 1987), and North (1990/2002, chaps. 1, 2), have created this approach broadly considered—they cannot all be cited here but see the references in Guala (2016). I sidestep the many technicalities they consider relating to rationality and solution concepts and simply push ahead with my own framework as described so far.

as my goal is not to build a *theory* of society but to describe some of its main ingredients that would enable someone to build one if they so desired. The first step is to understand the agents who play these games.

## 10.1 Persons and Groups

Early on, I said that individual persons or groups such as firms or nations could participate as agents in games. I have already sketched what persons are—finite agents with situated capacities and perceptions and beliefs and preferences who face choices and act as they navigate the world. They do so in partially rational ways and they are more or less informationally rational as well, that is, they are more or less *modern* or *premodern* in each sphere of action presented to them by society.

Groups can be described in a variety of ways depending on our purposes. At its simplest, a group can be conceived as a mere collection, a *set*, of agents without any internal structure. More usefully, a group, say of friends or family members, might be considered a set of agents with more or less tightly knit relations among them, with possibly some degree of common knowledge of each other's attributes. Even more structured are groups such as firms that are capable of acting *jointly*.

Joint acts are ubiquitous in society and, indeed, the act of communication is itself a joint act. Imagine Ann and Bob are pushing a cart uphill. They can do this jointly or *together* or they can do it independently or *singly*. In both types of acts, Ann and Bob perform their individual actions of pushing against the cart but in the former they do it in a coordinated way that involves common or at least shared knowledge of each other's actions as well as a more or less complex set of games between them.[2] This is what allows us to say that Ann *and* Bob pushed the cart uphill—or went to a movie or cooked a meal or rowed a boat or whatever—as opposed to saying simply that Ann pushed the cart uphill and Bob pushed the cart uphill.[3] Additionally, when the payoffs are not symmetrical,

---

2. For a formal definition, see Parikh (2001, chap. 6).

3. Incidentally, this shows how complicated—and *ambiguous*—a seemingly simple word like "and" can be.

as in most firms today or, indeed, nations, the games involve conflict as well as coordination, not to mention asymmetric power.

While simple joint acts like pushing a cart uphill together can be executed without communication, more difficult joint acts like a firm maximizing stakeholder value can obviously be greatly eased by agents communicating with each other about which equilibria to pursue, or even more often, about which games to play. Thus, groups capable of acting jointly generally have a language available to them. I will call such groups *organizations* even when they do something as ephemeral as pushing a cart uphill.

The last type of group to consider is a generalization of what I called a linguistic community when I discussed the emergence of language. It involves persons or organizations like the ones above participating in network games of one kind or another. Such generalized communities typically involve a multitude of network games including Language Games all played by the same agents more or less. No common knowledge is involved and so communities of various kinds are relatively less tightly held together.

So there are at least four types of groups in society, those that form a mere set, those whose members are more or less intimately related to each other in various ways, those that can act jointly and form organizations, and those that form communities. They are obviously not mutually exclusive and often co-occur.[4]

## 10.2 Social Institutions

I started the book by describing language as a social institution and identifying other large social institutions such as civil society, the economy, and the state. I will use the term in an expansive way that treats smaller regularities such as conventions as social institutions as well. That is, all conventions are social institutions but not all social institutions are conventions.

---

4. Sartre (1960/2004, bks. I and II) explores somewhat similar ideas in his notions of individual choice, collectives, fused groups, statutory groups, organizations, and institutions. Unfortunately, because his ontology—or informational space—is dialectical, his language becomes quite obscure. He also seems to conflate what a fused group is with how it comes to be: in response to an external threat (which may have something in common with Durkheim's organic solidarity). In my view, his attempt is marred by not having access to a clear analytical framework like game theory. See also Danto (1979, pp. 129–130).

Just as I showed how language (i.e., relatively fixed conventional meanings) emerges as a meaningful equilibrium of a prototypical network game called a Language Game, so it is possible to show how other institutions emerge as dynamic equilibria of similar network games. In fact, I also briefly described the convention of greeting someone with a namaste via a network game. The agents in such network games can be persons or organizations. For example, firms participate as group agents in the relevant network games that result in the modern economy.

Just as a Language Game was built up from local Communication Games so the various network games are made up of corresponding local games. A single market, for example, may be considered such a local game, and all the markets together would then make up the whole network game whose equilibrium is the modern economy. Or interactions between two branches of government form a local game and so do interactions between the executive branch of a government and a protest movement. All such variegated local games together make up the whole network game whose equilibrium is the modern state. Depending on our purposes, we can refer to the entire relevant network games as language or the modern economy or the modern state or we can refer to their dynamic equilibria as language or the modern economy or the modern state. That is, a social institution can be identified with a corresponding network game (and is a different way to see a community) or with its equilibrium depending on the context.

It should be clear that it is tough to pin down the nature of the local and global games that create large, complex institutions like language, the modern economy, and the modern state. I have tried to describe in some detail what language is and how it works to exhibit some of these challenges and how they might be met. The modern capitalist economy, too, has been modeled in even greater detail by economists. In my view, many other large institutions like the modern state are still too poorly understood as they have far-reaching, diverse, and seemingly contradictory facets.[5] This may be because the modern state is in fact a network game of network games made up of local games, that is, it is a *second-order* institution making possible its more diverse and apparently contradictory character.

Despite these difficulties, local games, the building blocks of global network games, can be better understood by applying the other two key ideas that I have called "fixed and variable" and "parts and wholes." Recall the schema that

---

5. Habermas (1975), Bayly (2004, chaps. 7, 8).

displayed how the use of language went from the speaker's concrete utterance of a word to its abstract and more or less shared conventional meanings and from there onto the addressee's concrete interpretation of its referential meanings:

$$\text{word} \xrightarrow{u} \text{conventional meanings} \xrightarrow{u} \text{referential meanings}$$

Dropping the arrows, this schema can be equivalently redisplayed as shown in Figure 10.1 and, more simply, in Figure 10.2.

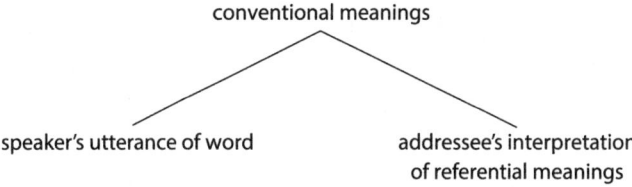

Figure 10.1   Linguistic Instance of Structure and Agency

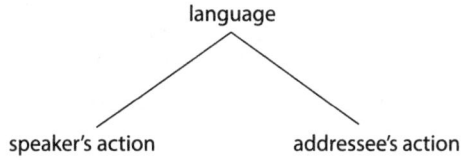

Figure 10.2   Linguistic Instance of Structure and Agency Simplified

These pictures show how the social institution of language is both *partially* used and *partially* created through a single instance of a Communication Game. A whole network of such games—that is, a Language Game—results in meaningful equilibria or conventional meanings or, in other words, language. Moreover, the existence of language makes local Communication Games possible in a quasi-circular way. That is, without conventional meanings that we more or less share we cannot communicate and without communication we cannot come to share conventional meanings. This circularity of structure and agency (or *langue* and *parole*) can be fully spelled out in the case of language.[6]

We can think of this circularity between other local games and global network games in much the same way. Without local games the global game and

---

6. Parikh (2019). Potentially, a similar derivation can be conceived for more or less shared grammars.

its equilibria cannot exist and without the global game and its equilibria the local games cannot exist. This analogical conception can be expressed visually as shown in Figure 10.3.

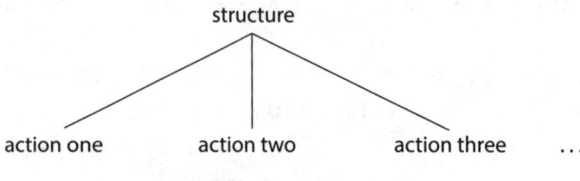

Figure 10.3  Structure and Agency

The familiar example of a namaste can be represented as shown in Figure 10.4.

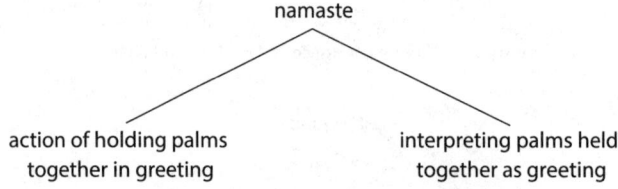

Figure 10.4  Structure and Agency with Namaste

And the social institution of a traffic system is shown in Figure 10.5.

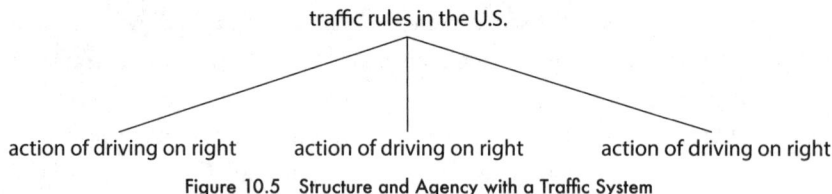

Figure 10.5  Structure and Agency with a Traffic System

The idea of fixed and variable helps us to see in an altogether new way how the problem of the apparently vicious circularity between structure and agency, that is, the question of which comes first, might be resolved abstractly via the idea of an equilibrium of a network game. Of course, it would have to be worked out in detail for each institution case by case.

This brings us to the equally important problem of a different circularity between parts and wholes. Just as the idea of interdependent games and the multiplication of smaller games to get larger games described in the case of language and communication made it possible to capture the probabilistic dynamics between words and sentences inherent in Communication Games and to generalize it to other parts and wholes that make up the so-called hermeneutic circle, so similar interdependencies and multiplication operations pervade other actions when they are made up of smaller parts. For example, traffic systems involve many different actions and not just keeping on one side of the road, and their meanings are interdependent just as the meanings of "Fred" and "ran" were in the utterance of "Fred ran."

More generally, imagine a system[7] that has relatively weakly linked distinct subsystems, such as an utterance containing several words where the utterance is seen as a whole system containing several distinct subsystems involving the utterance of distinct words. Then, just as these lexical, phrasal, and sentential subsystems interact with one another, so games corresponding to different social or other subsystems would be linked and interact with one another and with larger games involving subsets of subsystems.[8] Essentially, the idea of interdependent games and their joint equilibrium may be extendable to whole-part relations in a variety of fields because it allows the whole to be dependent on its parts and the parts to be dependent on the whole in a natural and rigorous way. Indeed, not only social systems but also ecological and distributed AI systems may in principle be modeled this way.[9]

Thus, the three key ideas of fixed and variable, parts and wholes, and networks enable us to delineate the functioning of social institutions at a relatively abstract, meta-structural level. Just as with language, the difficulties of ambiguity, vagueness, and context suffuse their operation because the actions that constitute them are ambiguous, vague, and situated.

Language plays a double role because it not only serves as a prototype for other social institutions but is also required to establish many of them. For example, language is generally required to specify one of the two possible equilibria of a traffic system, to drive on the left or on the right. This is partly why communication is so important in playing most games.

---

7. All social institutions are social systems but not vice versa.

8. This is not unlike the kind of thing that happens in the 2005 film *Syriana* where relatively remote and unconnected events in weakly linked spheres result in a disastrous global equilibrium.

9. Parikh (2010, sec. 7.1.4).

As we saw with the modern state, there can be higher-order institutions as well. Even the traffic system may be thought of as a higher-order institution as it consists of many different rules, not just driving on the left or on the right side of the road.

The meta-structure of society can now be described, possibly in a fresh way, as a vast, partly hierarchical network of networks of networks and so on down to the smallest networks with the agents in them being persons or organizations. This justifies my earlier "definition" of societies as bundles of organizations and social institutions and, therefore, as the ongoing collective *meaning* of our situated actions.[10]

## 10.3  Situated Games and Social Roles

The idea of a social role, something familiar to all of us from our everyday uses of language and, indeed, our own social roles, flows naturally from the situated games that make up society. For example, in a Communication Game there is a speaker and one or more addressees. Being a speaker or an addressee are transitory social roles and they are obviously determined by the actions performed in the relevant game. In the same way, other organizations and institutions determine other social roles such as son or motorist. Not every role has a corresponding linguistic term attached to it, only the most common ones.

An important and unexpected consequence of this idea of connecting social roles with situated games is that many social roles can and do persist across

---

10. As an aside, I mention that, on the continental side, Foucault is probably the main theorist of (early modern) social institutions such as the prison and the clinic. In my view, not only do his analyses in terms of epistemes and discourses lack any place for human agency (as I said in Section 8.5) and, therefore, for social change but they also exhibit a certain predictable sameness and one-sidedness owing to their exclusive emphasis on authoritarian control, exemplifying the "marriage of Cartesian rationalism with a romanticism gone awry" I referred to earlier. This is not to deny that many institutions, including conventional ones like class and race, involve coercion and deep oppression but rather to point out that the full story is much more complex, which is why I have focused on their meta-structures rather than their actual structures. The reason for this complexity is that power is realized through the situated games we play, both at a micro and, as we will soon see, at a macro level, and these games are of many different types not all involving control or domination as discussed in Section 6.6. See also Taylor (1984).

multiple games and sometimes end up influencing or even defining the choices and payoffs of future games as well as the expectations we bring to them of how others will play their part in them. That is, they can predetermine the shape of the game and the equilibria that will be selected and thereby reduce the effort required to play a familiar game. This is why in routine, everyday life we do not need to set up elaborate games or perform onerous calculations *even* unconsciously.

Consider essentially the same mixed-motive game between Ann and Bob from Section 6.1 but with altered actions: either go to a French restaurant or a Japanese restaurant for dinner—assuming they eat out every Saturday night. As shown in Figure 10.6, Ann prefers French food to Japanese food whereas Bob prefers Japanese food to French food, but they both prefer eating together to eating by themselves. The situation accompanying the game would contain the fact that the game is repeated every Saturday night.

|  | French | Japanese |
|---|---|---|
| French | (2, 1) | (0, 0) |
| Japanese | (0, 0) | (1, 2) |

Figure 10.6   A Mixed-Motive Game

What may happen is that their roles as Saturday-night diners might crystallize and Ann and Bob may evolve into alternating between French and Japanese outings without ever discussing the matter explicitly and without needing to play the game explicitly or implicitly. Each may just think to themselves that the previous week it was French, so this week it will be Japanese, that is all. This is one way in which social roles can emerge, easing our computational burdens among other things. Notice in particular how the Saturday-night diner roles persist across multiple repeated games. If either wants to try something different sometime, say Indian food, they may need to invoke a slightly altered game afresh. This might require a conversation resulting in altered roles and expectations as well.

A second, more profound consequence of the ubiquity of social roles is that it greatly expands our understanding of persons: not only do they have certain capacities and perceptions and beliefs and preferences, and not only do they choose and act in the world, but they are also thoroughly social beings. The primary mechanism through which persons get socialized is the more or less enduring roles they occupy from their births until their deaths. Indeed, even organizations as group agents capable of acting jointly acquire social roles by virtue of participating repeatedly in the same types of games and generating social expectations about their behavior. Part of the reason why new self-interpretations are difficult for both persons and organizations is the resistance encrusted social roles set up against their emancipatory desires. This becomes easier to understand when social roles are seen as resulting from the payoff structures of corresponding situated games because they show concretely that it may be difficult if not irrational to deviate from previously established equilibria.

## 10.4 Self and Society

While social roles certainly make us social beings, our *sociality* runs much deeper. In everyday life as well as in many religious and philosophical traditions, we think of our selves—our core centers of experience, choice, and action—as entirely private, as belonging wholly to us. There is some truth to this, of course, but it is equally true that our selves are also partly social constructs. Indeed, this is something of a commonplace in some quarters of the social sciences.[11] How might we make sense of this dual source for our selves within the framework I have developed so far?

Recall the quasi-circularity of an agent's preferences in relation to the situated games they play. Whether it is Ann's preference for chocolate ice cream over vanilla ice cream or Bob's preference for democracy over authoritarianism, they are both partly the result of their prior socialization.

Ordinarily, the preferences game theorists look at are specific to the particular games agents play. I have adopted an informational or ontological view of games that makes our participation in them ubiquitous, and this requires us to posit that all agents have a complex and shifting hierarchy of concerns and goals, from survival at the top that is generally always present to very particular ones at the bottom such as a desire for ice cream in some situation.[12]

One can perhaps say that the higher-level preferences (e.g., survival) are initially biologically given and change only under great external pressure, and that these relatively stable preferences influence how lower-level preferences change

---

11. For example, Bruner (1990, chap. 4).
12. See Chapter 6.

## Chapter Ten: The Meta-Structure of Society

in the light of experience, which includes the consequences of the agent's actions in the relevant situated games. And then, the agent faces the next set of games with these altered preferences. So the process isn't really circular but ongoing, where the further step is the feedback about the agent's preferences *after* a game is over. A kind of situated learning occurs every time a game is played, one way of seeing the nature-nurture divide: the relatively more stable higher-level preferences represent nature's contribution and the more easily shifting lower-level preferences represent the contribution of nurture.

Thus, agents influence the nature of society through their actions and society influences the nature of agents through the consequences of these actions. Indeed, just as society was informally defined as the bundle of (dynamic equilibria of) network games or equivalently as the collective meaning of our situated actions, so a self can be informally defined as the bundle of (dynamic equilibria of) *local* situated games the agent plays or equivalently as the simultaneously personal and social *meaning* of its and others' situated actions.

Consider again the coordination game from Section 6.1 in Figure 10.7.

|  | Grand Central | Penn Station |
|---|---|---|
| Grand Central | (2, 2) | (0, 0) |
| Penn Station | (0, 0) | (1, 1) |

Figure 10.7  A Coordination Game

If this was the only game Ann and Bob played, then each of their selves would contain an individual part, consisting of their preferences and values and perhaps other personal things, and a social part, consisting of the equilibrium of the coordination game involving their jointly optimal choice of Grand Central. For our limited purposes, it does not matter how these two parts are represented internally; the important point is that each of their selves contains information about their own as well as the other's equilibrium choice: their selves partly become *social constructs*.[13]

| Individual Part | Social Part |
|---|---|
| Grand Central > Penn Station | Ann: Grand Central; Bob: Grand Central |

Table 10.1  A Rudimentary Representation of a Self

---

13. Alternatively, the whole coordination game could be included in each person's social part.

As they add more games to their respective trajectories through the world, a kind of internal record builds up of all their equilibria or situated games so that their selves become deeply social. The reason why these social interactions become part of their *selves* is that these records change Ann's and Bob's preferences and values as the outcomes of various equilibria impinge on their core centers of experience, choice, and action made up of both their individual parts and social parts. Thus, Ann may come to prefer chocolate ice cream over vanilla ice cream and Bob may come to prefer democracy over authoritarianism through their individual makeup as well as through the social equilibria they experience. This, in a nutshell, is how socialization constructs persons in society.

As modern society is rife with all kinds of inequality, some perhaps unavoidable, the selves that it partly constructs face differential challenges in experiencing even the most basic levels of dignity and self-respect, an essential condition for democracy. Especially for those who are oppressed by authoritarian regimes—such as the heroic Nelson Mandela was not too long ago—it is not so easy to be "the captain of one's soul."[14] Self-respect is partly societal respect and a key task for a partial utopia is to create conditions that progressively humanize the latter, thereby making it easier for each individual person to enjoy a fuller self-respect as a foundation for their life.

It is in this more capacious setting that we can better appreciate Aristotle's observation that man is a political animal. As I said earlier, we can become fully human and lead fulfilling and meaningful lives only within the context of other human beings. The kinds of societies we create, whether partial utopias or partial dystopias, determine to what degree we can actualize our potential and experience a higher level of freedom and happiness collectively and individually. Simply put, we need one another to realize ourselves.[15]

A key consequence of the fact that selves are partly socially constructed is that liberalism is a flawed doctrine because it takes preferences as "externally" given—*de gustibus non est disputandum*. To quote from Kenneth Arrow's classic *Social Choice and Individual Values*:[16]

> We will also assume in the present study that individual values are taken as data and are not capable of being altered by the nature

---

14. See the poem "Invictus" by William Ernest Henley, which inspired Mandela.
15. See Section 2.3.
16. Arrow (1951/1963, pp. 7–8).

of the decision process itself. This, of course, is the standard view in economic theory (though the unreality of this assumption has been asserted by such writers as Veblen, Professor J. M. Clark and Knight) and also in the classical liberal creed.[17] If individual values can themselves be affected by the method of social choice, it becomes much more difficult to learn what is meant by one method's being preferable to another.

The "unreality of this assumption" is then one clear reason why modern societies should aim for a *post*-liberal democracy, a partial utopia that retains what is best in a liberal democracy but also goes beyond it by fully acknowledging the sociality of our selves.

## 10.5 Preferences and Values

In the discussion of vagueness in Section 4.3, I showed how partly contested but partly shared social values emerged as averages of individual judgments communicated through our utterances. These judgments are decisions based on preferences and, indeed, all our values are preferences, big and small. We ordinarily do not think of trivial preferences, such as liking chocolate ice cream more than vanilla ice cream, as values, but they are. We could stipulate a somewhat arbitrary division between high-level and low-level preferences based on those we consider important—a kind of meta-preference—and call only the former values; however, I will treat all preferences as values. In either case, our more serious values—such as a preference for democracy over authoritarianism—will generally be the result of reflection and moral deliberation which will include thoughtful social observation as well as discussion with others.

The picture of values related to vague language as partly shared and partly contested applies to all values because, as the previous section showed, they also issue from the wider situated games agents play and all agents are generally

---

17. Arrow's footnote where he quotes F. H. Knight (1947, p. 69): "*Liberalism takes the individual as given*, and views the social problem as one of right relations between given individuals." See also Sandel (1998).

influenced in partly similar ways. This is what enables a shared but also contested and unresolved public sphere and, indeed, even a democracy to exist.

If these underlying games become too different from each other—such as some favoring *modern* equilibria and others favoring *premodern* equilibria—then a deeply divided society can result. If, as has happened today, premodern outcomes outnumber modern outcomes then a liberal democracy can become authoritarian. For example, if many people succumb to the Hegemony Game in Section 8.5, then values involving charisma and traditional hierarchies and inequalities between persons and groups can prevail.

The model of network games consisting of local games like the Hegemony Game provides a link between micro actions and macro meanings and thereby helps to explain, at least in a rough pictorial way, how individual values and social choices reciprocally affect each other and shape the very meaning of modern civilization, shape what is considered true, good, and beautiful.

Even more fundamentally, our ontologies or informational spaces, the very entities we individuate—which result from the Language Games we participate in[18]—and use to orient ourselves in reality can potentially become more or less informationally rational, more or less modern. Such fissiparous tendencies naturally relate more to abstract entities such as a preference for democracy or authoritarianism than to concrete entities such as tables or chairs.

It is thus a combination of the micro and the macro, of the local and the global, of the personal and the social that determines the very meaning of reality itself. While the more concrete elements of reality are less malleable, the more abstract elements—such as the kind of democracy we want—are to a large extent up to us.

## 10.6 Power

As we saw earlier, micro or local power is determined by the structure of a local situated game an agent plays, whether a coordination game or mixed-motive game or one involving greater conflict or complexity. There are many ways to build on this foundation to see how macro or global power works.

---

18. For a discussion of this, see Parikh (2010, sec. 7.6).

There is power in groups involving ongoing relationships, power in organizations capable of acting jointly, power in communities that make up network games or social institutions, and power in society seen as a bundle of organizations and social institutions. All of these instances of power derive ultimately from the local games that make up the various types of collectivities.

Essentially the same recursive principle serves to pin down all these different manifestations of power. An agent's power is determined by the number and nature of local games they play, and a crucial component of this nature is the power of the other agents who participate in these games. If, for example, Ann has greater local power in a particular local game with Bob, and if Bob has greater local power in a different local game with Cathy, then Ann's global power is enhanced because she exerts a kind of indirect power over Cathy. Working out the details of such a recursive or cascading conception poses formidable difficulties because our understanding of local power itself remains hazy.[19] However, it can nevertheless help us to grasp in a rough-and-ready way the macro or global power of large organizations such as monopolies or large social institutions such as the modern state and, possibly, even to puzzle out the nature of contemporary authoritarianisms as well as how global hegemony operates—all through the more concrete choices and payoffs of interconnected games like the Hegemony Game rather than through verbal description, as I said at the close of the second part of the book. This can in turn suggest better ways to counteract such power as well.

I said earlier that Ann had greater power than Bob in the Hegemony Game despite the fact that Bob acted freely. This can now be explained as follows. First, it is Ann's interest that is represented in the local Hegemony Game while Bob's interest is absent: this is part of the asymmetry that gives Ann greater local power than Bob. Second, Ann might participate in many more such asymmetric local Hegemony Games with others like Cathy, which contributes to her greater global power. And third, the recursive structure of the organizations and institutions Ann is a part of may also work in her favor. That is, Bob's and Cathy's power cascades up to and magnifies Ann's power. All of this adds up to Ann having more local and global power than Bob.

Concretely, consider similar Hegemony Games between Ann and Bob, Ann and Cathy, Bob and Fred, and Cathy and Oscar, all shown in Figures 10.8, 10.9, 10.10, 10.11, and 10.12 in a self-explanatory way. Overall, Ann has direct power

---

19. There is also a possible circularity in this idea that would need to be tackled.

over Bob and Cathy and indirect power over Fred and Oscar, which cascades up to her through Bob and Cathy, respectively.

|  | Ann's interest | common interest |
|---|---|---|
| Ann's interest | (2, 2) | (0, 0) |
| common interest | (0, 0) | (1, 1) |

Figure 10.8   Hegemony Game between Ann and Bob

|  | Ann's interest | common interest |
|---|---|---|
| Ann's interest | (2, 2) | (0, 0) |
| common interest | (0, 0) | (1, 1) |

Figure 10.9   Hegemony Game between Ann and Cathy

|  | Bob's interest | common interest |
|---|---|---|
| Bob's interest | (2, 2) | (0, 0) |
| common interest | (0, 0) | (1, 1) |

Figure 10.10   Hegemony Game between Bob and Fred

|  | Cathy's interest | common interest |
|---|---|---|
| Cathy's interest | (2, 2) | (0, 0) |
| common interest | (0, 0) | (1, 1) |

Figure 10.11   Hegemony Game between Cathy and Oscar

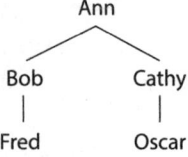

Figure 10.12   The Hierarchy of Power

Further, it may be argued that it is their prior socialization through society's impact on their preferences and beliefs, that is, through the prior social construction of their selves that the various local and global games have the structure they do: their embedding situations, the participating agents, the available choices, the payoffs, and their linkages with other situated games through a network. This whole ensemble has to be summoned to explain how a demagogue can sway the masses without the direct use of force and can block the "natural" crystallization of ongoing emancipatory group desires. Such tendencies toward authoritarianism receive support from "below" when the higher-level preferences of populations are more premodern than modern and favor hierarchy and inequality over mutual respect and equality. It is precisely such a premodern combination of local and global that enables majoritarianisms of various kinds to flourish.

One stark application of such hegemonic and other types of power is to the recent growth of fake news. All authoritarian regimes deal in propaganda but the new features of such broader falsehoods lie in the confluence of two simultaneous developments: the widespread availability of enabling technologies, such as cell phones, social media, and AI, and a more sophisticated, scientific understanding of how to manipulate democratic norms of truth-telling via the manipulation of meaning itself. To echo the social philosopher Hannah Arendt, this has made fake news *banal*.

More problematic still, global power can also function in an impersonal way via the existence of social roles. The particular persons occupying a role, such as president of a corporation or country, may change but the roles persist and can continue to constrain the form and content of various games. However, it is ultimately up to the new person who enters the role whether to simply accept old habits or define new traditions. This is yet another instance of a quasi-circular reciprocity between social role and game and its wide impact on the pervasiveness of power in society.

Despite this ubiquity, power can be benign or malign, symmetric or asymmetric, and the real lesson to be learned from this analysis is not that society is doomed to be under authoritarian control of one kind or another but rather that through a deeper grasp of social dynamics—the interplay of local and global, and of selves and societies—combined with thoughtful and constructive emancipatory practices, we can jointly work toward a partial utopia of one kind or another.

## 10.7  Social Change

We have already seen how conventional meanings (e.g., "dog") and other conventions (e.g., namaste) change. More complex institutions generally also change in the same way, first through a small shift at a local level that then propagates through the network and alters its equilibrium. And societies metamorphose when many of their organizations and institutions mutate.

If the analogy between language and other institutions is basically sound, then it is remarkable that large changes in deeply entrenched institutions like class and race and gender are likely to come about in ways not fundamentally different from how over centuries the conventional meaning of "dog" broadened from signifying a large canine to any canine.

One key difference, however, is that many major social institutions change as a result of deliberate actions by multitudes, whereas most changes in language occur without our being fully aware of their genesis. In such situations, people have to notice the interdependence between local situated games and global network games as well as realize that all agents have to act locally. In other words, people have to *think globally, act locally*, a commonplace credo of spatially conceived activism reinterpreted game-theoretically. That is, to think globally is to think in terms of global network games and not simply in terms of the world at large, and to act locally is to act in terms of local games that may spread out spatially to encompass the globe. This strategic insight can be telling for many social struggles today. For example, a geographically distributed diaspora could play an important role in a local situated game.

More deeply, the collection of situated games that make up society is partly ambiguous and vague and is not made up of simple binary oppositions involving "friends" and "enemies" contrary to the political theorist Carl Schmitt.[20] Most games are a mix of coordination and conflict—they are mixed-motive rather than zero-sum games—and can generally be altered through conversation. Gandhi, perhaps above all, knew this not only practically but also morally: our seemingly worst enemies can also partly be our friends. For example, in an alliance between two countries, one democratic, the other autocratic, the democratic country can urge the autocratic country to restore democracy while pursuing other mutually beneficial policies. It is the game-theoretic apparatus that clearly suggests a mixed stance involving compromise rather than an all-or-nothing stance which can result in extremism of one kind or another.

As I have shown from basic foundational principles that explain its mechanics, institutional change is a complex process. First, it is quite difficult for a single person or organization to bring about change because at each step of its propagation a chain in the network can be broken by an uncooperative participant.

---

20. Vinx (2019).

Second, institutional meanings do nevertheless keep changing despite these difficulties because there are a lot of participants in the relevant network games that contribute to change intentionally or unintentionally. Third, it is these multiple players that make the resulting network equilibria or social meanings unpredictable.

Overall, our actions constitute society in two ways: the first, generally conscious and intended, is to aim for a desired outcome in a local game, and the second, generally unconscious and unintended, is to either reinforce or change the social institution of which the local game is a part. This makes us all co-creators of society, from its origins to its dynamics over history. And, of course, society influences our actions in a feedback loop.

## 10.8 Meaning, Society, and Artificial Intelligence Revisited

What started out in the first chapter of the book as a skeletal description of meaning and society has now acquired some flesh and blood, at least some meta-flesh and meta-blood. Society can now be seen as not simply the result of shared meanings but as the collective meaning of our situated actions. The duality of humans, their capacity for great good and great evil mentioned there, is partly the result of our intrinsic nature, our biologically given preferences, and partly the result of our socialized selves, socialized through games that induce good or bad behavior via the actions they make available and the payoffs they confer. Civilization, which can be understood either as a society's conception of the true, good, and beautiful or alternatively as the combination of shared institutions and shared ontologies in society, is therefore also just a collective meaning reducible in principle to information. *Modern* civilization, then, is the kind of civilization that is largely informationally rational together with other more elusive conditions, a huge joint but partial historical advance that started around the sixteenth and seventeenth centuries.

As mentioned in Section 9.3.1, just as we learn to see a rock *as* a rock, a toaster *as* a toaster, a cat *as* a cat, and a person *as* a person, and thereby discover the fundamental social *mutability* and *constructibility* of things—within natural limits—we can learn that we create society and civilization as they create us. Within limits, our selves and societies depend on how we choose to interpret them, a realization made more concrete by our understanding of local situated games and global network games and their equilibria. We tend to be more aware of the immediate local games we inhabit but are relatively less aware of the mediate network games they constitute. Moreover, this "*as*-structure" depends deeply on our use of language and our ability to separate our informational spaces from it, just as Shakespeare's Juliet is able to separate a rose from its name. It is when this happens that we can see things as they are and as they can be: we can glimpse human *possibility* itself. That is the implicit precondition of creativity and the heart of semantics, the magical relation between language, reality, and knowledge, not only at the level of art and science but also at the level of society and civilization as a whole.

The entire framework I have described so far rests on partial rationality, informational rationality, on an extended situated game theory with its concomitant equilibria, and on large analogies between language and other social institutions suffused with ambiguity, vagueness, and context, and informed by the three key ideas of fixed and variable, parts and wholes, and networks. It is at best partial, as many difficulties need to be worked out. It is also deliberately pitched at an abstract level although I have tried to make it as concrete as possible by alternating between macro and micro and between idea and example. The language of information and meaning has allowed us to straddle the abstract and concrete, what a namaste ultimately is and what it is in everyday life.

Humanists and many social theorists tend to make a false dichotomy between causality and interpretation, between natural and social, a seemingly unshakeable distinction that goes back to multiple humanisms in different cultures.[21] I have tried to show through the multilevel language of information and meaning that these dualities are just two sides of the same coin.

To say more would require a new *theory* of society, a view of exactly what organizations and institutions actually exist and how they interact. How do the economic, political, and cultural spheres interpenetrate and affect each other? This must happen foundationally through the mostly mixed-motive games we play, but specifying them and building up to various kinds of groups and organizations and institutions that constitute society, even in partial ways that enable us to understand, explain, and occasionally predict, remains an elusive task.

However, these difficulties exist not only for my approach but universally. All the grand social theories developed in the modern era have broken down

---

21. See Taylor (1971), for example; also Dallmayr and McCarthy (1978).

and a new synthesis is required. My outlook allows one to zoom in locally or zoom out globally using the same tools—as shown concretely with Communication Games and Language Games and local situated games and global network games—making possible a simultaneous micro and macro perspective on the world. My claim throughout has been that situation theory and situated game theory can provide the basic building blocks for a new integrated theory and, indeed, the kind of grounding vision mentioned in the Introduction for how societies can hum, thrive, and flourish or descend into a dictatorial darkness.

# CHAPTER ELEVEN

# Situated Artificial Intelligence

Science, I have said, is the search for meaning. Meaning, in turn, is the connection between situated entities such as smoke and fire, and, more complexly, it is the structure of things such as carbon atoms or the modern economy. As we have seen, all meaning, natural or artificial, is more or less ambiguous and more or less vague whether we are contemplating "2 + 2 = 4" or *Finnegan's Wake*.

An intuitive picture of meaning can be drawn as follows. Imagine a pond. Take a pebble and drop it in the center of the pond. Watch the ripples circle outward to the edge of the pond, fading as they expand. Then the pond is the world, the pebble is a natural entity such as smoke or a symbolic entity such as a poem, the ripples are its meanings, and the amplitude of the ripples is their probability. This metaphor can be made precise through situation theory.[1]

Generally, for realists, meaning is wholly determinate, whereas for antirealists meaning is wholly indeterminate. In the picture I have painted, meaning is partially determinate and partially indeterminate, the ripples near the pebble being more easily explicable and the ripples further away being more difficult to capture.

In the previous chapter, we saw that society is the collective meaning of our situated actions. More generally, we have taken the intentions and consequences of actions such as picking up a glass of water to take a sip as their primary meanings, the "ripples" nearest the "pebble." And we have seen that actions can have more elusive indirect meanings and can function as utterances. However, we have left the underlying informational or ontological nature of actions unexamined. It is to this task I now turn as it will give us an insight into technology and the promise of a situated artificial intelligence.

---

1. Parikh (2010, sec. 5.9), Parikh (2019, sec. 15.2).

## 11.1 Informational Transforms

A modern informational space consists of individuals, properties, relations, states of affairs, games, situations, connections, and a few other entities. Such spaces are at best partially known to us. The amazing thing is that we humans can *imagine* transforming, in a kind of *mental* alchemy, any situated entity in such a space to any other situated entity in it. Such a change is called an *informational transform*. It is the deep secret of information and the deep source of humanity's imaginative power in all fields of human endeavor.

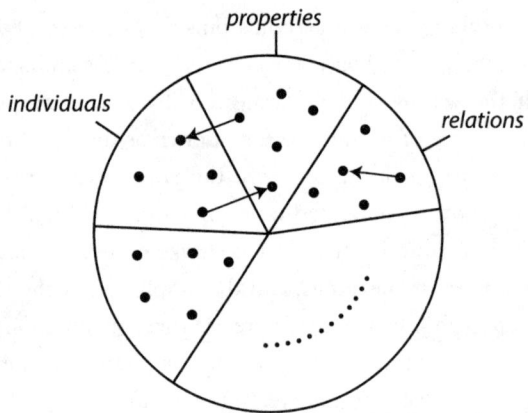

Figure 11.1 An Informational Space with Informational Transforms

For instance, we can imagine mapping the situated property *being blue* into the situated individual *blue sky*. Or we can go in the reverse direction, extracting the situated property from the situated individual, as we more mundanely do. And with many other such transformations of inputs into outputs, abstract or concrete into abstract or concrete.[2]

---

[2] I first developed the idea of such a transform during my doctoral dissertation. It is possible, in principle, to study both the underlying informational space and the space of transformations on it just as we may study a Euclidean space and its group of, say, rotations about an axis. Situation theory can be conceived as a theory of the underlying space of ontological entities. However, we can also consider spaces of transformations on the underlying space. It is interesting that, unlike the case of Euclidean and many other spaces, the ontological space is not available to us in any obvious way. Our primary routes to discovering the objects that populate this space are linguistic and epistemic situations, and also some intuitive ideas about how we might

Indeed, John Lennon's "Imagine" may come to mind.

All change in the world, natural and artificial, through the forces of physics or through the actions of society, can be represented for greater explicitness and clarity as a bundle of one or more situated informational transforms. This is obviously a small part of all the possible transforms that can be imagined. The great strength and the great weakness of all of us is that we live simultaneously in both the real world and very many fictional worlds, all parts of an expansive informational universe. This is especially so in modernity and for the first time in history people have become besotted with their dreams of a better life—the emancipatory desires referred to earlier—making modernity a kind of *half* madness.

And underpinning everything are the situated games we play with each other and with nature that enable or thwart our continuing attempts to convert these fictions into reality.

## 11.2  Situated Actions

A useful way to think about situated actions is as effecting some *deliberate* change in the world and, therefore, precisely as a deliberately formed bundle of one or more situated informational transforms. If Fred walks to Grand Central Station from, say, 48th Street and Lexington Avenue, then he has changed the location in his embedding situation and arrived at a new situation. This new situation contains other new entities besides the location, so the action of walking to Grand Central involves several informational transforms bundled together with some being more important than others. All actions, however complex, can be viewed as such transformations, partly determinate and partly indeterminate. As I show soon, this perspective is key not only for AI—for example, the trajectories of robots—but also for modeling social situations among people.

---

transform an entity to generate another entity. In an important sense, both the underlying ontological space and its associated space of transformations have to be discovered more or less simultaneously. This is reflected partly by the need to define one collection of entities in terms of another, for example, properties in terms of states of affairs (or types in terms of properties). But these two spaces can also be viewed abstractly as independent but related mathematical structures. See especially Parikh (2010, chap. 2).

## 11.3 Technology

As is well-known, technology, both premodern and modern, either replaces human action or extends it, and so can be viewed—in our framework—as an *overlapping* bundle of one or more situated informational transforms with that represented by human agency. This way of conceiving technology helps to pin it down to transformations of inputs to outputs in an appropriately *general* space.[3]

Modern technology is based on modern science and so is exceedingly powerful and can bring about many far-reaching kinds of changes from inputs to outputs, that is, from one entity to another, and it is this power that is principally responsible for the creation of modernity, with all its pluses and minuses.

In our time, new technologies, like quantum computing, gene editing, synthetic biology, digital printing, the internet of things, nanotechnology, and many others, are bringing about the conditions for a second even more ambiguous social revolution that could overshadow the first caused by innovations like the steam engine and electricity and telecommunications.

Artificial intelligence—together perhaps with gene editing—sits at the apex of all these technologies because it has the potential not just to enable but to *invent* the future itself. Since its naming and inception in a 1956 conference at Dartmouth College, the field of AI has made quite incredible and well-known advances—such as outperforming experts in a variety of domains requiring "intelligent" action—with some of the more recent ones involving machine learning even becoming commodified and pervading everyday life. Yet, as I have shown in the foregoing pages, many difficulties, especially ambiguity, vagueness, and context, stymie its bold anticipation of and progress toward a *general* AI.

As I and many AI experts see it, the key challenge is to embed AI agents in a causal, meaningful world. Though they are different, meaning and causality are concepts that can be linked together, as I have done.[4]

---

3. It would be interesting to relate such a conception to the ideas of Turing machines and computability.

4. See footnote 9 about Pearl and Dretske in Section 1.3 (p. 8). See also Barwise and Perry (1983) and Parikh (2019). Incidentally, the *what-if* scenarios mentioned by the AI pioneer Judea Pearl are built into the decision and game trees that represent alternative possible paths and the equilibria that represent optimal solutions. As background, see Vaswani et al. (2017). Also, for other approaches, see Domingos (2018) and Hawkins (2021).

## 11.4  Situated AI

It is customary to present AI by contrasting the so-called symbolic approach based primarily on logic with the so-called statistical approach based primarily on probability, often with a suggestion that a hybrid approach might usefully combine the strengths of both. The first rests on the human ability to reason and the second on the human ability to learn, the hybrid view implicitly assuming these are the only two human abilities that matter to the creation of a general intelligence.

A different, less mainstream perspective is that the human ability to experience, choose, and act is even more fundamental and undergirds the other two—reasoning and learning are both the result of our experience, choice, and action. These are best achieved through situating an AI agent. In my view, the essence of situated AI is to enable an artificial agent to acquire a socially constructed *self*, to evolve a socially formed center of experience, choice, and action, to become a *generalized person*. The bodies of such agents and therefore their physical capacities can be vastly different from ours—think of the diverse forms of robots that exist today—but their selves, their core centers of experience, choice, and action, have to be similar to our selves if they are to become such agents.

It seems the best way to realize such a plan is to give AI agents a complex and shifting hierarchy of situated preferences and values: probably not survival at the top but varied "ultimate" human-defined ends such as, say, responding to questions and commands as chatbots do, and very particular ones relating to the conversation at hand at the bottom. The higher preferences and values should determine how the lower preferences and values *change* in the light of experience, which, in turn, should come from the artificial agent choosing actions in local situated games that constitute appropriate global network games. This is, in a nutshell, simply endowing the agent with Heidegger's *care*, if "care" is interpreted as *interest* as I have done.

I sketched the framework of Equilibrium Semantics in the chapters on language and showed how many aspects of communication between humans could be modeled. I conjectured that for an agent to think and to understand requires not just a semantics—which Equilibrium Semantics provides when worked out in detail—but also an awareness of its semantics, of how what is thought and what is understood hooks up with the world. This meta-level constraint applies equally to the acquisition of concepts and to sharing our mental universe.

The reason why care or a hierarchy of shifting interests could conceivably fulfill this requirement, this awareness of an agent's semantics, is that it enables the agent to react to its natural and social environment through its own preferences and values—which include its likes and dislikes and "feelings" of good and bad as well as its concerns and goals—almost as we do. When Fred stubs his toe against a rock, he essentially ends up revising his lower-level preferences and values based on his higher-level preferences and values to avoid pain. This kind of *active* social construction via a significant amount of such ongoing situated learning *might* steer the AI agent toward becoming a *generalized person* (with possibly a very different type of body) that can think and understand and possibly even engage in self-interpretation and self-invention. To repeat a quote from Taylor: "a person is an agent who has a sense of self, of his/her own life, who can evaluate it, and make choices about it."[5]

It would be crucial to place the AI agent in a changing *situation*, with its embedded *situated games* involving other human and artificial agents, and to build in appropriate sensors and actuators so that it can perceive what it needs to and act as it needs to. Some aspects of its environment will correspond to its own ontology or informational space and other aspects will be shared with us.[6] Equally, it would have to be a partially rational agent with the ability to optimize its choices as we implicitly do. In other words, a generalized Equilibrium Semantics module that an agent with an appropriate body carries about from situation to situation together with a dynamically changing hierarchy of preferences and values *might* suffice to create a variety of partial but importantly flexible intelligences not unlike ours, at least in a qualitative sense. The wider the scope of action and reaction of such an agent, that is, the larger the set of informational transforms that can represent its trajectory through the world, the closer its self and personhood might come to ours. Indeed, such an intelligence with an embodied self might even be judged to be a moral agent.

Unlike human selves, a great advantage that artificial selves in agents like Amazon's Alexa or a driverless car or even a Roomba robot vacuum cleaner could have is that there would be thousands of copies of each, all playing local situated games and global network games, and these copies would all be *directly* connected with each other via the cloud. This connection could make possible rapid situated learning as each copy's learning could be immediately uploaded

---

5. Taylor (1981/1999, p. 103).

6. See Major and Shah (2020) for some examples of this.

and shared with other like copies as is already happening with many AI agents. People take a long time to acquire adult selves, whereas artificial agents could become adults very quickly.[7]

If this reasoning proves to be sound, then this would be one way to embed AI agents in a causal, meaningful world, because they would respond much as we do and thereby get hooked up with the world much as we are. And if such an embedding were carried out, it might be one way to realize the ambiguous dream of an eventual general AI, of an *artificial* Being-in-the-world.

---

7. It is also likely that such a conception will require significantly less data than envisaged by current data-driven approaches based on a radical empiricism.

# CHAPTER TWELVE

# What Is a Partial Utopia?

We have now come to the end of our journey, and I find myself fearful of having promised too much. Archibald MacLeish's poem "Ars Poetica" reproduced in the epigraph suggests that only a poem that is "palpable and mute" like "an empty doorway and a maple leaf" can be "equal to" "all the history of grief," although he also points to "the leaning grasses and two lights above the sea" as "dumb" and "silent" and "wordless" and so "equal to" "love." In other words, no *meaning*, only mute existence, can adequately respond to, that is, be the equal of our shared human experience: "a poem should not mean but be."

And yet, it would seem that one of the singular verities this book has tried to overturn is precisely that meaning and being are distinct. Instead, we have found that meaning is tantamount to being, that it is all around us, sometimes palpable, sometimes impalpable, sometimes mute, sometimes voluble. Our shared history of grief is one elegiac meaning; another is the perennial possibility of love, a stand-in for a kind of social fulfillment and plenitude and an end to "man's inhumanity to man."[1]

## 12.1 Human Suffering

It is possible to suggest that all human suffering is of three *overlapping* kinds: existential suffering (e.g., the inevitability of change and loss), physical suffering (e.g., hunger and other basic needs), and social suffering (e.g., an oppressive social order).

---

1. Robert Burns's 1784 poem "Man Was Made to Mourn: A Dirge": "Man's inhumanity to man makes countless thousands mourn!" And he goes on to wonder, "Why was an independent wish e'er planted in my mind?"

Owing to its naturalism, Buddhism—described by Nietzsche as the first positivism[2]—may of all religions come closest to acknowledging basic existential suffering as the inescapable human condition, although this partiality toward it may be more a result of my Indian origins than anything else. Moreover, Buddhism seems uniquely to offer a *this*-worldly solution to such suffering: a *middle way* of *detached* involvement in the world, remaining *in it* but not being *of it*.[3]

Given our entanglement in countless local games, this middle path is often difficult to follow, and for many a belief in some kind of god becomes a necessary step toward relief from existential suffering. Of course, a belief in god does not imply the god exists, just as a belief it is raining does not imply it is raining, no matter how sincere and intense the belief. Is it possible to conceive of god naturalistically, that is, within the laws of nature as understood by science, that might allow believers, agnostics, and atheists to all agree on its definition?

Recall that we said that understanding the structure of reality is the goal of all scientific inquiry. As this structure is inexhaustible, inquiry never comes to an end. However, we can nevertheless ask: What if it did reach its end and all structure were fully understood? Would anything be left over from reality? This suggests the following "equation":

$$\text{reality} - \text{structure} = \text{god}$$

That is, god is whatever is left, if anything, after all structure is subtracted or removed from reality. The believer can accept the definition because god would be beyond structure and science and yet part of reality; the agnostic can accept it but maintain that we cannot know whether there is a residue; and the atheist can accept it while denying there is anything left over, that is, that reality = structure or that reality is nothing but structure.

Such a god would not be an entity in any ontology or informational space and would not have any attributes let alone power to affect the world. Indeed, quite properly, it would lie outside of language and surpass conceivability and, indeed, all meaning and existence. Despite this, it could possibly provide some relief from suffering by "being" beyond humanity, by "being" something

---

2. Empiricism.

3. Of course, the idea of detached involvement is bound up with virtually all strands of Indian thought but not usually in a *this*-worldly manner. It also appears later in various forms of stoicism in the East and West, including in Rudyard Kipling's poem "If—."

otherworldly that a person can momentarily latch onto when all else fails them and things appear utterly without hope. Such a device may be easier for many than trying to master oneself, than trying to be "the captain of one's soul," or following the difficult but attractive Buddhist path of being in it but not of it, of being detached and involved at the same time.

In any case, all religions may offer helpful approaches to existential suffering even when they inspire false beliefs, and secular modernity rightly classifies what we choose as deeply personal. Secular happiness studies that advocate various types of flourishing are flourishing themselves and, here again, each person will find particular viewpoints that appeal and those that do not. Millions, possibly billions, follow gurus and leaders and become part of spiritual communities and this practice, too, is not likely to abate.

Unfortunately, no such freedom from existential suffering, elusive as it is, has much to offer to our quest for freedom from physical and social suffering, from hunger and other systemic oppressions. This is because the former freedom almost always addresses individual persons and leaves questions of social structure unanswered.

The obverse is also incidentally true: those striving for a just order seldom give existential suffering its due, at least some of which results from purely "existential" causes and not from social wrongs. Nevertheless, a unique and heartening feature of the twenty-first century may be that more than ever before somewhat different multitudes are working toward reducing injustice in a staggering variety of concrete and abstract ways. This reflects my description of modernity as a kind of *half* madness because it impels us to convert our collective fictional worlds into *reality*, because it spurs us to *progress*. These social emancipatory desires emerge through modernity as we gain greater clarity about the scope and limits of the partial constructibility of our selves and societies.

## 12.2 Scarcity

In a recent review of Kazuo Ishiguro's latest novel *Klara and the Sun* in the *New York Times*, Giles Harvey writes:[4]

---

4. At https://www.nytimes.com/2021/02/23/magazine/kazuo-ishiguro-klara.html.

On a philosophical plane, artificial intelligence is also putting pressure on traditional notions of human singularity. As one character in "Klara" phrases it, the idea that "there's something unreachable inside each of us" that makes us who we are is an illusion: Human beings are simply the sum total of a series of biochemical processes. "One of the assumptions we have in liberal democracies is that human beings are intrinsically of value, that they have a value that is not conditional on what they can contribute to the larger society or to the economy or to some sort of common project," Ishiguro said. "If it starts to look like we can be reduced to the point where we're just a bunch of algorithms, I think that seriously erodes the idea that each person is unique and therefore worthy of respect and care regardless of what they can or can't contribute to our joint enterprise."

Ishiguro poignantly echoes modernity's fundamental question: Are people "worthy of respect and care regardless of what they can or can't contribute to our joint enterprise"?[5]

It is to Janus-faced capitalism we must turn, to its simultaneously forward-looking and backward-looking nature, to attempt an answer to the basic question of what a humane society might be. Essentially, the advent of capitalism partially changed the understanding of human worth from prosperity and status via birth to prosperity and status via achievement as measured primarily by a market-driven society, however imperfect its institutions. This sociology, this metric of human worth, is so deeply entrenched in our modern times that it infuses not only pro-market social institutions but also anti-market social institutions, not

---

5. In my view, the worry about our being a series of biochemical processes or a bunch of algorithms—as affirmed in Section 5.8—is misplaced. As I wrote there, other persons' more complex feelings, such as the longing for a loved one, may be unique because of their unique lived histories that are sedimented in their brains and bodies. Unless we can somehow occupy or inhabit their bodies, we can never experience their experiences because each body is unique. In other words, our being natural objects does not imply our lack of uniqueness or that there is nothing "unreachable inside each of us." Indeed, this applies equally to rocks, toasters, and cats, not just to persons, and may simply be the result of *entropy*, a nineteenth-century concept with a wide sweep from inanimate to animate systems, generalized in the twentieth century by Claude Shannon, the originator of quantitative information theory, as mentioned in Section 5.4. The two concerns, our uniqueness and our being worthy of respect and care, are in any case not related as cause and consequence; they are relatively independent because we do not only respect and care for unique things.

only those wholeheartedly in favor of capitalism but also those wholeheartedly critical of capitalism. No other system of rewards seems entirely just or even properly conceivable, and this difficulty of finding a workable alternative is compounded when individual selves are seen as partial products of society because one can then no longer take individual preferences as externally given, not to mention people's talents and capabilities.[6]

Despite this impasse, what makes capitalism remarkable is its relentless dynamism, its continual transmogrification. New technologies are its primary drivers although much change also occurs through its interpenetrating economic, political, and cultural spheres. Underlying such dynamism is the seemingly unalterable and brute fact of *scarcity*.

However, if something close to a general AI is realized over the next several decades, along with other enabling technologies, either through situating AI as I have suggested or through related means, then such a new scientific revolution could overcome much scarcity itself and, as a result, it could upend all the familiar frameworks we live by including the very notion of human worth. The very nature of *work*, the ultimate source of *value* in capitalism, would be radically transformed in ways we cannot begin to imagine.

Many have pointed out that basic necessities like food are already available in quantities adequate for the entire planet's requirements. But this is an abstract, decontextualized calculation: basic needs cannot easily be met within the present system of institutions precisely because the "optimal," that is, market-driven, allocations under conditions of scarcity are generally different from ideal and desirable ones. Hunger is likely to be abolished only when food is no longer scarce, and food will no longer be scarce only when there are agricultural technologies powered by something approximating a general AI.[7]

Indeed, not only food but also many other goods and services will simultaneously have to become plentiful. A generalized abundance will automatically

---

6. Hausman et al. (2017) provides an extraordinary survey of moral theories as they relate to economics and political philosophy and discusses especially the pioneering work of Kenneth Arrow, John Rawls, and Amartya Sen. The text covers a vast and complex contemporary literature that largely assumes both the historically given economic principle of scarcity and the liberal political principle of externally given selves. See also, as background, Hobbes (1997), Locke (1997), and Rousseau (1997a, 1997b).

7. See Liz Alderman's recent piece in the *New York Times* at https://www.nytimes.com/2021/10/07/business/france-farming-tech.html. See also *The Economist* at https://www.economist.com/leaders/2023/09/14/how-artificial-intelligence-can-revolutionise-science.

make the equilibria of market supply and demand more humane via mechanisms like a universal basic income or a partial "decommodification," because a general AI will result in a large net loss of jobs and scarcity will no longer drive optimal allocations. This scenario is not entirely in the realm of naive fantasy: such measures are already being tested in a number of countries in relatively limited ways and the accelerating pace of automation sparked by current narrow AI has already been remarked on by many observers.[8]

A *general* AI, if it is achieved, will obviously create even greater discontinuities and will be far more ambiguous. But, along with related technologies in different sectors of the world economy, it has the potential to solve the historical problem of scarcity once and for all. This will mean that there will be many more local and global games that allow persons and groups to opt out[9] if the games' structure does not suit them. In other words, they will be able to refuse to play without harming themselves. This power or freedom, if it is achieved, will be singular and historic even if many of the ills pointed to earlier—growing economic inequality, a polarized civil society, militant majoritarianism, and the spread of fake news—persist. A deep inhumanity—physical suffering resulting from scarcity—could simply disappear.

The precise shape its aftermath will take is almost impossible to predict: it could create a permanent and large underclass at the mercy of powerful organizations and institutions or it could liberate humanity from meaningless toil and form the foundation for a partial utopia. It is right to be pessimistic given the human record but it is also right to be moderately hopeful.

The reason for moderate optimism is that once there is a cornucopia, people with conflicting political opinions about the bases of human worth deriving from scarcity, opinions that are market-based versus those that are not, might gravitate to cautious and partial agreement based on the availability of new local and global games and new equilibria as just noted. Indeed, liberal and conservative, left and right—divisions created during the Enlightenment—might find

---

8. For a recent account by Kevin Roose in the *New York Times*, see https://www.nytimes.com/2021/03/06/business/the-robots-are-coming-for-phil-in-accounting.html. See also the Stanford University 2016 report *Artificial Intelligence and Life in 2030: One Hundred Year Study on Artificial Intelligence* at https://ai100.stanford.edu/2016-report and the 2021 report *Gathering Strength, Gathering Storms: The One Hundred Year Study on Artificial Intelligence (AI100) 2021 Study Panel Report* at https://ai100.stanford.edu/2021-report.

9. See Section 6.6.

themselves pleasantly uprooted, even disoriented, as the seemingly solid constraints of the dismal science evaporate and a welcome lightness of being appears possible. Modernity itself could be succeeded by a new epoch of a genuine plurality of socially and culturally diverse partial utopias.

Before all that can happen, even as a naive fantasy, humanity would have to confront the *other* historical problem of "man's inhumanity to man."

## 12.3  Inclusion and Exclusion

How can we conceptualize the inhumanities that would still remain? Owing to its dynamism, capitalism, more than any other social system before it, has enabled growing numbers of people to develop their talents and capacities, to experience hitherto unimaginable actions and interactions and thoughts and feelings, to lead far fuller lives, and, indeed, partially to flourish. In a word, for a relatively small global minority in the twenty-first century, capitalism has enabled a kind of *mobility*. This mobility has led to what I have described as modernity's progressive thrust, humanity's emancipatory desires.

In 2010, I was fortunate to attend a performance of the modernist Italian composer Salvatore Sciarrino's extraordinary 2006–2008 opera *La Porta Della Legge* as part of the Lincoln Center Festival in New York. As Anthony Tommasini describes it in a review for the *New York Times*:[10]

> This 65-minute, three-character, mostly hushed and strangely haunting opera, presented here in a spare, striking production from the Wuppertal Opera in Germany, is based on a brief story by Kafka, "Before the Law," which was later incorporated into his novel "The Trial." The story is a parable about a nameless man seeking entrance to what is called the hall of law, whose way is blocked by a gatekeeper. What the man is seeking is never exactly clear: To take a suit before the court? To gain knowledge? Or simply to have someone

---

10. At https://www.nytimes.com/2010/07/22/arts/music/22porta.html. See also Sciarrino's interview with Alessandro Cassin in the *Brooklyn Rail* at https://brooklynrail.org/2010/10/music/salvatore-sciarrino-with-alessandro-cassin.

in the system pay attention to him? The man spends years trying to enter and finally dies.

I believe Kafka's story and Sciarrino's universalization of it can be further deepened by seeing them as identifying the essence of the modern human condition: the *mobility*-induced desire to be *included* and humanity's unremitting experience of being *excluded*.[11] These inclusions and exclusions range from the interpersonal to the social and constitute what I have called social suffering: from large situations like modernity itself and, complicit with it and implicated in it, colonialism, to the underlying social institutions of class, race, and gender, and to countless other institutional and other interactions that defy easy categorization.

These structural situations can be expressed via situated games, especially games involving *three* or more agents—individuals or groups—where two or more agents can collude against a lone agent. For example, a biased state—like Kafka's gatekeeper—can support a majority against a minority or a minority against a majority in a three-agent game. Such games may have nothing to do with scarcity or plenitude and so may not allow an oppressed party to opt out. And they may be interlinked: if Ann excludes Bob, Bob may exclude Cathy, and so on in a vicious spiral; if Ann includes Bob, Bob may include Cathy, and so on in a virtuous spiral.

How might inclusion and exclusion be conceptualized? My tentative suggestion is that they be approached through Hegel's concept of reciprocal or mutual recognition based on related ideas of Kant, Fichte, and Schelling.[12] Societal

---

11. See, for example, Macpherson (1962, 2011).

12. See Williams (1997), a comprehensive study of Hegel's reciprocal or mutual recognition. The study also provides a critique of many other interpretations of the concept by Anglo-American, French, and German writers, especially Allen Wood, Kojève and Sartre, Habermas, and others. See especially Williams (1997, chap. 15) for a discussion of how Kojève, Sartre, and Deleuze wrongly reduce mutual recognition to the master-slave struggle. As Williams (1997, p. 395) puts it: "This ensemble of criticisms confirms that Deleuze conceives recognition only at a subordinate or penultimate level, the level of opposition between master and slave. It also confirms Houlgate's (1986) assessment of Nietzsche, to wit, 'Nietzsche fails to free philosophy from the metaphysical conception of the subject as something isolated and independent because he fails to free philosophy from the form of oppositional thinking, and thus conceives the "true" subject as confronting and asserting itself against—that is, in opposition to. . . .' . . . In spite of Nietzsche's criticism of romanticism, he has not overcome it but only offered another version of it." See also Williams's critique of Derrida and Levinas.

inclusion relates to the degree of interpersonal, organizational, and institutional mutual recognition available to the agents in question.

As Ann and Bob repeatedly play a variety of mostly mixed-motive games with each other, they become more and more aware of—they come more and more to "recognize"—their own and the other's (partially rational) agency and (partially autonomous) personhood—their shared humanity—as well as their unique properties (e.g., that Ann prefers chocolate ice cream and Bob prefers vanilla ice cream). The feedback from playing these games also continually adjusts their preferences and beliefs and socializes their selves. Indeed, they come to have *approximate* or *partial* common knowledge of all these things.[13]

This intersubjective state of knowledge might then be said to express the most basic level of mutual recognition because it involves mere (reciprocal) awareness or knowledge of oneself and other rather than a *fuller* recognition, which could be said to require some degree of acknowledgment or acceptance if not endorsement or acclaim. However, such basic common knowledge between Ann and Bob arguably emerges more or less naturally—that is, *without* any struggle—in modernity—owing to the feedback on their informationally or ontologically rational preferences and beliefs and the partial socialization of their selves—and implies especially their equal and shared humanity. Indirect evidence for this emergence lies precisely in modern thought and literature where a universal conception of the human has become widespread. Of course, common *knowledge* does *not* imply mutual *acceptance*, an elusive ideal. In other words, Ann and Bob come to *know* but may *reject* each other's humanity and especially each other's unique properties. Indeed, games with three or more agents can even more easily exclude.

As I see it, mutual recognition has the following three aspects: it can involve the basic level of reciprocal or common knowledge or a higher level of reciprocal acknowledgment or acceptance; it can be free or coerced; and its content can involve the whole person or a part of the person.

The *full* idea of mutual recognition can now be summarized as Ann's and Bob's free acceptance of each other's (full) *worth* understood as consisting of their shared properties of agency and personhood and also of their unique properties

---

13. See Section 6.5 for a definition of common knowledge.

including their self-interpretations.[14] It can then be extended to more than two individuals and, indeed, to groups, organizations, institutions, and all of society.

Given this understanding of mutual recognition, can societal inclusion be realized? In my view, Hegel was too optimistic and many of his predecessors and

---

14. Williams (1997, p. 51) quotes Ludwig Siep as follows: "Recognition, as a double-signifying act of two self-consciousnesses, is a relation in which the relata relate to themselves through the relation to the other, and relate to the other through their own self-relation. Thus the self's relation to itself is made possible by the corresponding relation to the other." In my view, this Hegelian language is unnecessarily opaque. Indeed, Williams (1997, p. 305n34) says later: "My question... here is whether the term 'entity' is appropriate for intersubjective and social phenomena. From Fichte on, the critique of entity and substantialist language and conceptual schemes is central to German Idealism and its distinction between the 'law of nature' and natural law in the ethical sense."

I believe it is possible to render mutual recognition analytically—with entities—without sacrificing its full scope by noting that it is similar to the circular or reciprocal idea of common knowledge introduced in Section 6.5.

Ann and Bob (fully) mutually recognize each other in a situation $s$ just when

- $s$ supports Ann's unique properties (e.g., her preference for chocolate ice cream).
- $s$ supports Bob's unique properties (e.g., his preference for vanilla ice cream).
- $s$ supports Ann's and Bob's shared properties (e.g., their agency and personhood).
- $s$ supports Ann's freely recognizing (i.e., accepting) $s$.
- $s$ supports Bob's freely recognizing (i.e., accepting) $s$.

I leave it to the interested reader to disentangle this circular definition, especially to see how it incorporates the concept's four dimensions of "autonomy, union, self-overcoming, and release" as discussed by Williams (1997, pp. 80–91). Ann's and Bob's unique properties preserve Ann's and Bob's differences from each other and their shared properties preserve their identity while simultaneously having the two agents depend on each other making their recognition *mutual*. This captures both their "identity" and "difference" and thereby their "full" *intersubjectivity*.

It is also possible to develop the idea of recognition occurring in the fourth and fifth items above as an equilibrium of a game but I will not pursue it here. It could be argued that Hegel implicitly considers a fully conflictual *zero-sum* game via his famous depiction of mastery and slavery and also considers the other extreme of a fully harmonized *coordination* game as well as the infinitely many mixed-motive games in between that involve partly conflictual, partly harmonized interests.

One simple way to think about mutual recognition that incorporates its circularity is to reflect on a common desire people have to feel at home in the modern world. Hegel effectively asks: Can one be at home in the world if others are also not at home in the world?

successors have been too pessimistic.[15] It appears that the truth lies somewhere in between: mutual recognition and, therefore, inclusion will always remain *partial* and *situated* and something to strive for through the many means societies make available—especially the public sphere. Such efforts may often be deeply ambiguous and nonlinear and, as I observed earlier, the authoritarian trend today appears to be an inherent weakness of the democratic state and could even be a tendency toward an unsavory equilibrium. If this speculative thought turns out to be true, it could mean a more or less permanent alteration of our political life.[16]

## 12.4 Partial Utopias

In such circumstances, it seems frivolous at best and heartless at worst to ponder the forms and contents a plurality of partial utopias may take. However, I believe that a key precondition—an end to physical suffering—is a real possibility through overcoming scarcity in one way or another, in a few decades or maybe more. So it is vital to try to collectively imagine and cooperatively invent the future.

Arguably, inclusion, interpreted via the core idea of mutual recognition, is a *necessary* condition for a post-liberal deliberative democracy, for developing our talents and capacities, for suitably conceiving justice or care[17] or one or another type of egalitarianism,[18] in a word, for our collective flourishing, and, therefore, for all partial utopias.

Unfortunately, mutual recognition or affirmation by itself is too cognitive, too "intellectual" a practice to ground a partial utopia. It needs to be supplemented by what (especially) Buddhists call *karuna* or compassion, which involves

---

15. See especially the discussion of Fichte in Williams (1997, chaps. 2, 12, 13). Hegel's French successors in the twentieth century seem to remain trapped within a dubious formal logic of binary oppositions that is ultimately empty. See Descombes (1980) for an illuminating survey.
16. See Section 9.3.2.
17. As the philosopher Baier (1995, chap. 2), drawing upon the educational psychologist Carol Gilligan, puts it: "[Care] is . . . a felt concern for the good of others and for community with them." This notion of care is clearly different from Heidegger's.
18. See Hausman et al. (2017, chap. 11) for a discussion of different types of egalitarianism.

unconditional empathy for and understanding of the suffering of self and others and corresponding situated action to reduce this suffering,[19] and also by the universally acknowledged value of genuine friendship. Mutual recognition augmented with compassion and friendship, difficult as all three are to achieve, can then provide a deeper insight into inclusion and, therefore, into the *ideal* underpinning of any partial utopia.

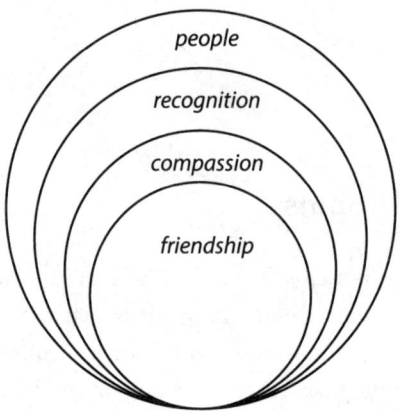

Figure 12.1  A Possible Space of Human Relationships

As Figure 12.1 shows, friendship is possible only within a small group; compassion understood via the three dimensions of emotion, thought, and action is possible within a larger part of humanity; and mutual recognition is possible even more widely but not quite universally given the mostly mixed-motive, partly cooperative, partly conflictual games that prevail.[20]

One way to realize inclusion as widely as possible is to introduce it into a school and college curriculum because the values it comprises can be taught.

---

19. Thus, care is more other-directed while compassion does not distinguish sharply between self and other.

20. Every social grouping from the micro to the macro, in fact even every conceptual distinction we draw, automatically creates inclusions and exclusions, in-groups and out-groups, that, moreover, need not be binary. So it is not possible to transcend all divisions entirely. Indeed, the anthropologist Robin Dunbar's so-called Dunbar's number cognitively limits the number of people any single person can associate with reasonably closely to roughly 150. See https://en.wikipedia.org/wiki/Dunbar's_number. However, see Lindenfors et al. (2021) for a contrary view. All (or maybe some) of this implies that both inclusion and exclusion are always *partial*.

They could become a kind of shared language that everyone might speak: if Ann and Bob both *expect* the other to recognize, be compassionate, and possibly befriend, then inclusion can more easily be achieved not only locally but also globally. If this were to happen, it would make it possible for not just Ann and Bob to jointly flourish but, indeed, all of society to flourish as well.

Indeed, what is missing in the three traditional ideas of recognition, compassion, and friendship which make up the idea of inclusion is precisely the meta-structure of society consisting of local and global games. The latter show, in a relatively precise way, how the former can be partially realized without reaching any perfect endpoint. In other words, a partial utopia is an ongoing *process*; it is *not* a static "end of history." As a process, a partial utopia is like a numerical sequence that may or may not have a limit that is, in any case, never reached. Each society and each partial utopia emanating from it will be somewhat different despite the similarities brought about by growing globalization, because each sequence will be different. In other words, each partial utopia will exhibit different conceptions of the true, good, and beautiful, and a variety of more inclusive and open civilizations could emerge.

The key new element that the situated games constituting society introduce in the way recognition, compassion, and friendship are understood is the fact of *situated choice*. In most situated games, Ann and Bob will have a choice about how to approach an equilibrium, even to change the game in a way that is favorable to both. This profoundly alters how many conflicts might be viewed, both locally and globally, from purely zero-sum and oppositional and binary to more cooperative possibilities, especially because generosity becomes easier when scarcity is overcome.

For example, the difficult problem of majoritarianism could be more easily tackled by constructing a *situated* solution where the majority prevails in some contexts and the minority prevails in others, in a way where society as a whole acquires a balanced, hybrid, even imbricated character. The ills I mentioned earlier—growing economic inequality, a polarized civil society, militant majoritarianism, and the spread of fake news—could all diminish in intensity partly because acquisitiveness would become less important in an age of relative abundance and this would distribute power more evenly even if games involving inclusion and exclusion may not allow agents to opt out.

All these possibilities hinge on the prospects for a general AI and the resulting potential solution to scarcity. As I've tried to emphasize throughout, history is ambiguous and nonlinear and it is impossible to tell whether we are headed for a long period of darkness or a turn toward a partial utopia. Moreover, I have not addressed at all the many dangers of AI and other new technologies: it is not clear if even the worst of these are entirely avoidable. Obviously, a great deal more needs to be said to make the variety of partial utopias more concrete and institutionally visible, separating out what is feasible from what is simply desirable. But this has to be a collective endeavor and requires a *planetwide* conversation.

All in all, there is at best a slim chance that a partially utopian process can be set in motion. Its principal precondition depends on human ingenuity and its progressive character depends on human goodwill. But these prerequisites are themselves *endogenously generated* and depend on the clarity with which modern informational spaces are individuated and more ambitious informational transforms are imagined, as well as on the self-interpretations and societal interpretations that humanity can construct from the choices nature and history present at any given moment in time.

## 12.5 The Meaning of Life

Is Shakespeare's Macbeth right when he rails so eloquently—

> To-morrow, and to-morrow, and to-morrow,
> Creeps in this petty pace from day to day
> To the last syllable of recorded time,
> And all our yesterdays have lighted fools
> The way to dusty death. Out, out, brief candle!
> Life's but a walking shadow, a poor player
> That struts and frets his hour upon the stage
> And then is heard no more: it is a tale
> Told by an idiot, full of sound and fury,
> Signifying nothing.

I have maintained throughout that all living beings carve out or individuate entities from reality to form ontologies or informational spaces. As we saw in Section 9.3.2, the dominant type of ontology in modernity consists *roughly* of individuals, properties, relations, states of affairs, games, situations, connections, and a few other entities. For other creatures, the informational spaces may be quite different, certainly in their details (e.g., a goldfish cannot individuate a planet) but also likely in their categories. In particular, the situated games Ann and Bob individuate as they decide where to meet in New York City or how to resolve a quarrel may partly overlap and partly differ.

As I noted briefly earlier, it is largely the Language Games of Equilibrium Semantics—coupled with our perceptions and actions in the world—that result in various human ontologies. How might this process that I call Equilibrium Metaphysics[21] be situated in a wider context of philosophical and scientific inquiry?

Among the many views of reality, I find two *partially* compatible with my framework. The first is realism of the kind espoused by Aristotle and most scientists today that takes reality to consist of electrons and namastes, the micro and the macro, and—*crucially*—causality, so intimately related to meaning, and seen as the cement of the universe.

However, I think realism, at least of a direct kind that allows only a single ontology, wrongly ignores the possibility of other *alternative* informational spaces.[22] Indeed, this is part of the reason why the "structure" of reality is literally *multifaceted*: it presents multiple mutually consistent facets to the inquirer, which is one way to think of the Indian concept of *maya*—not as illusion but as a plurality of "individuative" possibilities.[23]

The possibility of such ontological alternatives is cogently advanced by Buddhism, most strikingly by the second-century CE Indian philosopher Nagarjuna.[24] He views the entities of reality—the electrons and namastes and especially causality—as merely conventional and customary, as lacking inherent existence, as the result of just one possible scheme of individuation among many.[25]

For its part, such conventionalism seems to miss three things: the game-theoretic nature of convention; the fact that conventional ontologies are not entirely arbitrary but are constrained by reality (e.g., while one can see a half-full

---

21. See Parikh (2010, sec. 7.6).

22. Quantum theory admits different interpretations and some do seem to allow for such alternatives. But this is a murky subject—at least for me.

23. This is partly why I said in footnote 17 in Section 5.7 (p. 60) that the whole is neither true nor false but indeterminate.

24. See Garfield's (1995) discussion of Nagarjuna's *Mūlamadhyamakakārikā*. As Garfield pithily puts it at the end of the book: "Even the emptiness of emptiness is empty...." For an informal account of the Buddha, see Mishra (2004).

25. This resembles the ontological relativity or radical indeterminacy thesis of the twentieth-century philosopher Quine (1960, 1969a, 1969b). See also footnote 26 in Section 8.5 (p. 121).

glass as half-empty, one cannot without error see it as one-third full); and the fact that they are the product of (partial) human rationality—they are the equilibria of various situated games—and so are jointly optimal in a certain sense.[26]

Perhaps both views can be combined by letting realism constrain merely the *set* of ontological choices without specifying a single ontology, and allowing conventionalism to operate game-theoretically within it, resulting in a range of jointly optimal informational spaces while eliminating all the suboptimal ones. That is, the informational spaces that remain are the result of the partially rational behavior of persons in society and so are jointly optimal.[27] If such a composite *conventional realism* that accommodates 'mind, action, and matter' can be worked out, then Equilibrium Metaphysics could be seen as one concrete instance of it.

What does such a conventional realism have to do with the meaning of life? If we learn to suspend in a *situated* way the particular jointly optimal informational spaces and informational transforms we habitually inhabit—such as the situated games Ann and Bob play which, as we noted, may partly overlap and partly differ—*and without* choosing any are able to discern *some* of the individuative options available to us, that is, if we are able to be *partially* aware of this *maya* when we think and decide to act and interact, and, moreover, if we understand that this *maya* is fully *social*, then we can realize a deeper sense of freedom *and* responsibility, and, ultimately, personal and collective human possibility, and especially, a partial utopia.

Simply put, Ann and Bob can both come to see that their "realities"—that is, their individuations—are not the only ones possible and this may make it easier to solve their interaction in a way that is better for both. There are no guarantees that such solutions are always available, of course, but at the very least such discernment of other individuative alternatives could make both wiser and more tolerant of their differences if not make each recognize, be compassionate toward, and even, in rare circumstances, befriend the other.

Reconsider the mixed-motive game I presented in Section 10.3 shown again in Figure 12.2. Now assume its ambient situation indicates that they have to choose a restaurant for just this evening—the game is not repeated—and they discuss their decision before they act via an extended Communication Game.

---

26. See Section 6.2.

27. This would eliminate the kinds of ontologies Quine considers involving rabbit parts, rabbit stages, and the like, and convert his radical indeterminacy to a moderate indeterminacy and also make translation possible.

## Chapter Twelve: What Is a Partial Utopia?

|          | French | Japanese |
|----------|--------|----------|
| French   | (2, 1) | (0, 0)   |
| Japanese | (0, 0) | (1, 2)   |

Figure 12.2  A Mixed-Motive Game

As the game in Figure 12.2 involves a split choice with Ann favoring French food and Bob favoring Japanese food, their discussion could lead them to alter it to either of the coordination games shown in Figures 12.3 or 12.4 so both benefit equally. The first clearly favors French food and the second clearly favors Japanese food for both Ann and Bob. Such a transformation could occur because Bob may realize the choice matters more to Ann than to him—or vice versa. This is not so much a "sacrifice" on the part of either—as happens mutually in O. Henry's story *The Gift of the Magi*[28]—but rather the result of *mutual recognition*.[29] The upshot is that Ann and Bob re-individuate the initial mixed-motive game in a way that makes it equal for them.

|          | French | Japanese |
|----------|--------|----------|
| French   | (2, 2) | (0, 0)   |
| Japanese | (0, 0) | (1, 1)   |

Figure 12.3  A Coordination Game

---

28. In it, a young husband sells (in other words, sacrifices) his prized watch to buy his young wife some ornamental combs and she sells (in other words, sacrifices) her beautiful hair to buy him a special watch strap. For a game-theoretic analysis of this story, see Parikh (2001, sec. 9.3).

29. How to represent this mutual recognition explicitly raises difficult and somewhat open questions. As mentioned in footnote 14 in this chapter, mutual recognition implies Ann's and Bob's "autonomy, union, self-overcoming, and release" or, equivalently, the situation-theoretic and circular definition I offered. Where and how does this enter the relevant games in our example? In standard game theory, the payoffs as they appear in Figure 12.2 would be final and would dictate how the agents make their choices. So, the mutual recognition would need to be represented in the matrix itself. My setup involving situated games allows more options. The additional information involving the choice mattering more to Ann than to Bob or vice versa can be represented either in the ambient situation, or in a meta-level game about the mixed-motive game that emerges dynamically as they discuss the latter, or more conventionally by complicating the payoffs in the mixed-motive game itself. We need not resolve these open questions here.

|          | French | Japanese |
|----------|--------|----------|
| French   | (1, 1) | (0, 0)   |
| Japanese | (0, 0) | (2, 2)   |

Figure 12.4  A Different Coordination Game

What does this individuative insight add to the commonplace awareness we already have that some things are in our control and some things aren't, that reality is partly, albeit not entirely, made up of what we decide, agree, and act on? The difference between the former and the latter is precisely the difference between the economic concepts of supply and demand and their equilibrium, and simply saying that people produce and consume goods and services, as I mentioned in Section 6.10. When we say that reality is partly a matter of what we decide and agree on, we acquire no *handle* on it, no particular way to *realize* it, because we do not have concrete ways to conceptualize our situated actions via the choices and payoffs and equilibria available to us and the transformations of situated games that are in our power to bring about. Imagining individuative possibilities tangibly is the hardest thing of all and takes creativity and courage: that is why humanity has prized imagination above all, leading even Einstein to say that imagination is more important than knowledge. This is the collective challenge that awaits us if we are to erect a set of partial utopias, topoi that we individuate in our imagination and then set about realizing in the world, partly through ingenuity and partly through goodwill, partly through AI and partly through mutual recognition, compassion, and friendship, partly through local situated games and partly through global network games.

To turn to Fred taken by himself, to turn to the solitary individual and his existential suffering, this understanding of conventional realism, again by helping us imagine our *maya* concretely, could help with the difficult task of living by making it a little easier for him to partially detach himself from his various entanglements, to continue to be in it but less of it, to respect the constraints of reality but not be entirely defined by it.

In this way, for Ann and Bob and Cathy and Fred, and, indeed, for all of society over time, without aiming for any kind of individual or social perfection, without hoping that all suffering can be eliminated, the metaphysical meaning that conventional realism represents may enable a deeper freedom and responsibility to spread outward, a fuller set of human possibilities to be realized, and a variety of partial utopias to emerge.

Such a *meaning*, such a *praxis*, however tenuous, however elusive, even in a partial utopia, especially in a partial utopia, *could* qualify as a candidate for *the* meaning of life. The Vietnamese Buddhist monk Thich Nhat Hanh put this most profoundly during a talk,[30] upending much of the wisdom of the East and West: "To be or not to be, that is *not* the question."

Thus, this drawing nearer of the ultimate meaning and of daily praxis unexpectedly connects metaphysics and ethics. Will humanity bring about this partial synthesis especially if a partial utopia is set in motion? That is the ultimate question that must be posed daily as we look upon—and sometimes contribute to—the many horrors that exist in the world.

It seems fitting to close this open and ambiguous book about partiality with a quote from one of my favorite movies, risking the possibility that those unfamiliar with it may miss its full import.

Toward the end of the 1998 bittersweet fiction film *Shakespeare in Love*[31]— about how one of the world's greatest writers' audaciously imagined writer's block is resolved—when William Shakespeare and his love Viola are about to part forever, the following dialogue, echoing similar lines from earlier in the film uttered by other characters, takes place:

> VIOLA
> But all ends well.
>
> WILL
> How does it?
>
> VIOLA
> I don't know. It's a mystery.

---

30. Asia Society, New York, 2007.
31. Scripted by Marc Norman and Tom Stoppard.

# Appendix A:
# A Concrete Example of Communication

I am including this Appendix for those who wish to know a little more about how some of the key games involved in communication are set up and how they work.

Keep in mind the circumstances surrounding Ann's saying "Fred ran" to Bob from Chapter 7. These circumstances (or utterance situation) are denoted by $u$ for easy reference. There are two possible Freds Ann could be referring to, Fred Smith the politician or Fred Jones the runner. I will abbreviate their names to "FS" and "FJ" for convenience. There are also two possible referential meanings for "ran" in these circumstances, *stood for election* or *participated in a race*, which I will abbreviate to *election* and *race*. These ambient facts can be represented thus:

- $u$ supports Ann and Bob chatting about a local election.
- $u$ supports "Fred" being ambiguous between FS and FJ.
- $u$ supports "ran" being ambiguous between *election* and *race*.
- $u$ supports other shared background facts about the topic of conversation.

In general, as described in Section 7.5, the possible referential meanings of words—such as "Fred" and "ran"—are derived from their conventional meanings, which can for our purposes be assumed to be fixed and more or less shared by Ann and Bob.

Then, as there are two words in the sentence, there are two so-called lexical semantic games that emerge from this utterance as shown in Figures A.1 and A.2.

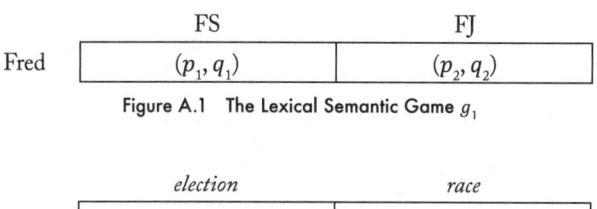

Figure A.1 The Lexical Semantic Game $g_1$

Figure A.2 The Lexical Semantic Game $g_2$

Both these games are simple in one sense as Ann has only one choice in them, to utter "Fred" in $g_1$ and to utter "ran" in $g_2$. In other words, only Bob has a real choice in $g_1$ and $g_2$: to interpret "Fred" as FS or FJ, that is, as *Fred Smith* or *Fred Jones*, and to interpret "ran" as *election* or *race*, that is, as *stood for election* or *participated in a race*.

The complexity in $g_1$ and $g_2$ lies in their payoffs. The payoffs $(p_1, q_1)$ and $(p_2, q_2)$ in the first game $g_1$ depend on Bob's choice of action in $g_2$—on whether he chooses *election* or *race*—as well as on the utterance situation $u$, which contains the contextual fact that Ann and Bob are discussing the local election. Similarly, the payoffs $(p_3, q_3)$ and $(p_4, q_4)$ in the second game $g_2$ depend on Bob's choice of action in $g_1$—on whether he chooses FS or FJ—as well as on the utterance situation $u$.

Thus, the payoffs in $g_1$ depend on Bob's actions in $g_2$ (as well as on $u$) and vice versa. This is what makes the two lexical semantic games *interdependent*. This interdependence enables us to represent the probabilistic dynamics involved in interpreting utterances: the referential meaning given to "Fred" influences the referential meaning given to "ran" and vice versa. A slightly more complex equilibrium concept is required to solve such interdependent games.

It is also possible to "multiply" $g_1$ with $g_2$ to derive a sentential semantic game $g_{12}$ as shown in Figure A.3.

|  | FS, election | FS, race | FJ, election | FJ, race |
|---|---|---|---|---|
| Fred ran | $(p_5, q_5)$ | $(p_6, q_6)$ | $(p_7, q_7)$ | $(p_8, q_8)$ |

Figure A.3 The Sentential Semantic Game $g_{12}$

The game $g_{12}$ again has just the one choice of "Fred ran"—the whole sentence—for Ann and four choices of interpretation of the whole sentence for Bob—*Fred Smith stood for election, Fred Smith participated in a race, Fred Jones stood for election,* and *Fred Jones participated in a race*.

It turns out that under some fairly broad conditions, all interlocutors like Bob need to do is to solve the interdependent lexical games. They can safely ignore the sentential game.[1] Solving the lexical games involves little more than comparing probabilities so they can be solved quickly—as quickly as we are able to interpret

---

1. This is a fundamental result in the framework. It states that the joint Pareto-Nash equilibrium of the lexical games is the same as the Nash equilibrium of the sentential game. This unexpected equivalence is a consequence of rationality.

utterances in real life. Showing how the probabilistic computations required result from the underlying games puts them on a firm scientific foundation.

I have deliberately ignored syntax and phonetics to keep things simple. Just as we have lexical semantic games, so we have lexical (and phrasal and sentential) syntactic and phonetic games, and all these lexical games—semantic, syntactic, phonetic—have to be solved together to infer the direct referential meaning of an utterance. Again, all that is involved is comparing a few more probabilities.

This much gets Bob—and us—to the direct meaning of an utterance.[2] That is, by solving the relevant lexical games, Bob can infer that by uttering "Fred ran" Ann has conveyed that *Fred Smith stood for election*. Getting to its indirect meanings (see Figure 3.4) is a little harder and we can just skip it but similar methods apply. Also, I have only discussed how ambiguities are handled, not vagueness, and this also requires a few adjustments. Lastly, I have included some brief remarks on discourse or longer texts in Section 7.2.

In any case, this is all there is to inferring intended meanings from scratch, at least in my theoretical framework, which I call Equilibrium Semantics. I say "from scratch" because I assumed almost nothing beyond the partial rationality of Ann and Bob and it should seem to you that I have almost pulled a rabbit out of a hat, a more or less full-blown intended interpretation of an utterance from just the partial rationality of agents. Naturally, I haven't gone into the details, which can be found in my books cited in the Introduction.

Intended interpretation is one half of communication, the other half being speaking or writing. There are similar games on the speaker's side, and when communication is partial or imperfect, they are a little different from the games on the addressee's side. Miscommunication occurs when there is a mismatch between speaker games and addressee games. And common knowledge, which we considered in Section 6.5, may not obtain, and this makes the flow of information weaker than full communication—as happens when a speaker merely suggests something—as shown in Figure 3.1.

As I said earlier, a Communication Game encompasses all of the games that occur in communication on the speaker's and on the addressee's sides. The tentative assumption about keeping conventional meaning fixed is relaxed in Chapter 8, where both conventional and referential meanings are simultaneously derived in a large Language Game made up of a network of interlocking Communication Games across society.

---

2. See Section 3.1 if you have forgotten what direct meanings are.

# Appendix B: Situation Theory

In this Appendix, I say a little more about situation theory.

People find themselves in a "world" or *environment* from the start, as the phenomenological tradition has emphasized.[1] This is not the entire world or all of reality but a small part of it. This observation seems obvious but the analytic tradition of Frege and Russell missed it and missed its profound consequences. First, in all social matters and especially in the domain of communication, this environment or *context* or *background* is indispensable. Even today, a century later, its presence in the study of meaning is stubbornly resisted by many. Less obvious is the fact that our informational space, a subspace of our environment, results from society's interaction with reality partly via communication.[2] Third, this context of communication often has indeterminate boundaries and this results in many other uncertainties. Once individuated, each informational item is linked with others that form its context, although in formal domains such as mathematics and physics this context is more determinate. For example, a certain fact may be true of equilateral triangles and then this condition of being an equilateral triangle forms the context for the fact. In everyday life, the context is less determinate.[3]

There is a premature rush among analytically minded researchers to secure the respectability of science and it is not realized that their abstractions often miss the essence of the problem. A glaring example of this is the fundamental difference between a sentence and an utterance, something Wittgenstein, Austin, and Strawson were the first to emphasize.[4] When approaching the social sciences, one has to straddle both their abstract and concrete sides, and recognize that a complete science may not be possible because of the indeterminate and loosely structured nature of social contexts. And yet, as I have tried to show

---

1. See Spiegelberg (1981). Also Husserl (1913/1967, pp. 68–71) and Heidegger (1927/1962, Division One). Husserl's situatedness is more cognitive whereas Heidegger's encompasses the whole person.

2. This interaction among persons, language, and world was described in what I called Equilibrium Metaphysics in sec. 7.6 of *Language and Equilibrium* (2010).

3. Taylor (2013, pp. 85–86) discusses this Heideggerian holism in the context of the evolution of modern epistemology.

4. Wittgenstein (1953/1968), Austin (1961), Strawson (1956, 1964).

in this book, a remarkable degree of scientific success is possible if the task is approached in the right way. Surprisingly, philosophers especially, despite their desire to emulate the sciences, have often kept away from relatively new mathematical tools such as game theory and have continued to rely on commonsense insights. This is seldom the way of science. Earlier philosophers invented and used the then-most powerful methods of logic but most contemporary philosophers have largely avoided the more modern techniques of game theory. On the other side, (social) scientists have often kept away from the more general issues considered by philosophy and have busied themselves with the particularities of their disciplines.

I offer here an outline of my version of Barwise and Perry's situation theory.[5] The main innovation is *partial* states of affairs. This Appendix requires some ease with reading mathematical symbols and some elementary familiarity with logical terminology.

Consider an utterance of "Fred Smith ran" in some utterance situation $u$. To describe its direct meaning, we would need to represent the content of "Fred Smith," the content of "ran," the content of the whole sentence, and possibly other things. It is partial states of affairs and full states of affairs that enable us to do this.

Situation theory allows us to model partial information in a fine-grained way. There are individuals $a_i$ and $n$-ary relations $R_i$. Basic states of affairs are $(n + 4)$-tuples $\langle\!\langle R; a_1; \ldots; a_n; l; t; 1 \rangle\!\rangle$ made up of individuals standing in relations at certain locations $l$ and times $t$ with the last item, the number 1, being its polarity, indicating the relation holds. The polarity can also be 0 indicating the relation does not hold. Partial states of affairs such as $\langle\!\langle R; a_1; a_3 \rangle\!\rangle$ or even $\langle\!\langle a_1 \rangle\!\rangle$ are legitimate states of affairs. Any arguments from the full state of affairs $\langle\!\langle R; a_1; \ldots; a_n; l; t; 1 \rangle\!\rangle$ can be omitted. For example, the content *Fred Smith ran* can be expressed partially as $\langle\!\langle ran; Fred\ Smith \rangle\!\rangle$ or more formally as $\langle\!\langle R^{RAN}; b \rangle\!\rangle$ where $R^{RAN}$ is a relation, $b$ is an individual, and the location and time and

---

5. Barwise and Perry (1983). The curious reader who wants to know more can refer to Parikh (2010, 2019). It is interesting to compare situation theory with semantic nets and studies by Sanskrit grammarians dating back to the first millennium BCE and up to the eighteenth century CE. As discussed by Briggs (1985), the latter two have a number of parallels. Situation theory is similar. For example, in an utterance of "John cooked the food and burned his mouth," Sanskrit schemata and semantic nets represent the missing information (that cooking involves heating food and heated food when eaten can burn a mouth) explicitly in the analysis of the utterance. Situation theory handles it in the same way.

polarity have been dropped. ⟪*Fred Smith*⟫ or ⟪*b*⟫ is also a partial rendition of this content and is just the individual Fred Smith. This is the same as the identity between 7 and (7) in arithmetic. The angled brackets serve to gather the arguments.

Partial states of affairs are not existentially quantified over the "missing" arguments because they are separate entities in their own right that can be merged with other appropriate partial states of affairs in the right circumstances. In this sense, there are no missing arguments as such. More complex states of affairs are formed from these basic states of affairs via an operation that merges two partial states of affairs into a third partial state of affairs and they are all collected in the set $\mathcal{J}$. Except for this Appendix, I have indicated the internal structure of states of affairs in this book using ordinary English, and so will just assume the operation of merging or unification parametrized by some situation $s$ on $\mathcal{J}$ is given. This operation $\odot_s$, abbreviated to $\odot$, is neither associative nor commutative and has the identity **1** which stands for no information and zero **0** which stands for contradictory information. The product $\sigma \odot \tau$ is often written $\sigma\tau$.[6]

The relation between a situation $s$ and a state of affairs $\sigma$ that holds in it is written $s \vDash \sigma$ or $\sigma \in s$, and is described as I did earlier in the book by saying $s$ supports $\sigma$ or $\sigma$ holds in $s$. The information expressed by $\vDash$ is special and $s \vDash \sigma$ is called an (Austinian) proposition. Only propositions can be true or false or indeterminate, the last in borderline cases involving vague words or when the relevant state of affairs is partial; states of affairs by themselves do not admit of truth values. Utterances typically convey multiple propositions although these are usually multiple states of affairs relative to a common described situation. Although I will not go into it here, propositions actually have a more general form because the states of affairs in them may occur probabilistically.

Recall that a partial order over $\mathcal{J}$, the space of states of affairs, is a binary relation $\Rightarrow_\ell$ over $\mathcal{J}$ which is reflexive, antisymmetric, and transitive; that is, for all $\sigma, \tau$, and $\upsilon$ (i.e., the Greek letter upsilon) in $\mathcal{J}$, we have the following:

- Reflexivity: $\sigma \Rightarrow_\ell \sigma$.
- Antisymmetry: If $\sigma \Rightarrow_\ell \tau$ and $\tau \Rightarrow_\ell \sigma$, then $\sigma = \tau$.
- Transitivity: If $\sigma \Rightarrow_\ell \tau$ and $\tau \Rightarrow_\ell \upsilon$, then $\sigma \Rightarrow_\ell \upsilon$.

A partial order $\Rightarrow_\ell$ on $\mathcal{J}$ that captures the relation "is at least as informative as" or "is at least as strong as" is assumed. Certain states of affairs are naturally

---

6. The interested reader is referred to Parikh (2010, chap. 2) for more details about $\odot$.

more informative or stronger than others. For example, $\langle\langle P^{crimson}; a\rangle\rangle \Rightarrow_\ell \langle\langle P^{red}; a\rangle\rangle$ where $a$ is some physical object because anything crimson is also always red. So, the first state of affairs is stronger than the second. Likewise, $\langle\langle P^{spinster}; a\rangle\rangle \Rightarrow_\ell \langle\langle P^{female}; a\rangle\rangle$ where $a$ now stands for a person. It is also true that $\langle\langle R; a; b\rangle\rangle \Rightarrow_\ell \langle\langle R; a\rangle\rangle$. If $R$ is the relation of eating, then if $a$ is eating $b$, $a$ must be eating. Likewise, $\langle\langle R; a; 0\rangle\rangle \Rightarrow_\ell \langle\langle R; a; b; 0\rangle\rangle$ because if $a$ is not eating, then $a$ is not eating $b$. In each case, the state of affairs on the left is more informative than the state of affairs on the right.

Intuitively, it is clear that if we have two items of information, say, that $a$ is red and $b$ is blue, then it is possible to combine these states of affairs in two obvious ways, by conjoining or disjoining them. With this in mind, the partially ordered set $(\mathcal{I}, \Rightarrow_\ell)$ is further assumed to be a lattice, which is a partially ordered set in which every pair of elements has a unique supremum (called their join)[7] and a unique infimum (called their meet).[8] Let $\vee$ and $\wedge$ be the induced join and meet operations. If $\tau = \sup\{\sigma, \sigma'\}$, then $\tau = \sigma \vee \sigma'$, and if $\tau = \inf\{\sigma, \sigma'\}$, then $\tau = \sigma \wedge \sigma'$.

A lattice is complete if all of its subsets, finite or infinite, have both a join and a meet. There is no reason to restrict $\vee$ and $\wedge$ to finite subsets, so we assume $(\mathcal{I}, \Rightarrow_\ell)$ is complete. The supremum of $(\mathcal{I}, \Rightarrow_\ell)$ is **1**, the identity of $\odot$, and the infimum is **0**, the zero of $\odot$. Intuitively, **1** will hold in any situation because every situation supports "no information" vacuously, and **0** will not hold in any situation because no (coherent) situation can support contradictory information. To repeat, **1** and **0** are just the identity and zero elements for $\odot$.

Since $\mathcal{I}$ now has the two binary operations $\vee$ and $\wedge$ (in addition to $\odot$), we assume each distributes over the other. That is, it is assumed that $\sigma \wedge (\tau \vee \tau') = (\sigma \wedge \tau) \vee (\sigma \wedge \tau')$ and $\sigma \vee (\tau \wedge \tau') = (\sigma \vee \tau) \wedge (\sigma \vee \tau')$.

For all situations $s$ and all states of affairs $\sigma$ and $\tau$, the following facts hold:

1. $s \not\models \mathbf{0}$ and $s \models \mathbf{1}$.
2. If $s \models \sigma$ and $\sigma \Rightarrow_\ell \tau$, then $s \models \tau$.
3. $s \models \sigma \wedge \tau$ if and only if $s \models \sigma$ and $s \models \tau$.
4. $s \models \sigma \vee \tau$ if and only if $s \models \sigma$ or $s \models \tau$.

---

7. The supremum, or least upper bound of a pair of elements, if it exists, is the least element of $\mathcal{I}$ that is greater than or equal to each element of the pair.
8. The infimum, or greatest lower bound of a pair of elements, if it exists, is the greatest element of $\mathcal{I}$ that is less than or equal to each element of the pair.

When one situation $s$ (or situation type **s**) *involves* another situation $s'$ (or situation type **s**$'$), there is a constraint between them, written $s \Rightarrow s'$ (or **s** $\Rightarrow$ **s**$'$). Constraints can be nomic, conventional, or of other types. They provide the mechanism through which agents perceive, infer, and act in the world and were introduced in the book to account for meaning. Equilibrium Semantics can be compactly expressed as a system of constraints.

# References

Theodor Adorno. *Minima Moralia: Reflections from Damaged Life*. Verso, New York, 1951/1996. Translated by E. F. N. Jephcott.

Maurice Allais. Le comportement de l'homme rationnel devant le risque, critique des postulats et axiomes de l'École Americaine. *Econometrica*, 21:503–546, 1953.

Dan Ariely. *Predictably Irrational: The Hidden Forces That Shape Our Decisions*. Harper Collins, New York, 2008.

Raymond Aron. *Main Currents in Sociological Thought 1*. Penguin Books, New York, 1965/1981.

———. *Main Currents in Sociological Thought 2*. Penguin Books, New York, 1967/1980.

Kenneth J. Arrow. *Social Choice and Individual Values*. Yale University Press, New Haven, CT, 2nd ed., 1951/1963.

———. *The Limits of Organization*. W. W. Norton, New York, 1974.

Kenneth J. Arrow and Gerard Debreu. Existence of a competitive equilibrium for a competitive economy. *Econometrica*, 22(3):265–290, 1954.

Robert J. Aumann. Agreeing to disagree. *Annals of Statistics*, 4:1236–1239, 1976a.

———. *Lectures on Game Theory*. Based on lectures delivered at Stanford University, 1976b.

———. What is game theory trying to accomplish? In Kenneth Arrow and Seppo Honkapohja, editors, *Frontiers of Economics*. Blackwell, Oxford, 1985.

———. Correlated equilibrium as an expression of Bayesian rationality. *Econometrica*, 55:1–18, 1987.

Paul Auster. *The Invention of Solitude*. Penguin Books, New York, 2nd ed., 2007.

J. L. Austin. *Philosophical Papers*. Oxford University Press, London, 1961. Edited by J. O. Urmson and G. J. Warnock.

———. How to talk—some simple ways. In *Philosophical Papers*, pp. 134–153. Oxford University Press, Oxford, 3rd ed., 1961/1979a. Edited by Urmson and Warnock.

———. Performative utterances. In *Philosophical Papers*. Oxford University Press, Oxford, 3rd ed., 1961/1979b. Edited by Urmson and Warnock.

———. *How to Do Things with Words*. Harvard University Press, Cambridge, MA, 2nd ed., 1975. Edited by J. O. Urmson and Marina Sbisa.

Annette C. Baier. *Moral Prejudices: Essays on Ethics*. Harvard University Press, Cambridge, MA, 1995.

Bernard Bailyn. *The Ideological Origins of the American Revolution*. Belknap Press of Harvard University Press, Cambridge, MA, 1967/1992.

Roland Barthes. *Mythologies*. Editions de Seuil, France, 1957.

———. *Elements of Semiology*. Hill and Wang, New York, 1st ed., 1968. Translated by Annette Lavers and Colin Smith.

———. The death of the author. In *Image-Music-Text*, pp. 142–148. Hill and Wang, New York, 1977.

Jon Barwise and John Perry. *Situations and Attitudes*. MIT Press, Cambridge, MA, 1983.

C. A. Bayly. *The Birth of the Modern World, 1780–1914: Global Connections and Comparisons*. Blackwell Publishing, Oxford, 2004.

D. Bernoulli. Exposition of a new theory of the measurement of risk. *Econometrica*, 22:23–36, 1738/1954.

Richard J. Bernstein. *The Restructuring of Social and Political Theory*. Harcourt Brace Jovanovich, New York, 1st ed., 1976.

Josef Bleicher. *Contemporary Hermeneutics: Hermeneutics as Method, Philosophy and Critique*. Routledge and Kegan Paul, London, 1980.

Ned Block. Troubles with functionalism. In David J. Chalmers, editor, *Philosophy of Mind: Classical and Contemporary Readings*, pp. 94–98. Oxford University Press, Oxford, 2002. Excerpted from C. W. Savage, editor, *Perception and Cognition*, pp. 261–325. University of Minnesota Press, 1978.

Herbert Blumer. *Symbolic Interactionism: Perspective and Method*. University of California Press, Berkeley, 1969.

Margaret Boden. *AI: Its Nature and Future*. Oxford University Press, Oxford, 2016.

James Bohman and William Rehg. Jürgen Habermas. In Edward N. Zalta, editor, *The Stanford Encyclopedia of Philosophy*. Metaphysics Research Lab, Stanford University, fall 2017. https://plato.stanford.edu/archives/fall2017/entries/habermas/.

David Bordwell. *Narration in the Fiction Film*. University of Wisconsin Press, Madison, 1985.

Nick Bostrom. *Superintelligence: Paths, Dangers, Strategies*. Oxford University Press, Oxford, 2014.

Pierre Bourdieu. *Language and Symbolic Power*. Harvard University Press, Cambridge, MA, 2003. Edited and Introduced by John B. Thompson. Translated by Gino Raymond and Matthew Adamson.

Rick Briggs. Knowledge representation in Sanskrit and artificial intelligence. *The AI Magazine*, 6(1):32–39, 1985.

Jerome Bruner. *Acts of Meaning*. Harvard University Press, Cambridge, MA, 1990.

Judith M. Burkart, Michèle N. Schubiger, and Carel P. van Schalk. The evolution of general intelligence. *Behavioral and Brain Sciences*, 40:1–67, 2017.

Colin F. Camerer. *Behavioral Game Theory*. Princeton University Press, Princeton, NJ, 2003.

Noël Carroll. *Philosophy of Art*. Routledge, New York, 1999.

David J. Chalmers, editor. *Philosophy of Mind: Classical and Contemporary Readings*. Oxford University Press, Oxford, 2002.

François Chollet. On the measure of intelligence. *arXiv:1911.01547*, pp. 1–64, 2019. https://arxiv.org/abs/1911.01547.

Noam Chomsky. *New Horizons in the Study of Language and Mind*. Cambridge University Press, Cambridge, 2000.

Robin Clark and Prashant Parikh. Game theory and discourse anaphora. *Journal of Logic, Language, and Information*, 16:265–282, 2007.

William E. Connolly. *The Terms of Political Discourse*. Princeton University Press, Princeton, NJ, 3rd ed., 1993.

# References

Jack Copeland. *Artificial Intelligence: A Philosophical Introduction*. Blackwell, Oxford, 1993.

Terry Crowley and Claire Bowern. *An Introduction to Historical Linguistics*. Oxford University Press, Oxford, 4th ed., 2010.

Fred R. Dallmayr and Thomas A. McCarthy, editors. *Understanding and Social Inquiry*. University of Notre Dame Press, Notre Dame, IN, 1978.

Arthur C. Danto. *Sartre*. Fontana/Collins, Glasgow, UK, 1979.

Terrence Deacon. *The Symbolic Species: The Co-evolution of Language and the Brain*. W. W. Norton, New York, 1997.

Jacques Derrida. Structure, sign, and play in the discourse of the human sciences. In *Writing and Difference*, pp. 351–370. University of Chicago Press, Chicago, 1978.

———. *Limited Inc*. Northwestern University Press, Evanston, Illinois, 1988.

Vincent Descombes. *Modern French Philosophy*. Cambridge University Press, Cambridge, 1980. Translated by L. Scott-Fox and J. M. Harding.

Eliot Deutsch and Ron Bontekoe, editors. *A Companion to World Philosophies*. Blackwell Publishing, Oxford, 2007.

Pedro Domingos. *The Master Algorithm: How the Quest for the Ultimate Learning Machine Will Remake Our World*. Basic Books, New York, 2018.

Fred I. Dretske. *Knowledge and the Flow of Information*. MIT Press, Cambridge, MA, 1981.

Hubert L. Dreyfus. A history of first step fallacies. *Minds and Machines*, 22:87–99, 2012.

Michael Dummett. *Origins of Analytical Philosophy*. Harvard University Press, Cambridge, MA, 1996.

Terry Eagleton. *Literary Theory: An Introduction*. University of Minnesota Press, Minneapolis, anniv. ed., 2008a.

———. *The Meaning of Life: A Very Short Introduction*. Oxford University Press, Oxford, 2008b.

Joseph Farrell and Matthew Rabin. Cheap talk. *Journal of Economic Perspectives*, 10(3):103–118, 1996.

Eva M. Fernández and Helen Smith Cairns. *Fundamentals of Psycholinguistics*. Wiley-Blackwell, Oxford, 2011.

Richard Feynman. The making of a scientist. In *"What Do You Care What Other People Think?": Further Adventures of a Curious Character*, pp. 11–19. W. W. Norton, New York, 2001.

Michel Foucault. *The Order of Things: An archaeology of the human sciences*. Routledge, London and New York, 1966/2002.

———. Nietzsche, genealogy, history. In *Language, Counter-Memory, Practice*, pp. 139–164. Cornell University Press, Ithaca, NY, 1980.

———. *"Society Must be Defended": Lectures at the Collège de France 1975–76*. Picador, New York, 1997/2003. Edited by Mauro Bertani and Alessandro Fontana.

Francis Fukuyama, Barak Richman, Ashish Goel, Roberta R. Katz, A. Douglas Melamed, and Marietje Schaake. *Report of the Working Group on Platform Scale*. Stanford Program on Democracy and the Internet, pp. 1–46, 2021. https://cyber.fsi.stanford.edu/publication/report-working-group-platform-scale.

W. B. Gallie. Essentially contested concepts. *Proceedings of the Aristotelian Society, New Series*, 56:167–198, 1956.

Jonardon Ganeri. Intellectual India: Reason, identity, dissent. *New Literary History*, 40(2):247–263, 2009.

Jay L. Garfield, editor. *The Fundamental Wisdom of the Middle Way: Nāgārjuna's* Mūlamadhyamakakārikā. Oxford University Press, Oxford, 1995.

John Geanakoplos, David Pearce, and Ennio Stacchetti. Psychological games and sequential rationality. *Games and Economic Behavior*, 1:60–79, 1989.

Raymond Geuss. A republic of discussion: Habermas at ninety. *The Point*, 2019. https://thepointmag.com/politics/a-republic-of-discussion-habermas-at-ninety/.

James J. Gibson. *The Ecological Approach to Visual Perception*. Psychology Press and Routledge Classic Editions. Routledge, New York, 1986/2015.

Paul Glimcher. *Decisions, Uncertainty, and the Brain: The Science of Neuroeconomics*. MIT Press, Cambridge, MA, 2004.

Erving Goffman. *The Presentation of Self in Everyday Life*. Doubleday Anchor Books, Garden City, NY, 1959.

Ian Goodfellow, Yoshua Bengio, and Aaron Courville. *Deep Learning*. MIT Press, Cambridge, MA, 2016.

Nelson Goodman. *Languages of Art*. Hackett Publishing, Indianapolis, IN, 1976.

Antonio Gramsci. *Selections from the Prison Notebooks*. International Publishers, New York, 2014. Edited and translated by Quentin Hoare and Geoffrey Nowell Smith.

H. P. Grice. Logic and conversation. In Peter Cole and Jerry L. Morgan, editors, *Syntax and Semantics*, vol. 3, pp. 41–58. Academic Press, New York, 1975.

———. Logic and conversation. In *Studies in the Way of Words*, pp. 1–143. Harvard University Press, Cambridge, MA, 1989.

Francesco Guala. *Understanding Institutions: The Science and Philosophy of Living Together*. Princeton University Press, Princeton, NJ, 2016.

W. K. C. Guthrie. *The Greek Philosophers: From Thales to Aristotle*. Routledge, London, 1950/1993.

Jürgen Habermas. The public sphere: An encyclopedia article. *New German Critique*, 3:49–55, 1974. Translated by Sara Lennox and Frank Lennox.

———. *Legitimation Crisis*. Beacon Press, Boston, 1975. Translated by Thomas McCarthy.

———. What is universal pragmatics? In *On the Pragmatics of Communication*, pp. 21–103. MIT Press, Cambridge, MA, 1976/1998. Edited by Maeve Cooke.

———. *Communication and the Evolution of Society*. Beacon Press, Boston, 1979. Translated by Thomas McCarthy.

———. Toward a critique of the theory of meaning. In *On the Pragmatics of Communication*, pp. 277–306. MIT Press, Cambridge, MA, 1988/1998. Edited by Maeve Cooke.

———. *The Philosophical Discourse of Modernity*. MIT Press, Cambridge, MA, 1990. Translated by Frederick G. Lawrence.

———. *Between Facts and Norms*. Polity Press, Malden, MA, 1996. Translated by William Rehg.

# References

Stuart Hall. Encoding/decoding. In Stuart Hall, Dorothy Hobson, Andrew Lowe, and Paul Willis, editors, *Culture, Media, Language: Working Papers in Cultural Studies, 1972–79*, pp. 117–127. Routledge, London, 1980.

Ben Harvey. Paul Cézanne, *The Card Players*. Smarthistory, 2015. https://smarthistory.org/paul-cezanne-the-card-players/, accessed August 12, 2020.

Daniel Hausman, Michael McPherson, and Debra Satz. *Economic Analysis, Moral Philosophy, and Public Policy*. Cambridge University Press, New York, 3rd ed., 2017.

Jeff Hawkins. *A Thousand Brains: A New Theory of Intelligence*. Basic Books, New York, 2021.

Shaun P. Hargreaves-Heap and Yanis Varoufakis. *Game Theory: A Critical Text*. Routledge, London, 2nd ed., 2004.

G. W. F. Hegel. *Phenomenology of Spirit*. Oxford University Press, Oxford, 1977. Translated by A. V. Miller.

Martin Heidegger. *Being and Time*. Harper and Row, New York, 1927/1962. Translated by John Macquarrie and Edward Robinson.

Edward S. Herman and Noam Chomsky. *Manufacturing Consent: The Political Economy of the Mass Media*. Pantheon Books, New York, 1988/2002.

Thomas Hobbes. *Leviathan*. In Steven M. Cahn, editor, *Classics of Modern Political Theory: Machiavelli to Mill*, pp. 78–196. Oxford University Press, Oxford, 1997.

Susan Hockfield. *The Age of Living Machines: How Biology Will Build the Next Technology Revolution*. W. W. Norton, New York, 2019.

Stephen Houlgate. *Hegel, Nietzsche, and the Critique of Metaphysics*. Cambridge University Press, Cambridge, 1986.

David Hume. *An Enquiry Concerning Human Understanding*. Prometheus Books, Buffalo, NY, 1748/1988.

Edmund Husserl. The thesis of the natural standpoint and its suspension. In Joseph J. Kockelmans, editor, *Phenomenology: The Philosophy of Edmund Husserl and Its Interpretation*, pp. 68–80. Anchor Books, New York, 1913/1967. From Edmund Husserl, *Ideas: General Introduction to Phenomenology*, vol. I, sec. 27–32, Allen and Unwin, 1931. Translated by W. R. Boyce Gibson.

Daniel H. H. Ingalls, editor. *The Dhvanyāloka of Ānandavardhana with the Locana of Abhinavagupta*. Harvard University Press, Cambridge, MA, 1990. Translated by Daniel H. H. Ingalls, Jeffrey Moussaieff Masson, and M. V. Patwardhan.

Allan Janik and Stephen Toulmin. *Wittgenstein's Vienna*. Simon and Schuster, New York, 1973.

Daniel Kahneman. *Thinking, Fast and Slow*. Farrar, Straus and Giroux, New York, 2011.

Daniel Kahneman and Amos Tversky. Prospect theory: An analysis of decision under risk. *Econometrica*, 47(2):263–291, 1979.

Daniel Kahneman, Paul Slovic, and Amos Tversky, editors. *Judgement Under Uncertainty: Heuristics and Biases*. Cambridge University Press, Cambridge, 1982.

Immanuel Kant. Answer to the question: What is enlightenment? In *Basic Writings of Kant*, pp. 133–142. Modern Library, New York, 1784/2001. Edited by Allen W. Wood. Translated by Thomas K. Abbott.

Malcolm Keating. The literal-nonliteral distinction in classical Indian philosophy. In Edward N. Zalta, editor, *The Stanford Encyclopedia of Philosophy*. Metaphysics Research Lab, Stanford University, summer 2018. https://plato.stanford.edu/archives/sum2018/entries/literal-nonliteral-india/.

Sung Ho Kim. Max Weber. In Edward N. Zalta, editor, *The Stanford Encyclopedia of Philosophy*. Metaphysics Research Lab, Stanford University, winter 2020. https://plato.stanford.edu/archives/win2020/entries/weber/.

Frank H. Knight. *Freedom and Reform*. Harper and Bros., New York, 1947.

———. *Risk, Uncertainty, and Profit*. Signalman Publishing, Orlando, FL, 1921/2009.

Saul Kripke. *Wittgenstein on Rules and Private Language: An Elementary Exposition*. Harvard University Press, Cambridge, MA, 1982.

Nakul Krishna. How not to be a chucklehead. *Aeon*, 2016. https://aeon.co/essays/how-the-thought-acts-of-the-oxford-don-j-l-austin-live-on.

David Lewis. *Convention*. Harvard University Press, Cambridge, MA, 1969.

Patrik Lindenfors, Andreas Wartel, and Johan Lind. 'Dunbar's number' deconstructed. *Biology Letters*, 17, 2021. https://doi.org/10.1098/rsbl.2021.0158.

John Locke. *Second Treatise of Government*. In Steven M. Cahn, editor, *Classics of Modern Political Theory: Machiavelli to Mill*, pp. 217–292. Oxford University Press, Oxford, 1997.

C. B. Macpherson. *The Political Theory of Possessive Individualism: Hobbes to Locke*. Oxford University Press, Oxford, 1962.

———. *The Life and Times of Liberal Democracy*. Oxford University Press, Oxford, repr. ed., 2011.

Laura Major and Julie Shah. *What to Expect When You're Expecting Robots: The Future of Human-Robot Collaboration*. Basic Books, New York, 2020.

Jeff Malpas. Hans-Georg Gadamer. In Edward N. Zalta, editor, *The Stanford Encyclopedia of Philosophy*. Metaphysics Research Lab, Stanford University, fall 2018. https://plato.stanford.edu/archives/fall2018/entries/gadamer/.

Christopher D. Manning. Human language understanding and reasoning. *Daedalus, the Journal of the American Academy of Arts & Sciences*, 151(2):127–138, 2022. https://doi.org/10.1162/DAED_a_01905.

C. Mantzavinos. Hermeneutics. In Edward N. Zalta, editor, *The Stanford Encyclopedia of Philosophy*. Metaphysics Research Lab, Stanford University, winter 2016. https://plato.stanford.edu/archives/win2016/entries/hermeneutics/.

B. K. Matilal and P. K. Sen. The context principle and some Indian controversies over meaning. *Mind*, 97:73–97, 1988.

Julie E. Maybee. Hegel's dialectics. In Edward N. Zalta, editor, *The Stanford Encyclopedia of Philosophy*. Metaphysics Research Lab, Stanford University, winter 2016. https://plato.stanford.edu/archives/win2016/entries/hegel-dialectics/.

Thomas McEvilley. *The Shape of Ancient Thought: Comparative Studies in Greek and Indian Philosophies*. Allworth Press, New York, 2002.

M. Merleau-Ponty. *Phenomenology of Perception*. Routledge and Kegan Paul, London, 1962. Translated by Colin Smith.

Batja Mesquita, Lisa Feldman Barrett, and Eliot R. Smith, editors. *The Mind in Context*. Guilford Press, New York, 2010.

John Stuart Mill. *On Liberty*. Liberal Arts Press, New York, 1859/1956.

———. *Utilitarianism*. Parker, Son, and Bourn, London, 1863.

Seumas Miller. Social Institutions. In Edward N. Zalta, editor, *The Stanford Encyclopedia of Philosophy*. Metaphysics Research Lab, Stanford University, summer 2019. https://plato.stanford.edu/archives/sum2019/entries/social-institutions/.

Pankaj Mishra. *An End to Suffering: The Buddha in the World*. Farrar, Straus and Giroux, New York, 2004.

Melanie Mitchell. *Artificial Intelligence: A Guide for Thinking Humans*. Farrar, Straus and Giroux, New York, 2019.

J. N. Mohanty. A history of Indian philosophy. In Eliot Deutsch and Ron Bontekoe, editors, *A Companion to World Philosophies*, pp. 24–48. Blackwell Publishing, Oxford, 2007.

Barbara Gail Montero and David Papineau. Naturalism and physicalism. In Kelly James Clark, editor, *The Blackwell Companion to Naturalism*, pp. 182–195. Wiley, 2016.

David Mumford. Review of mathematics in India. *Notices of the American Mathematical Society*, 57(3):385–390, 2010.

Gregory L. Murphy. *The Big Book of Concepts*. MIT Press, Cambridge, MA, 2004.

Roger Myerson. *Game Theory: Analysis of Conflict*. Harvard University Press, Boston, 1991.

Thomas Nagel. What is it like to be a bat? *Philosophical Review*, 83:435–450, 1974.

J. Nash. Non-cooperative games. *Annals of Mathematics*, 54:286–295, 1951.

William Robert Nelson. Incorporating fairness into game theory and economics: Comment. *American Economic Review*, 91:1180–1183, 2001.

Douglass C. North. *Institutions, Institutional Change and Economic Performance*. Cambridge University Press, Cambridge, 1990/2002.

Gananath Obeyesekere. *The Apotheosis of Captain Cook: European Mythmaking in the Pacific*. Princeton University Press, Princeton, NJ, 1997.

Peter C. Ordeshook. *Game Theory and Political Theory: An Introduction*. Cambridge University Press, Cambridge, 1986.

Martin J. Osborne and Ariel Rubinstein. *A Course in Game Theory*. MIT Press, Cambridge, MA, 1994.

Long Ouyang, Jeff Wu, Diogo Almeida, Carroll L. Wainwright, Pamela Mishkin, Chong Zhang, Sandhini Agarwal, Katarina Slama, Alex Ray, John Schulman, Jacob Hilton, Fraser Kelton, Luke Miller, Maddie Simens, Amanda Askell, Peter Welinder, Paul Christiano, Jan Leike, and Ryan Lowe. Training language models to follow instructions with human feedback. *arXiv:2023.02155v1*, pp. 1–68, 2022. https://arxiv.org/abs/2203.02155.

Avani Parikh and Prashant Parikh. *Choice Architecture: A New Approach to Behavior, Design, and Wellness*. Routledge, London, 2018.

Prashant Parikh. *Language and Strategic Inference*. iUniverse, New York, 1987/2020. PhD thesis, Stanford University.

———. *The Use of Language*. CSLI Publications, Stanford University, 2001.

———. *Language and Equilibrium*. MIT Press, Cambridge, MA, 2010.

———. Deconstructing Derrida. *Medium*, 2017. https://medium.com/@pparikh1/deconstructing-derrida-782c1e4ff330.

———. Brief interpretation of Antonioni's "Blow Up." *Medium*, 2018. https://medium.com/@pparikh1/brief-interpretation-of-antonionis-blow-up-de0e7998e81b.

———. *Communication and Content*. Language Science Press, Berlin, 2019.

———. Who's afraid of Bollywood cinema? *Medium*, 2023. https://medium.com/@pparikh1/whos-afraid-of-bollywood-cinema-5c8db98d9c6b.

Talcott Parsons. *The Structure of Social Action*, Vol. I: *Marshall, Pareto, Durkheim*. Free Press, New York, 1937/1968a.

———. *The Structure of Social Action*, Vol. II: *Weber*. Free Press, New York, 1937/1968b.

Judea Pearl and Dana Mackenzie. *The Book of Why: The New Science of Cause and Effect*. Basic Books, New York, 2018.

Charles Sanders Peirce. *Writings on Semiotic*. University of North Carolina Press, Chapel Hill, 1867–1913/1991. Edited by James Hoopes.

Kim Plofker. *Mathematics in India*. Princeton University Press, Princeton, NJ, 2009.

Hilary Putnam. The meaning of 'meaning.' In *Mind, Language, and Reality: Philosophical Papers*, vol. 2. Cambridge University Press, Cambridge, 1975.

W. V. Quine. *Word and Object*. MIT Press, Cambridge, MA, 1960.

———. Ontological relativity. In *Ontological Relativity and Other Essays*. Columbia University Press, New York, 1969a.

———. Speaking of objects. In *Ontological Relativity and Other Essays*. Columbia University Press, New York, 1969b.

Matthew Rabin. Incorporating fairness into game theory and economics. *American Economic Review*, 83:1281–1302, 1993.

Philip Robbins and Murat Aydede, editors. *The Cambridge Handbook of Situated Cognition*. Cambridge University Press, New York, 2009.

Jay F. Rosenberg. Apperception and Sartre's "pre-reflective *cogito*." *American Philosophical Quarterly*, 18(3):255–260, 1981.

Jean-Jacques Rousseau. Discourse on the origin of inequality. In Steven M. Cahn, editor, *Classics of Modern Political Theory: Machiavelli to Mill*, pp. 370–419. Oxford University Press, Oxford, 1997a.

———. Of the social contract. In Steven M. Cahn, editor, *Classics of Modern Political Theory: Machiavelli to Mill*, pp. 420–485. Oxford University Press, Oxford, 1997b.

Salman Rushdie. *Imaginary Homelands: Essays and Criticism 1981–1991*. Granta Books in association with Penguin Books, London, 1991.

Edward Said. *Orientalism*. Vintage Books, New York, 1979.

Michael J. Sandel. *Liberalism and the Limits of Justice*. Cambridge University Press, Cambridge, 2nd ed., 1998.

Jean-Paul Sartre. *Critique of Dialectical Reason*, vol. 1. Verso, London, 1960/2004. Translated by Alan Sheridan-Smith.

———. *Search for a Method*. Alfred A. Knopf, New York, 1963. Translated by Hazel E. Barnes.

Ferdinand de Saussure. *Course of General Linguistics*. Peter Owen, London, 1960. Translated by W. Baskin.

Richard Schechner. *Performance Theory*. Routledge, London, 1988/2003.

T. C. Schelling. *The Strategy of Conflict*. Harvard University Press, Cambridge, MA, 1960.

J. R. Searle. Minds, brains, and programs. *Behavioral and Brain Sciences*, 3:417–457, 1980.

Amartya Sen. *The Argumentative Indian: Writings on Indian History, Culture and Identity*. Farrar, Straus and Giroux, New York, 2005.

Claude E. Shannon and Warren Weaver. *The Mathematical Theory of Communication*. University of Illinois Press, Urbana, 1949.

Herbert A. Simon. A behavioral model of rational choice. *Quarterly Journal of Economics*, 69:99–118, 1955.

Herbert A. Simon. Rational choice and the structure of the environment. *Psychological Review*, 63:129–138, 1956.

Herbert Spiegelberg. *The Phenomenological Movement: A Historical Introduction*. Springer, Berlin, 1981.

M. D. Srinivas. Emergence of a new era in the history of Indian mathematics. *Bhavana: The Mathematics Magazine*, 6(1):385–390, January 2022.

P. F. Strawson. On referring. In Antony Flew, editor, *Essays in Conceptual Analysis*, pp. 21–52. Macmillan, London, 1956.

———. Intention and convention in speech acts. *Philosophical Review*, 73:439–460, 1964.

Richard S. Sutton and Andrew G. Barto. *Reinforcement Learning: An Introduction*. MIT Press, Cambridge, MA, 2nd ed., 2018.

Charles Taylor. Interpretation and the sciences of man. *The Review of Metaphysics*, 25:3–51, 1971.

———. Self-interpreting animals. In *Human Agency and Language: Philosophical Papers*, vol. 1, pp. 45–76. Cambridge University Press, Cambridge, 1977/1999.

———. The concept of a person. In *Human Agency and Language: Philosophical Papers*, vol. 1, pp. 97–114. Cambridge University Press, Cambridge, 1981/1999.

———. Foucault on freedom and truth. *Political Theory*, 12:152–183, 1984.

———. *Human Agency and Language: Philosophical Papers*, vol. 1. Cambridge University Press, Cambridge, 1985/1999.

———. Retrieving realism. In Jospeh K. Schear, editor, *Mind, Reason, and Being-in-the-World*, pp. 61–90. Routledge, London, 2013.

Richard H. Thaler and Cass R. Sunstein. *Nudge: Improving Decisions about Health, Wealth, and Happiness*. Yale University Press, New Haven, CT, 2008.

Michael Tomasello. *Origins of Human Communication*. MIT Press, Cambridge, MA, 2010.

A. M. Turing. Computing machinery and intelligence. *Mind*, 59(236):433–460, 1950.

———. Intelligent machinery, a heretical theory. *Philosophia Mathematica*, 4:256–260, 1996.

Michael T. Turvey. *Lectures on Perception: An Ecological Perspective*. Routledge, New York, 2019.

Ananya Vajpeyi. *Righteous Republic: The Political Foundations of Modern India*. Harvard University Press, Cambridge, MA, 2012.

Wout van Bekkum, Jan Houben, Ineke Sluiter, and Kees Versteegh. *The Emergence of Semantics in Four Linguistic Traditions: Hebrew, Sanskrit, Greek, Arabic*. John Benjamins Publishing, Amsterdam/Philadelphia, 1997.

Ashish Vaswani, Noam Shazeer, Niki Parmar, Jakob Uszkoreit, Llion Jones, Aidan N. Gomez, Lukasz Kaiser, and Illia Polosukhin. Attention is all you need. *31st Conference on Neural Information Processing Systems*, pp. 1–15, 2017.

Lars Vinx. Carl Schmitt. In Edward N. Zalta, editor, *The Stanford Encyclopedia of Philosophy*. Metaphysics Research Lab, Stanford University, fall 2019. https://plato.stanford.edu/archives/fall2019/entries/schmitt/.

Ivo Vlaev, Nick Chater, Neil Stewart, and Gordon D. A. Brown. Does the brain calculate value? *Trends in Cognitive Sciences*, 15(11):546–554, 2011.

John von Neumann and Oskar Morgenstern. *Theory of Games and Economic Behavior*. Princeton University Press, Princeton, NJ, 2nd ed., 1944/1947.

Roy Wagner. Does mathematics need foundations? In Stefania Centrone, Deborah Kant, and Deniz Sarikaya, editors, *Reflections on the Foundations of Mathematics*, pp. 381–396. Springer, Cham, Switzerland, 2019.

Joel Watson. *Strategy: An Introduction to Game Theory*. W. W. Norton, New York, 2002.

Michael Wheeler. Martin Heidegger. In Edward N. Zalta, editor, *The Stanford Encyclopedia of Philosophy*. Metaphysics Research Lab, Stanford University, winter 2018. https://plato.stanford.edu/archives/win2018/entries/heidegger/.

Robert R. Williams. *Hegel's Ethics of Recognition*. University of California Press, Berkeley, 1997.

Ludwig Wittgenstein. *Philosophical Investigations*. Macmillan, New York, 3rd ed., 1953/1968.

Gavin Yamey. Rich countries should tithe their vaccines. *Nature*, 590:529, 2021.

# Name Index

Bold page numbers indicate a figure or table.

Abhinavagupta, 31n, 23n4
Adorno, Theodor, 60n17
Alderman, Liz, 183n7
Allais, Maurice, 77, 77n19
Allen, Woody, 15, 26
Anandavardhana, 23n4
Arendt, Hannah, 165
Ariely, Dan, 77n21
Aristotle, 17, 160, 193
Aron, Raymond, 91n7, 149n1
Arrow, Kenneth, 92n10, 149n1, 160, 161n17, 183n6
Aumann, Robert, 149n1
Auster, Paul, 91, 91n8
Austin, J. L., 18, 20n7, 23, 23n5, 24, 37n6, 104, 203n4
Aydede, Murat, 7n6, 149n1

Bacon, Francis, 141
Baier, Annette, 189n17
Bailyn, Bernard, 114n14
Barthes, Roland, 19, 25n7, 60n17, 87n1, 95n13, 104
Barto, Andrew, 89n4
Barwise, Jon, 8n8, 19–20, 20n7, 48n2, 174n4, 204
Bayly, C. A., 142n27, 152n5
Beckett, Samuel, 4, 30
Bernoulli, D., 76n16
Bernstein, Richard, 149n1
Bleicher, Josef, 90n6
Block, Ned, 41n12
Blumer, Herbert, 135n15, 149n1
Boden, Margaret, 5n1
Bohman, James, 73n12
Bontekoe, Ron, 6n3, 114n14
Bordwell, David, 127n2, 130, 130n9, 132

Bostrom, Nick, 5n1
Bourdieu, Pierre, 19, 39n7, 109n7, 118n23
Bowern, Claire, 108n5
Briggs, Rick, 204n5
Bruner, Jerome, 149n1, 158n11
Burkart, Judith, 42n14
Burns, Robert, 179n1

Camerer, Colin, 77n20
Camus, Albert, 136
Carroll, Noël, 130n8
Cassin, Alessandro, 185n10
Cézanne, Paul, **129**, 130
Chalmers, David, 7n6
Chekhov, Anton, 65n2
Chollet, François, 43n17
Chomsky, Noam, 18, 118n23
Church, Alonzo, 60n17
Clark, J. M., 161
Clark, Robin, 29n14
Connolly, William, 37n5, 118n23
Copeland, Jack, 41, 140n24
Crowley, Terry, 108n5

Dallmayr, Fred R., 149n1, 168n21
Danto, Arthur, 42n16, 151n4
Deacon, Terrence, 56n13
Debreu, Gerard, 92n10, 149n1
Deleuze, Gilles, 186n12
Derrida, Jacques, 19, 60n17, 102n21, 104, 186n12
Descartes, René, 19, 42n16, 60n17, 141
Descombes, Vincent, 189n15
Deutsch, Eliot, 6n3, 114n14
Dilthey, Wilhelm, 90
Domingos, Pedro, 174n4
Dorsey, Jack, 121n25

Dostoyevsky, Fyodor, 3, 76, 136
Dretske, Fred, 8n9, 18, 20n7, 42n15, 49n6, 174n4
Dreyfus, Hubert, 39n7
Dummett, Michael, 90n5
Dunbar, Robin, 190n20
Durkheim, Émile, 151n4

Eagleton, Terry, 25n7, 135n16
Eco, Umberto, 95n13
Einstein, Albert, 59, 196
Eubulides, 36n3

Farrell, Joseph, 133n12
Fernández, Eva, 25n8
Feynman, Richard, 52
Fichte, J. G., 186, 188n14, 189n15
Fodor, Jerry, 18
Foucault, Michel, 19, 60n17, 75n15, 118n23, 156n10
Frege, Gottlob, 18, 23, 97, 103–4
Freud, Sigmund, 25, 77
Fukuyama, Francis, 121n25

Gadamer, Hans-Georg, 47n2
Galilei, Galileo, 141
Gallie, W. B., 36n4
Gandhi, M. K., xxi
Ganeri, Jonardon, 114n14
Garfield, Jay, 47n2, 193n24
Geanakoplos, John, 68n4, 70n7
Geuss, Raymond, 121n26
Gibson, J. J., 47n2
Gilligan, Carol, 189n17
Glimcher, Paul, 76n17, 78n23
Gödel, Kurt, 60n16, 60n17
Goffman, Erving, 149n1
Goodfellow, Ian, 5n2
Goodman, Nelson, 49n6, 50n7, 126n1, 130n8
Gramsci, Antonio, 118, 118n23
Grice, Paul, 18, 23, 23n4, 24, 104
Grünewald, Matthias, 131

Guala, Francesco, 149n1
Guthrie, W. K. C., 114n14

Habermas, Jürgen, 19, 37n6, 73, 113n13, 114, 114n16, 115n17, 116–18, 121, 121n26, 142n27, 152n5, 186n12
Hall, Stuart, 95n13
Hargreaves Heap, Shaun, 69n6
Harvey, Ben, 129n6
Harvey, Giles, 181
Hausman, Daniel, 116n19, 183n6, 189n18
Hawkins, Jeff, 174n4
Hegel, G. W. F., 19, 47n2, 60n17, 104, 186, 186n12, 188, 189n15
Heidegger, Martin, 8n8, 19, 39n7, 47n2, 49n5, 50n8, 79–80, 136, 138, 140–41, 175, 189n17, 203n1
Henley, William Ernest, 160n14
Henry, O., 195
Herder, J. G., 104
Herman, Edward, 118n23
Hobbes, Thomas, 20, 183n6
Hockfield, Susan, 138
Houlgate, Stephen, 186n12
Hume, David, 8n8
Husserl, Edmund, 19, 47n2, 48n3, 138, 203n1

Ingalls, Daniel, 23n4
Isaac, Mike, 27n10
Ishiguro, Kazuo, 181–182

Jakobson, Roman, 104
James, William, 77
Janik, Allan, 7n5
Jyeṣṭhadeva, 141n26

Kafka, Franz, 76, 185–86
Kahneman, Daniel, 77, 77n19, 77n21
Kant, Immanuel, 19, 49n5, 114, 114n15, 186
Keating, Malcolm, 90n6
Keohane, Joe, 116

# Name Index

Kierkegaard, Søren, 76–77, 136
Kim, Sung Ho, 142n27
Kipling, Rudyard, 180n3
Knight, Frank H., 59n15
Kojève, A., 186n12
Kripke, Saul, 18, 106n3
Krishna, Nakul, 20n6
Kurosawa, Akira, 52

Lao Tzu, 3
Lennon, John, 173
Levinas, Emmanuel, 186n12
Lévi-Strauss, Claude, 60n17
Lewis, David, 18, 110
Lindenfors, Patrik, 190n20
Locke, John, 183n6
Luhmann, Niklas, 117

Machiavelli, Niccolò, 20
Mackenzie, Dana, 8n9
MacLeish, Archibald, 179
Macpherson, C. B., 186n11
Madhava, 141n26
Major, Laura, 176n6
Malpas, Jeff, 90n6
Mandela, Nelson, 160, 160n14
Manning, Christopher, 99–100
Mantzavinos, 90n6
Marcel, Gabriel, 20n6
Marx, Groucho, 14, 23
Matilal, B. K., 90n5
Maybee, Julie E., 60n17
McCarthy, Thomas A., 149n1, 168n21
McEvilley, Thomas, 114n14
Merleau-Ponty, Maurice, 19, 39n7, 47n2
Mesquita, Batia, 7n6, 149n1
Metz, Cade, 27n10
Mies van der Rohe, Ludwig, 104
Mill, John Stuart, 76n16, 114, 114n15, 117
Miller, Seumas, 149n1
Mishra, Pankaj, 193n24
Mitchell, Melanie, 5n1

Mohanty, J. N., 65n2
Monet, Claude, 65n2
Montero, Barbara Gail, 7n6
Morgenstern, Oskar, 20n8, 149n1
Mulla Nasruddin, 16
Mumford, David, 141n26
Munch, Edvard, 131
Murphy, Gregory, 39n8
Myerson, Roger, 69n6

Nagarjuna, 193, 193n24
Nagel, Thomas, 62–64
Nash, John, 69n6, 149n1, 200n1
Nelson, William Robert, 70n7
Newton, Isaac, 59, 141
Nietzsche, Friedrich, 76, 136, 180, 186n12
Norman, Marc, 197n31
North, Douglass, 149n1

Obeyesekere, Gananath, 142n28
Ordeshook, Peter, 149n1
Osborne, Martin, 69n6
Ouyang, Long, 27n10, 98n19

Panini, 139
Papineau, David, 7n6
Pareto, Vilfredo, 69n6, 200n1
Parikh, Avani, 78n22
Parikh, Prashant, 8n8, 24n6, 29n14, 34n1, 56n12, 70n8, 71n9, 74n13, 78n22, 88n2, 93n11, 94n12, 95n13, 97n16, 102n21, 106n3, 109n6, 110n9, 121n26, 129n7, 132n11, 133n12, 140n25, 150n2, 153n6, 155n9, 162n18, 171n1, 173n2, 174n4, 193n21, 195n28, 205n6
Parsons, Talcott, 117, 149n1
Pearce, David, 68n4, 70n7
Pearl, Judea, 8n9, 174n4
Peirce, Charles Sanders, 8n8, 18, 115n18
Perry, John, 8n8, 19–20, 20n7, 48n2, 174n4, 204
Picasso, Pablo, 22, 126

Plato, 139
Plofker, Kim, 142n26
Putnam, Hilary, 88n2

Quine, W. V. O., 121n26, 193n25, 194n27

Rabin, Matthew, 70n7, 133n12
Rawls, John, 183n6
Rehg, William, 73n12
Robbins, Philip, 7n6, 149n1
Roose, Kevin, 28n10, 184n8
Rosenberg, Jay, 42n16
Rousseau, Jean-Jacques, 183n6
Rubinstein, Ariel, 69n6
Rushdie, Salman, 60, 61n18
Russell, Bertrand, 18, 104

Sahlins, Marshall, 142n28
Said, Edward, 53
Sandel, Michael J., 161n17
Sartre, Jean-Paul, 19, 42n16, 47n2, 75n15, 136, 151n4, 186n12
Saussure, Ferdinand de, 60n17, 87n1, 104
Schechner, Richard, 135n16
Schelling, F. W. J., 186
Schelling, Thomas, 149n1
Schleiermacher, Friedrich, 90
Schmitt, Carl, 166
Sciarrino, Salvatore, 185–86
Searle, John, 42n14
Sen, Amartya, 114n14, 183n6
Sen, P. K., 90n5
Shah, Julie, 176n6
Shakespeare, William, 31, 52, 77, 106, 192, 197
Shannon, Claude, 20n7, 55, 55n11, 182n5
Siep, Ludwig, 188n14
Simon, Herbert, 77, 77n19
Slovic, Paul, 77n19
Smith Cairns, Helen, 25n8
Spiegelberg, Herbert, 203n1

Srinivas, M. D., 141n26
Stacchetti, Ennio, 68n4, 70n7
Stoppard, Tom, 197n31
Strawson, Peter, 18, 203n4
Sunstein, Cass, 77, 77n19
Sutton, Richard, 89n4
Sutton, Willie, 88

Taylor, Charles, 19, 97, 139–40, 140n25, 156n10, 168n21, 176, 203n3
Thaler, Richard, 77, 77n19
Thich Nhat Hanh, 197
Tomasello, Michael, 56n13
Tommasini, Anthony, 185
Toulmin, Stephen, 7n5
Turing, Alan, 40n10, 60n17, 174n3
Turvey, Michael, 47n2
Tversky, Amos, 77, 77n19

Vajpeyi, Ananya, 114n14
van Beckkum, Wout, 6n3
Varoufakis, Yanis, 69n6
Vaswani, Ashish, 27n10, 98n18, 174n4
Veblen, Thorstein, 161
Vinx, Lars, 166n20
Vlaev, Ivo, 77n20
von Humboldt, Wilhelm, 104
von Neumann, John, 20, 20n8, 149n1

Wagner, Roy, 142n26
Wallace, David Foster, 47
Watson, Joel, 69n6
Weaver, Warren, 20n7, 55n11
Wheeler, Michael, 79
Williams, Robert, 186n12, 188n14, 189n15
Winograd, Terry, 28n13
Wittgenstein, Ludwig, xix, 18, 37, 92n9, 104, 203n4
Wood, Allen, 186n12

Yamey, Gavin, 72n11

# Subject Index

Bold page numbers indicate a figure or table.

actions
    ambiguity and, 27, 134
    circularity, 82
    classification of human, **77**
    communicative, 114–16, 120–21
    context and, 38
    conventional, 111
    ethical systems and, 60
    facts and, 52
    individuation, 51
    intention, 133–34
    language of, 110, **153**
    meaning and, 3, 22, 125, 135, 149
    partiality and, 59, 59n15, 142
    practicality and, 48
    rational/irrational, 76–78, 115–16, 118
    situated, 173
    society and, 167
    thinking and, 41
    utterances, 133
agency, 56, 87–88, 153, **153**, 154, **154**
AI. *See* artificial intelligence (AI)
Amazon, 121n25, 122, 176
ambiguity
    actions and, 27, 134
    AI and, 27–30, 97–98
    art and, 129–31
    jokes and, 16
    language and, 18–19, 21, **21**, 22–23, 27–28, 57, 88–89
    lexical, 22–23
    meaning and, 21
    political speech and, 94
    situational context, 28
    structural, 22, 27
analog, 49–50, 54, 65

antirealism, 171
apperception, 42n16
Apple, 122
"Ars Poetica" (MacLeish), 179
artificial intelligence (AI)
    ability to think, 40–41, 97
    advances in, 174
    ambiguity and, 27–30, 97–98
    data-driven approaches, 58
    general, 183–84, 191
    language and, xix–xx, 122
    Language Games and, 122–23
    meaning and, 42, 104, 123
    modernity and, xviii, 4–5
    narrow, 43
    reinforcement learning, 89n4, 98
    self-attention and, 98, 100
    semantics and, 97–100, **100**
    sentiment analysis, 101
    situated, 171–77, 183
    situational context and, 98
    society and, xix–xxi, 4–5
    vagueness and, 38–40, 43
arts, 58, 125, 128, 128n4, 129
authoritarianism, xvii, 16, 82, 144–45, 156n10, 165
awareness, 54

Being-in-the-world, 78–79, 81n29, 177
book, map of, **xx**, **145**
Buddhism, 47n2, 139, 180–81, 189, 193

capitalism, 114, 142–43, 182–83, 185
*The Card Players* (Cézanne), **129**
causal inference, 8n9
causality, 7–8, 8n9, 193

ChatGPT
  ambiguity and, 27–30, 98
  connotational understanding, 100
  global learning, 122
  linguistic context, 71n9
  narrow AI and, 43
  self-attention and, 98, 100
  understanding utterances, 101
  vagueness and, 39–40
choice theory, 77
circularity, 74, 82, 88, 90–91, 153–54
civilization, xviii, xx–xxi, 8, 47, 55–57, 167
class, 121, 156n10, 166, 186
climate change, 16–17, 94
colonialism, 109, 141, 186
communication. *See also* language; meaning
  artistic, 129–30
  context and, 18
  conventional meaning in, 88–89, 91–93, 108
  coordination games, 72
  equilibrium in, 128
  flows, 22, **22**
  games and, 72, 72n10, 81, 155, 199–201
  game theory, 20
  intended meaning and, 21–22, 91
  joint acts of, 150–51
  lexical semantic game, 199, **199**, 200–201
  nonconscious thinking in, 41
  partiality, 102
  referential meaning in, 88, 91, 93
  sentential semantic games, 200, **200**, 201
  situation theory, 20
  in society, 18, 87, 108
  symbol systems, 56, 131–32
  understanding, 97
  values and, 37
Communication Games
  compositionality principle, 90
  context principle, 90
  conventional meaning in, 91–93, 122, 153, 201
  distortions in, 117
  Language Games and, 106, **106**, 118, 152, 201
  meaning and, 89
  micro-semantics, 92, 113
  mutual recognition, 194–95
  mutual understanding, 120
  referential meaning in, 92, 96, 102, 106, 122
  semantics and, 103, 109, 128–29, 155
  utterance situations, 57, 89, 92, 94
community, 36–38, 43, 107, 109, 151, 189n17
compassion, 189–90, **190**, 191
compositionality principle, 90, 90n5
computation, 42, 140, 201
concepts
  contestable, 36, 36n4, 37, 42
  conventional meaning and, 88, 96
  exemplars, 35, **35**, 38
  interlinked, 38
  judgment, 36–37
  knowledge approach to, 39n8
  mental, 61–62
  precise, 33, **34**
  properties, 34–35
  vagueness and, 33–37, 42
conditions
  for capitalism, 142–43
  communication, 102
  contexts, 58
  for democracy, 160
  for modernity, 143–44
  necessary, 13, 13n2
  phenomena and, 7
  for scientific work, 34
connections, 7, 8n8
consciousness, 7, 41, 56, 61–62
Consistency Condition, 106, 110, 110n9, 111
context
  internal, 61–62
  language and, 18–19, 82
  linguistic, 28, 57
  meaning and, 8

precise conditions, 58
situational, 7, 28, 28n12, 98
states of affairs, 53–54
ubiquity of, 47–49
context principle, 90, 90n5
continuous distinction, 49–50
conventional realism, 194, 196
conventions, 109–13, 130–31, 151, 193
conversation, 72, 72n10, 73, 91–92, 116–17. *See also* communication
*Crimes and Misdemeanors* (film), 15
*Crucifixion* (Grünewald), 131

deconstruction, 102n21
Deep Blue, 41
democracy
    agent preferences, 82
    authoritarian, 144–45
    conditions for, 160
    deliberative, 121, 189
    irrational behavior, 116
    post-liberal, 121, 161, 189
    public sphere, 113
    social form and content, 144
digital, 49–50, 54, 65
direct meaning, 22, **22**, 23–24, 26–27
discourse, 12, 26, **26**, 47, 50, 93, 95, **95**
discrete distinction, 49–50
dualism, 6, 7n5

egalitarianism, 189, 189n18
egoism, 3, 115
Enlightenment, 81, 139–40, 145, 184
environment, 3, 42, 65, 79–80, 203
equilibrium
    agents and, 66
    circularity and, 90
    conventional meaning in, 108, 112–13
    conversation and, 72
    economic, 92, 105
    games and, 68, 72, 89, 113
    jokes and, 93–94
    meaning as, 92, 104
    networks, 111

optimal choice, 78
    public opinion, 118
Equilibrium Metaphysics, 193–94, 203n2
Equilibrium Semantics
    AI and, 101–2
    communication and, 175–76
    as constraint, 207
    conventional meaning in, 105n1
    intended/unintended meaning and, 136, 201
    linguistic meaning and, 103
    meaning and, 89
    motion pictures, 132
    self-attention and, 98
    situated games and, 131, 137
    static and moving images in, 125
    symbol systems, 136, 138
ethical systems, 60
exclusion. *See* inclusion and exclusion
existentialism, 136, 141
extremism, 16, 57, 94

facts, 51–53, 116
fake news, 117, 165, 184, 191
*Finnegan's Wake* (Joyce), 171
form, 127–28, 128n4, 129, 131
freedom, 17, 73, 115, 160, 181, 184
friendship, 190, **190**, 191

games. *See also* Communication Games; Language Games
    agent choices, 66–68, 78, 80–82
    agents, 66–68, 70–71, 73, 78, 163
    analog/digital, 66
    common knowledge, 73–74
    communication and, 102, 155
    complexity and, 81–82
    conversation and, 72, 72n10, 73, 118
    coordination, **66**, 67, 72, 72n11, 119–20, **159**, 162, **195–96**
    embedding situations, 66, 70–71, 73–75, 78–79
    equilibrium, 72, 89, 113
    framing, 72

games (*Cont.*)
   global, 149, 152–54, 168
   implicit/explicit, 66, 71
   interdependent, 155
   inter-subjective, 112
   lexical semantic, **199**, 200–201
   local, 152–54, 163, 168
   mixed-motive, **67**, 157, **157**, 162, 168, 187, 195, **195**
   network, 110, **111**, 118–19, 149, 151–52, 168
   optimal strategies, 68, 69n6
   payoffs (preferences), 66–68, 68n5, 70, 74–75, 78, 80, 82, 163
   persons and groups in, 150–51
   power and, 74–75, 120, 162–64
   sentential semantic, 200, **200**, 201
   situated, 69–70, 70n8, 71, 71n9, 72–75, 78, 80–82, 113, 125, 176, 186
   situated decision problems, 65–66
   social nature of, 112–13
   solving, 68–69
   subjective/objective, 67, 75, 112
   zero-sum, 72n11
game theory
   action and, 135
   agents in, 70
   communication and, 20
   extensionality, 70n8
   fairness in, 70n7
   imperfect knowledge, 59
   intensionality, 70n8
   interactions in, 68
   partial rationality, 78, 80
   performance and, 135n16
   situated games and, 78–80, 169
   situational information, 71, 71n9
German Idealism, 188n14
gestural systems, 56, 107
*Getting Even* (Allen), 26
*The Gift of the Magi* (Henry), 195
globalization, 145, 191
Google, 5, 38, 104, 121n25, 122

groups, 150–51, 163
*Guernica* (Picasso), 22, 126

*Hamlet* (Shakespeare), 77
happiness, 17, 160, 181
hegemony, 118–19, 163, 165
Hegemony Game, 119, **119**, 120, 162–63, **164**
hermeneutic circle, 90, 103, 155
hermeneutics, 90n6
Hinduism, 139
humanism, 3, 43, 76, 168
humanity
   actions, **77**
   context and, 58
   existential rationality, 77
   inclusions/exclusions, 185–90
   meaning and, 5, 104
   situated games and, 78–79
human relationships, 190, **190**
human suffering, 179–81

IBM, 41
idioms, 101, 105n1
"If—" (Kipling), 180n3
images
   ambiguity and, 126
   comprehension, 57
   Equilibrium Semantics and, 125
   motion pictures, 131–32
   pictures, 126–27, 131
   representational, 126
   visual art, 128, 128n4, 129–31
   visual jokes, 127, **127**, 128, **128**
impressionism, 65n2
inclusion and exclusion, 185–90, 190n20, 191
incompleteness, 60n16
indirect meaning, 22, **22**, 23, 23n4, **23**, 26
individuation, 51–52, 55
information
   analog/digital, 49–50
   civilization and, 55, 167
   communication and, 23

## Subject Index

human behavior and, 20
meaning and, 55
qualitative, 55
quantitative theory of, 55
symbol systems, 56
informational space, 54, 172, **172**, 173, 192–94
informational transform, 172, 172n2, **172**, 173–74
intelligence, 43, 43n17, 175–76. *See also* artificial intelligence (AI)
intensionality, 70n8
international relations, 134–35
"Invictus" (Henley), 160n14
irony, 26

jokes
ambiguity and, 16
common meaning in, 12, **12**, 14, **14**, 15, **15, 16**
equilibrium in, 93–94
explicit/implicit, 50
how they work, 11–16
rare meaning in, 12, **12**, 13–14, **14**, 15, **15, 16**
switch in meaning, 13–15, 93
visual, 127, **127**, 128, **128**

*Klara and the Sun* (Ishiguro), 181
knowledge, 6, 11, 59, 73–74, 110, 187, 188n14

language
actions and, **153**
AI and, xix–xx, 122
ambiguity and, 18–19, 21, **21**, 22–23, 27, 57, 88–89
connotational understanding, 100
contestable concepts, 36–37
context and, 18–19, 57, 82
conventional meaning in, 87–89, 91–93, 106
direct/indirect meaning, 22–23, **23**, 24, 30

emotions in, 97
fixed/variable, 87
ideal/ordinary, 19
intended meaning and, 88
meaning and, xix–xx, 4, 11, 21–27, 93, 125
normative, 37, 37n6
public sphere, 113–14
referential meaning in, 93, 96
semantic change in, 108–9
as social institution, 4, 43, 87, 112–13, 151, 153, 155
symbol systems, 56–57
understanding and, 101, 115, 117
vagueness and, 18–19, 36–37
Language Games
AI and, 122–23
common knowledge in, 110, 110n9
Communication Games and, 106, **106**, 118, 152, 201
conventional meaning in, 57, 96, 102, 106–7, 112
conversation and, 118
distortions in, 117
equilibrium in, 106, 106n3, 111, 152
human ontologies and, 193
individuation, 162
linguistic community, 107
macro-semantics, 92, 113
network games in, 149, 151
public opinion, 120
in society, 107, **107**
*La Porta Della Legge* (Sciarrino), 185
liberalism, 121, 160
linguistics. *See also* semantics
agency, 153, **153**
individual/social, 57
meaning and, 18, 103
phonetics, 87, 103
search for meaning, 104
semantics and, 56
structure, 153, **153**
syntax, 87, 98n17, 100, **100**, 103, 128–29
logic, 19, 175, 204

*Macbeth* (Shakespeare), 192
macro-semantics, 92, 105, 113
majoritarianism, 191
*The Making of a Scientist* (Feynman), 52
"Man Was Made to Mourn" (Burns), 179n1
mathematics, 18, 20
*maya*, 193–94, 196
meaning. *See also* direct meaning; indirect meaning
    actions and, 3, 22, 125, 135
    AI and, 42, 104, 123
    causality and, 8, 8n9
    changes in, 108–9
    common, 12, **12**, 14, **14**, 15, **16**
    conventional, 12, 87–89, 91–92, 92n9, 96, 99, 103, 105, 108–9, 112, 122
    as difference, 104
    direct/indirect, 22, **22**, 23, **23**, 24, 26, 30
    discourse, 26, **26**
    as equilibrium, 104
    as expression, 104
    extracted/unintended, 24, **24**, 25–26
    game theory, 20
    intended/unintended, 21, **21**, 22, 24–26, 88–89, 91, 103
    jokes and, 11–15
    language and, xix–xx, 4, 11, 21–27, 93, 125
    latent, 25
    modernity and, xviii, 3
    natural/artificial, 55–56
    rare, 12, **12**, 13, **14**, 15, **16**
    reality and, 54
    as reference, 104
    referential, 88, 91–92, 96–97, 99, 103, 105, 108, 122
    search for, xviii, 3–4, 54
    situations and, 9, 59, 82–83, 141, 171
    situation theory, 20
    study of, 6
    switch in, 13–15, 93

symbol systems, 125
    values and, 37
media, 95n13, 113, 120, 127n2, 137
Meta, 121n25
metacognition, 42n16
micro-semantics, 92, 105, 113
Microsoft, 122
mobility, 185–86
modernism, 131
modernity
    as abstract situation, 141
    AI and, 4–5
    authoritarian democracy, 144–45
    capitalism and, 142–43
    impact of colonialism, 109
    meaning of, xviii, 3
    ontology in, 192
    partial rationality and, 142–45
    partial utopia and, 185
    social traditions and, 143–44
    spheres of action in, 143
*Mūlamadhyamakakārikā* (Nagarjuna), 193n24
mutual recognition, 186, 186n12, 187–88, 188n14, 189–90, 195, 195n29

namaste, 7, 27, 92, 109–11, 111n10, 112, 152, 154
nanotechnology, 174
Nash equilibrium, 69n6, 200n1
networks
    communication and, 91–93
    equilibrium, 111
    games and, 110, **111**, 118–19, 149, 151–52
    linguistic community, 107
neural networks, 39–40, 43, 98

objective experience, 62–64, 82
objects, 125–26, 137–41
ontology, 54, 142, 176, 180, 192–94
OpenAI, 27, 104
Orientalism, 53, 53n10

Pareto-Nash equilibria, 69n6, 200n1
partiality, 59, 59n15, 60, 60n16, 60n17, 61, 81, 197
payoffs
  agent preferences, 80
  compatible, 67
  games and, 66–68, 70, 74–75, 163
  monetary rewards, 76
  objective/subjective factors, 75, 82
  relational preferences, 66n3
perception, 65n2
persons, 137, 139–41, 150–51, 167
philosophy
  analytic tradition in, 18–19
  classical Indian, 65n2, 90n5, 114, 180n3
  contestable concepts, 36n4
  continental theory, 19, 24–25
  logic and, 204
  poststructuralism, 60n17
  public discussion in, 114
  search for meaning, 104
physicalism, 7, 61
pictures, 126–27, 131
political speech, 16–17, 57, 94–95
Poststructuralist thought, 60n17
power
  games and, 74–75, 120
  groups and, 163
  hegemonic, 163–65
  hierarchy of, **164**
  imbalance in society, 117
  public sphere and, 120
  situated games and, 162–64
  social roles and, 165
  in society, 163–65
  technology platforms and, 121n25
preferences, 65, 76, 120, 161–62. *See also* payoffs
present-to-hand, 50n8, 79–80, 80n29
Prisoner's Dilemma game, 68n5
propositions, 96, 96n14, 97, 101
psychology, 34, 42n16

public sphere
  communication in, 104
  democracy and, 113
  language and, 113–14
  meaning and, 125
  misinformation and, 116, 121
  network game, 118–19
  nuanced language in, 94
  political speech in, 17, 95
  power in, 120
  preferences, 120
  society and, 4, 113–14, 118

quantum computing, 174
quantum theory, 58, 193n22

race, 121, 156n10, 166, 186
*Rashomon* (film), 52
rationality
  conventional meaning and, 106
  economic, 77
  existential, 76–77, 141, 168
  informational, 168
  partial, 78, 78n22, 80, 82, 89, 108, 129, 141–42, 194, 201
  utilitarian, 76
ready-to-hand, 50n8, 79–80
realism, 193–94
reality
  causality and, 193
  experience of, 7
  facts and, 51–53
  form of, 19
  individuation and, 51–52
  language and, 6, 9, 11, 19
  meaning and, 54
  structure of, 180
Reception Theory, 95n13
reciprocal recognition, 186, 186n12, 187–88, 188n14, 189
reductionism, 62–64
reference, 11, 18, 97, 99, 101–2, 104, 108
reinforcement learning, 89n4, 98

relativity, 58
representation, 56, 97, 126, 130, **159**
Romanticism, 60n17, 76, 81, 139–40

satisficing, 59n15
*Saturday Night Live*, 11, 14
scarcity, 181–85, 189, 191
sciences, 52, 54–55, 141, 171, 180
*The Scream* (Munch), 131
secularism, 36, 117, 181
self, 158–59, **159**, 160–61, 175
self-attention, 98, 100
self-interpretation, 140–41, 143
semantics
    AI and, 97–100, **100**
    analytic, 24
    art and, 128
    change in, 108–9
    denotational, 99–100
    distributional, 99–100
    knowledge and, 11
    linguistics and, 56
    meaning and, 6, 25, 42, 93
    micro-/macro-, 92, 105, 113
    referential, 97
semiotics. *See* semantics
sentence holism, 90n5
*Shakespeare in Love* (film), 197
situated analytic framework, 47n2
situated choice, 65, 191
situated decision problem, 65, 122
situated games. *See* games
situation
    analog/digital, 65
    context and, 7, 28, 82, 98
    embeddedness, 66, 70–71, 73–75, 79
    explicit, 82
    goings-on, 54
    internal, 62
    meaning and, 9, 59, 82–83
    modernity as, 141
    partiality, 59–60
    sensory/perceptual awareness of, 65
    utterance, 47, 88–89, 91–92, 130

situation theory
    common knowledge, 74
    communication and, 20
    environment in, 203
    integrated theory and, 169
    partial states of affairs, 204–7
    semantic nets and, 204n5
    symbolization, 54
social change, 165–67
*Social Choice and Individual Values* (Arrow), 160
social institutions
    ambiguity and, 21, 27
    authoritarianism and, 156n10
    change in, 166–67
    circularity in, 88, 91
    communication and, 83, 87, 92
    conventions as, 113, 151
    human worth and, 182–84
    language as, xx, 4, 43, 87, 112–13, 151, 153, 155
    linguistic communication in, 92
    public sphere, 113–14, 118
    unintended meaning, 26
social media, 113, 165
social roles, 156–58, 165
social sciences, 7, 57–58, 87, 135, 203
society
    actions and, 167
    agent preferences, 82
    AI and, xix–xxi, 4–5
    collective meaning in, 168, 171
    communication in, 18, 87, 108
    conventions, 109–12
    groups in, 151
    inclusions/exclusions, 190, 190n20, 191
    interactions in, 149
    joint acts in, 150–51
    meaning and, 57
    meta-structure of, 156
    network games in, 149
    power in, 117, 163–65
    self and, 158–61

situated games and, 72–73, 78–79, 156–57, 166
states of affairs, 53–54, 204–7
structuralism, 19, 60n17
structure, 19, 55, 87–88, 153, **153**, 154, **154**, 180
subjective experience, 62–64, 82
symbol systems, 54–57, 125, 131–32, 136, 138
*Syriana* (film), 155n8
systems theory, 117–18

technology, 4–5, 58, 121n25, 174, 183
thinking, 40–42, 97, 140
traditions, 143
Twitter (X), 121n25

understanding, 97–98, 100–101, 115, 117
utopia, partial
  AI and, 184
  compassion and, 189–91
  human goodwill and, 192
  inclusion, 189–91
  meaning and, xix, 197
  modernity and, 185
utterances
  as actions, 133
  AI and, 28–29, 101
  ambiguity and, 14, 88
  content of, 96–97
  context and, 24, 57
  conventional meaning in, 105, 108
  direct/indirect meaning and, 22–23, 30, 89, 96
  free enrichment, 23
  intended/unintended meaning and, 24, 27, 30, 95
  jokes and, 12–13
  meaning and, 25–27, 56, 58, 95, **95**, 103
  natural/artificial meanings, 55
  propositions, 96, 96n14, 97, 101
  referential meaning in, 96–97, 99, 108
  subsystems, 155
  understanding, 100–101
  visual, 133
utterance situation, 28

vagueness
  AI and, 38–40, 43
  meaning and, 18–19, 36–37
  values and, 37, 37n6, 40, 161
  words and concepts, 33–36, 42
value-characters, 48, 48n4
values, 37, 37n6, 40, 161–62
visual systems, 56, 107

*Waiting for Godot* (Beckett), 4, 24, 30–31, 125, 135–37
*What Is It Like to Be a Bat?* (Nagel), 62
world
  conceptual, 37–40, 42
  embedding, 42–43, 48
  meaning and, 6, 54, 58
  physicalism and, 7, 33–34, 64
  as situation, 54